WISH YOU WERE HERE

JOHN ALLORE and **PATRICIA PEARSON**

WISH YOU WERE HERE

A MURDERED GIRL, A BROTHER'S QUEST
AND THE HUNT FOR A SERIAL KILLER

RANDOM HOUSE CANADA

PUBLISHED BY RANDOM HOUSE CANADA

www.penguinrandomhouse.ca

Library and Archives Canada Cataloguing in Publication

Title: Wish you were here : a murdered girl, a brother's quest and the hunt for a serial killer / John Allore and Patricia Pearson.
Names: Allore, John, author. | Pearson, Patricia, 1964– author.
Identifiers: Canadiana (print) 20200219715 | Canadiana (ebook) 20200219723 | ISBN 9780735277168 (softcover) | ISBN 9780735277175 (EPUB)
Subjects: LCSH: Allore, John. | LCSH: Allore, Theresa. | LCSH: Murder—Québec (Province)—Compton. | LCSH: Murder—Investigation—Québec (Province)—Compton. | LCSH: Serial murders—Québec (Province)
Classification: LCC HV6535.C33 C66 2020 | DDC 364.152/30971467—dc23

Text design by Talia Abramson
Cover design by Lisa Jager
Image credits: (field) Peter Oslanec, Unsplash; maps by Talia Abramson

Printed and bound in Canada

10 9 8 7 6 5 4 3 2 1

 Penguin
Random House
RANDOM HOUSE CANADA

For those who ask why

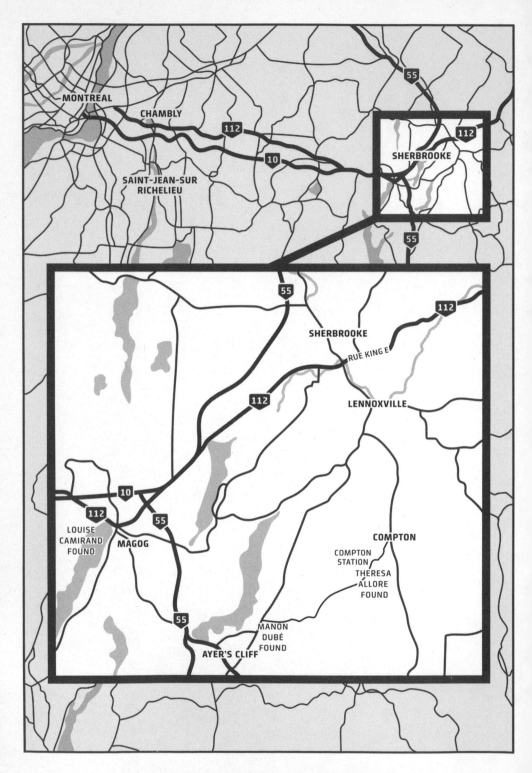

SHERBROOKE, QUEBEC, AND AREA (1978)

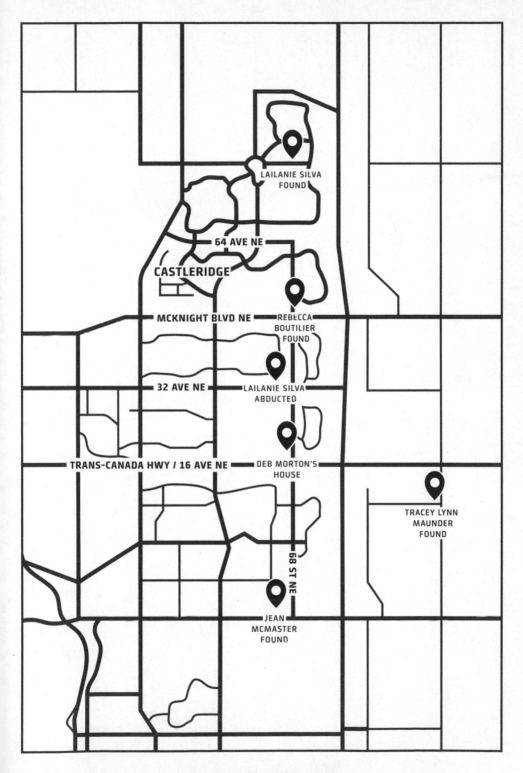

LAILANIE SILVA
FOUND

64 AVE NE

CASTLERIDGE

MCKNIGHT BLVD NE

REBECCA
BOUTILIER
FOUND

32 AVE NE

LAILANIE SILVA
ABDUCTED

TRANS-CANADA HWY / 16 AVE NE

DEB MORTON'S
HOUSE

TRACEY LYNN
MAUNDER
FOUND

68 ST NE

JEAN
MCMASTER
FOUND

NORTHEAST CALGARY, ALBERTA

CONTENTS

PROLOGUE

"Confusion now hath made his masterpiece"
—William Shakespeare, *Macbeth*

TEN O'CLOCK IN THE MORNING OF FRIDAY, APRIL 13, 1979.

For the many Catholic residents of Quebec, it is Good Friday, a day to ritually lament the death of the Messiah. Sorrow then yields to joy: Easter is coming, and so is the hesitant spring. Water trickles through lacy matrixes of ice. Mud squelches beneath boots. Plump red robins alight in the branches of maple and oak trees. In the southern reaches of the province, above the Vermont border, a thirty-year-old man named Robert Ride goes about his annual spring routine of setting and baiting muskrat traps before joining his family for lunch.

The furry rodents are abundant in marshy areas, fond of still or slow-moving water. Ride has been at it all morning, tucking small wire traps into the banks of the gentle Massawippi and Coaticook Rivers as winter softens its grip on their soils. In his pickup truck, he travels south from the town of Waterville to the village of Compton Station, which consists of little more than a grain elevator. From there, he heads east on chemin de la Station to the floor of the Coaticook Valley and pulls over near the entrance to a farm. In the summer and fall, the muskrats here nibble on the cornstalks adjacent to the shores of the Coaticook River, then burrow into its silted banks. Ride sets more traps and continues another fifty metres down the road, slowing his truck just before a small service bridge. Another good spot. There is a pond formed by the spring runoff draining from the fields. The rains have fallen hard this April.

Ride climbs over the guardrail and slide-walks down the steep embankment. He doesn't carry supplies. He has trapped here before, and leaves a stash of materials in the underbrush next to the pond. He walks a short distance from the road toward a large oak tree. To his left is the cornfield, with the farmhouse off in the distance. To his right are the edges of the pond, with the village of Compton thataway eastward a kilometre or so. Ride retrieves the cord of wire he uses for trapping from the base of the oak tree. He can see tiny paw prints in the mud. He begins to set traps. About thirty metres back from the road, Ride stops. A tree branch has broken off during a winter storm and collapsed down the bank. Trying to figure out a way around the large limb, Ride glances to the right and sees something in the water, tangled amongst the fallen branches. It is a mannequin, lying face down. The skin is grey. The hair is matted. It is clothed only in a bra and underwear. He is confounded. *Right some Jesus queer! Who would toss a department-store mannequin into a cornfield in the middle of nowhere? Some pranking kids?*

Leaning closer, he grapples with a more astonishing discovery. He is looking at a person. A dead woman. A woman died here and wasn't buried. She lies here in perfect stillness, without warm clothes on, accompanied by frost and muskrats and rain.

For thirty years, Robert Ride would be so disturbed by this wrongness, this sense of defilement against all that is sacred, that he believed the police would blame him, that by merely witnessing her here, it was—or should be—somehow his fault.

By noon, the pond had become a crime scene. Detectives Roch Gaudreault and Guy Lessard of the Sûreté du Québec, Eastern Townships division, stumped through the mud and cornstalks accompanied by Coroner Michel Durand and a mobile forensics unit. SQ Agent Normand Grégoire took photographs and drew a map: the bridge was precisely 17.8 metres long and 8.6 metres wide. Halfway between the bridge and the farm entrance, he sketched a tractor entrance that allowed access to the cornfield. The body lay exactly 34 metres back from the bridge, and 38 metres from the tractor entrance, on a straight trajectory. She had walked or been dragged from the road. Detectives broke into teams to search the field. They came across a green garbage bag, in which they found women's clothing, including a pink sweater. In the cornfield, they found two torn pieces of a knee-length green scarf. One piece lay 15.3 metres from the tractor entrance. The other lay 16.4 metres farther away, and 25.3 metres from the body.

A tractor entrance, a dropped scarf, a second scattered piece of scarf, and all of it along the same curving trajectory towards a body lying face-down in ten inches of spring runoff. There was a watch on her left wrist and a ring on her left forefinger. She wore earrings. There were, Coroner Durand observed and wrote down, what appeared to be marks of strangulation around her neck.

The coroner noted additional bruise marks under both armpits, suggesting that she had still been alive, if unconscious or dying, when she was dragged through the field. It was, he estimated, the body of a girl between seventeen and eighteen, about five foot five and weighing around 120 pounds. These details roughly corresponded with the age, height and weight of Theresa Allore, who had gone missing from her college residence in Compton on November 3, 1978. That would need to be confirmed.

As the body was whisked to the morgue in the nearby city of Sherbrooke, investigators tried to track down Theresa's brother Andre, who also attended Champlain College. But he was away for Easter, as were her close friends, so the Sûreté du Québec corralled three nervous students who barely knew her to gaze wincingly at the remains. Abruptly confronted with a water-soaked, decomposed corpse, the teenagers couldn't say—they didn't know. Finally, toward the supper hour, Corporal Gaudreault located Theresa's father, who was visiting family in the small Ontario town in which his daughter had been born nineteen years earlier: Trenton, a two-hour drive east of Toronto along the shore of Lake Ontario.

The detective told Bob Allore they'd found a body and thought it was his daughter. Gaudreault described the watch and the ring, the earrings. He didn't mention the strangulation marks. He never would, nor would any police officer. He asked

Mr. Allore to travel immediately to Montreal, where an autopsy would be performed once he had identified his only daughter.

So began one loving, thoughtful family's descent into hell. There would be no resurrection this Easter, only a story that would take forty years to unravel and tell.

PART ONE

ONE

SIMPLE TWIST OF FATE

"Fortune brings in some boats that are not steered"
—William Shakespeare, *Cymbeline*

WHEN I WAS SIXTEEN, I SLEPT IN THE BEDROOM OF A DEAD GIRL.

It is a strange notion, and of course she wasn't just a girl. Nor is this a ghost story. Or maybe it is, given how many people remain haunted by the mysterious violence that befell her.

What I remember are the hiking boots that stood neatly in the closet of that bedroom, a pair that nineteen-year-old Theresa Allore had acquired in Burlington, Vermont, four months before she died, in the hopes of scaling hills she would never encounter. I also remember the devastated silence of her mother, in the adjacent bedroom—a silence I didn't know how to make sense of. She retreated and took frequent naps, which was so different from my own energetic mother. How odd! I was a self-absorbed teenager who was dating her younger son, John. I slept in their turreted Victorian house, fronted by soft pink peonies, on weekend leave from our school, where I was a boarder because my father, a diplomat, had been posted abroad. I was hungry for a feeling of home, and so I embraced this gentle house with its kind parents who accepted my romance with their son and let me sleep in this high, soft bed covered in lace and pillows while John slept in his room one floor below.

Around the room were pictures of Theresa, showing her wavy auburn hair and dark, amused eyes. Her personality—intelligent, independent, witty—shone through. I recall being told she had gone missing from her college campus and been found six months later in a creek beside a cornfield, stripped down to her bra and panties. When I ventured into the realm of her ruined family nearly two years after her death, John told me the investigators in Quebec had advised the Allores that their daughter, a fearless girl who rock-climbed and skydived and was excelling in school, had overdosed on drugs (unspecified) and been taken (surely) from her dorm to the creek a mile or so away by panicked friends. They'd heard speculative talk of her choking on vomit, or perhaps having an allergic reaction. The friends must have dumped her, police explained, after stripping off her clothes and stealing her purse and tossing her wallet in a ditch. As friends do.

Two months after her body was found by the muskrat trapper, the Sûreté du Québec mailed her personal effects—her wallet, watch and earrings—to the family. Apparently, as far as the cops were concerned, Theresa had been pulled under by the riptide of seventies party culture. "Sooner or later, someone will talk," investigators assured the Allores. But in the ensuing years, no one had said a word.

. . .

In 2018, I stood outside that same house on Leinster Street in the port city of Saint John, New Brunswick, gazing up at Theresa's bedroom window. It was a cool, clear autumn day. John was with me. Our relationship had evolved over the decades from young lovers to wary friends to co-investigators into his sister's death—into the enduring silence—after I'd studied crime journalism at Columbia and written a book about murder, and he'd studied criminal justice at North Carolina State. Improbably, although I never met her, Theresa's fate had become a thread that bound us together, even though we sometimes lost touch for years.

In his fifties, John is still handsome, his dark-brown eyes accruing wrinkles now, his inky hair streaked grey. He has a habit of stroking his stubbly moustache, quick and contemplative whisks beneath his nose and on his chin. We have become comfortable old friends, each with daughters who have surpassed Theresa in age. What brings us here this autumn day is the lingering unfinished business of finding justice for her and, perhaps more importantly now that we're parents, asserting the fact that she was, she *was*, and she was loved.

"There's a 1978 calendar that hangs in my kitchen in North Carolina," John told me. "There was a family-run grocery store just up the street, where we used to live in the West Island of Montreal. Lalande's. It was the kind of place where my father would stop if Mom asked him to pick up a loaf of bread on the way home from work, maybe a case of beer and some hockey cards for us kids." The calendar includes a picture of the Lalande farm, adjacent to the store. It's an autumn photo, all reds and yellows, the pumpkin field newly harvested. The Allores would buy a pumpkin there each Halloween. "I recently drove by Lalande's.

It's still there, abandoned and boarded up. The farm is gone. The calendar used to hang above my father's workbench in the basement of this house." Where we now stand, where I knew him, as his girlfriend. "When my parents were downsizing, it was left there after the final cleanout, so I grabbed it, never fully realizing the power of objects. Now it's in my home." It's a tear-away calendar, the kind from which you peel away the months as they pass. But this one didn't get very far. "It is permanently stopped, at November 1978."

There are many turns in this story, and I've come to call John the "plot twist magnet." But as we stood in front of the old house in Saint John, we agreed that the tale must begin with the person at the heart of it, whom the trapper had perceived as a mannequin in the water, who was once a vibrant young woman: keen cyclist, mad David Bowie fan, science whiz like her engineer father, vivacious friend, Theresa Marie Allore. We walked across Leinster Street against a sharpening Atlantic wind and headed down one block, to the condominium building his aging parents had moved to a few years ago when the size of the home became too much for them. He left me there, went off for a walk, so that I could talk to his mother, Marilyn, whom I hadn't seen since I'd slept in her daughter's room.

She greeted me in a pale-pink cashmere robe over pajamas and slippers, her once-black hair pinned back in a loose but meticulous grey chignon. Bracelets jingled on her wrist. Her voice was light and melodic, her hosting effortless, neither overbearing nor inattentive. There's an ethereal softness and femininity to Marilyn Allore, a loving graciousness that combines with such thoughtful intelligence that the admixture is almost divine. She is a flow of sorrow and love who clutches a sword. I couldn't imagine what she took in of me, so changed by the years, a young woman who had wandered into and out of her life shortly after Theresa's death, leaving behind only a small cardboard box with pictures, a diary and some high school keepsakes, which Marilyn had kept safe for me, it turned out, for decades. Seeing her again felt awkward and delicate. I had so carelessly inhabited her home, and her grief, all those years ago. Now I was a grown-up, and also a mother. I understood what it was like to hold a daughter beloved. I recall, so vividly, a day spent at a beach, when I picked up a stick and reflexively wrote my child's name—Clara—rather than my own in the wet sand. Marilyn had been ambivalent about John continuing this quest for justice; she worried about his mental health. But she could never be conflicted about wanting her daughter, in the totality of her nineteen years on earth, to be known.

So we sat down in the Allores' small, decorous living room, featuring art and ceramics from retirement travels, to talk about who Theresa, her eldest child, had been before she was called so many random things by the Quebec police and the administrators of Champlain College—a druggie, a lesbian, a disturbed person, a knocked-up teen, a runaway—none of which was relevant or true. Let's not start with their words for Theresa. Let's begin with her mother's.

Theresa was born in 1959 on Thanksgiving Day, a year after Bob and Marilyn got married in Trenton, Ontario. "She was an easy baby. She walked at nine months, and travelled well," Marilyn said, offering me a glass of ginger ale with ice. "Once, we left her with my mother when we went to Montreal, but we missed her and she missed us. So I said, 'Never again.' I remember that." She paused, with her hands clasped loosely in her lap. "I remember when she was two, and I said, 'Wait here while I get your brother dressed.' Then the phone rang. And she went off. I found her knocking on a neighbour's door, wanting to know who lived there."

What Marilyn brings up without realizing it are moments of almost-loss. Her husband does the same. Bob, a man in his eighties with fierce ice-blue eyes, remembers a busy morning when he brought young Andre and Theresa out to his Buick in the driveway, placed them in the car and went around back of the house to put away the garbage. By the time he returned, the car was halfway across the road, with four-year-old Theresa calmly at the wheel, slowly coasting toward a steep hill. The speed with which he reached the driver's side door handle was almost cartoonish, as he described it. The recollection made him laugh.

The young family lived in the house where Bob grew up, surrounded by relatives on both sides. After Theresa, Andre was born in 1960, and John in '64. They took home movies of Christmas 1961 that reveal everything blessed about being middle-class white Canadians in that era. Around a beautifully decorated fir tree in a cozy living room sit the opened presents: a Popeye doll, a fire engine, a Raggedy Ann, a robot. Theresa and Andre hurry about in matching red outfits with candy-striped pants and Santa jackets, both smiling excitedly. As the siblings mount their new rocking horses, beside them is a seated boy doll, also in a red outfit, as if forecasting the baby brother yet to be born. One child still to come, who will long outlive the happy girl beside him and yet be completely overshadowed by her death.

"They were all very close," Marilyn told me, as I sipped my ginger ale in her condo and glanced at my laptop to ensure it was recording her very soft voice. "Andre has the ability to calm you and give you self-confidence. John will excite you. You need the two to balance it out, and Theresa was in between. She helped me a lot with the boys. If you were going out for an errand, you had to leave her with them so they wouldn't fight. She kept order."

I asked her what Theresa's passions were. "She loved ballet, and did really well at it. She also loved to cycle. When it came time for her to get a bicycle, I got her a girl's bike, and Andre of course got a boy's bicycle. She was so upset. Bob took her down to the shop to pick out a boy's model." Marilyn smiled. "She always wanted to have the boys' toys. Fire engines. Do you remember Johnny West, Chief Cherokee and Jane West?" I didn't, really. But I nodded. "Jane had a horse, like the others, but Theresa also wanted Johnny West's Jeep and trailer." We girls born in the late fifties and sixties had to account for any deviation from the norm, for preferring well-built bikes to Barbies. It was still a thing to remark upon. But Theresa was essentially action-oriented. Her most prized possession in her teens was an Italian racing bike.

Some of the happiest memories for the Allore family involved renting a summer cottage for a few years on Stony Lake, in Ontario. Marilyn recalls the three children putt-putting over to the marina in a little motorboat helmed by Theresa from their island cabin after she provided them with a grocery list; later, the proprietor told her how expertly Theresa considered the shopping, squeezing the bread and checking the price of the cheese. The cottage that they rented, by remarkable coincidence, stood just across the bay from my own family's. We were within echoey shouting distance in our respective wooden cabins perched on the rocky Canadian Shield. Ontario—four times the size of France—is filled with shimmering waterways, a place of infinite destination options for families on vacation. Even this particular lake has several marinas from which to launch to the dozens of islands. And yet we were summering on the same bay, our lives, unbeknownst to us, already entwining.

As five-year-olds, John and I might well have been at the Kawartha Park Marina on the same July afternoon in 1969, clutching our mums' hands, waiting for the cars to be unpacked and the suitcases and paper bags filled with hot dogs and peaches to get hauled by wheelbarrow down the gravel drive from the parking lot and over to boats with ten-horsepower engines, bobbing gently in their slips at the small public dock. I had a pink knit one-piece bathing suit with pompoms sewn at each thigh. There is a picture of me in the summer of '69 holding hands with my cousin Patrick on the bonfire rock on our shoreline, my blond hair trimmed like a serf's, severe bangs and a bowl cut. Behind us across the rippling water is the piney shore where the Allores summered.

Maybe I stood under the awning at the marina one day, mouthing a candy necklace, waiting for the grown-ups to finesse the transport to our cottage, while John, in his swim trunks and boxy red life jacket, skipped right past me, two kids in the safe harbour of loving families, anticipating the excitement of camp-fires and moss gardens and the patient capture of bullfrogs.

Between our cottages arose two small, round islands known as the Sisters, comprising rose-hued granite overgrown with blueberry bushes. We children would shriek in excitement and alarm as we took turns jumping from the highest point of one of the islands to splash into the cool lake below. (When my own sister lay dying, in 2008, she chose to imagine approaching death as summoning the bravery to jump from the Sisters. "Lots of people have done it before me," she whispered.)

Several years after the last of these family vacations, John and I would be back together at this lake without our mums, no longer contained within the sunlit stillness of childhood, where a day's adventure is the taste of clover honey on fresh white bread. Now I had slept in Theresa's room, and life was darker, even if we didn't understand it that way. Weren't all lives like this, with sand hollowing out beneath one's feet as tides of pain surged and receded?

As teenage lovers we moved along the shoreline recklessly, a bit unhinged, smoking hash oil smeared on cigarettes and drinking too much beer. I remember stumbling into a lichen-covered boulder and gashing both knees, which we found hilarious. I don't recall how we got there that summer, since neither of us had a car. I have no memory of John wanting to revisit his old family cabin rental on the far side of the Sisters. He says now that he didn't much think about it. It was as if he'd never been to Stony Lake.

A memory shared by Bob over dinner in Saint John in 2018: Theresa teaching John how to steer the boat at the lake. Bob laughed at how it went, the physical comedy of the two of them. The next day, after telling me his stories, he remained in bed.

"You don't realize how quickly you can lose control and get overwhelmed," John told me. "You can start with totally happy, innocent memories and then not recover for days."

In Montreal, after they moved from Trenton in the mid-1960s, the small-town family found their lives enriched in new ways by a big city. "Our neighbours all came from the Second World War in Europe," Marilyn told me. "They were every nationality, which made it exciting because you learned all kinds of things, and they were very friendly and very hard-working, and their children were nice to have in the house. We lived on a corner lot, so the other kids came over in the winter to skate in the back-yard, or put up tents in the summer. I was happy to have them because I knew what was going on." She laughed. "You just baked a lot of cookies at night. It was fun. The women in the neighbourhood helped one another. One of them had a car, and she'd drive any of us in an emergency. We babysat for each other. It was normal, it was good."

We are counting down the years, now, before nothing felt normal or good.

As Theresa entered her teens, she began to forge a path that other girls admired. One fan was her cousin Kathy, a petite woman with blue-green eyes and light-brown hair, cut in a bob, who later welcomed me into her neat house in Trenton. The extended Allore family had remained in this working-class city that mainly services a Canadian Forces Base. Growing up, Kathy told me, she had marvelled at her sophisticated Montreal cousin, who seemed so at home in the world. "She was special to me, like a sister,"

Kathy said, as we sat at her dining room table. "When I was confirmed [by the Catholic Church] in grade seven, I added her name into mine: Mary Kathleen Theresa..."

Kathy used to visit Theresa in the Montreal suburb of Pierrefonds, where the two girls would loll around on the floor of Theresa's cheerfully messy bedroom, eating peanut butter and jam sandwiches and listening to records. Theresa introduced Kathy to David Bowie, and took her to see the Frampton Comes Alive! concert in 1976 at the amphitheatre Place des Nations. They also nabbed box seats at the Montreal Forum to see Heart touring *Dreamboat Annie.*

Theresa, she said, taught her to disco dance and introduced her to her many friends, who seemed "so outgoing and street-smart" compared to what Kathy was used to. They all appeared to adore Theresa, who was "kind and funny and caring and adventurous." She was always open, always game. "If something was happening, she was right on it, meeting up with friends."

One of those friends during the Montreal high school period was Deborah Ferdinand, now a communications consultant near Toronto. "We listened to a lot of good music, we laughed a lot, we talked," Deborah told me. "Theresa was very cerebral. She had very strong values. She stood up for me against racism when somebody called me a name. But she was also very bubbly and playful. We used to call her Squeaky."

The 1970s marked the advent of the New Age, sparking interest in everything from occult séances to crystals. Theresa's Catholic social circle started playing around with intriguing taboos: tarot readings, Ouija boards. "Kids were really into levitating you off a chair," Deborah recalled. "Conversations arose after that. We talked about astro-travelling, which was new to me as a Roman Catholic. We'd go from that conversation to listening to David Bowie, a couple of joints, a few beers, and then back to discussing spirituality."

I began filling in the picture frame of this young woman, who was athletic, curious, extroverted. Mischievous. Her brother Andre remembers the home movie Bob filmed of Andre's high school graduation in Pierrefonds, how Theresa would seize the moment. "She saw that I had this black robe for graduation, and she got the movie camera and turned the whole thing into a skit. It ended with her donning Groucho Marx glasses and drawling, 'I hope you enjoyed the show.'"

After high school, sixteen-year-old Theresa began working at a ski factory in the Montreal suburb of Pointe-Claire, which was where she met her boyfriend, a handsome blond Czech émigré named Vlad Kulich. "We were pals in the autumn of 1977," he told me in his murmuring baritone, a voice that reminds me of Robbie Robertson, "once in awhile having a beer. I had a thing for her, but I was shy." Theresa, on the other hand, was assertive and dynamic. "She would vocalize what she observed in a very entertaining way. She was also knowledgeable and appreciative of every kind of art form, way more versed in culture than I was."

For a guy who would go on to a career in Hollywood, most recently as an actor on the series *Vikings*, Theresa's vivacity and sophistication was alluring. That spring, he had saved enough money to buy a used Pontiac convertible, which emboldened him to ask her if she'd like to take a little road trip south to

Burlington, Vermont. He remembers the romantic excitement of "our shoulders brushing in the car." They popped into some shops, one of which was selling a belt buckle that Vlad really liked, but couldn't afford. "Instead, I bought the record 'Wildfire' by Michael Martin Murphey." Anyone who grew up in the seventies would be familiar with that soft-rock AM radio hit. This was the time of John Denver and Al Stewart and America and "Muskrat Love," when romance in American music featured soft tenor voices and synthesizers. The day trip was exhilarating. "When I dropped Theresa off, she handed me a bag—and inside was the belt buckle."

As late spring flowed into summer, the two became an item. "We would go out and listen to bands and kiss." For Vlad, raised with a healthy dose of Eastern European cynicism, Theresa was everything he found good about Canada. "She was very open-minded, but she had her own convictions. She was an honest person; she would never fuck you over."

That summer, Bob and Marilyn made the move from Montreal to Saint John, and Theresa and Vlad decided to take a road trip along the south side of the border, through the States, to visit them in the family's new digs on Leinster Street. "I bought an old Ford for a hundred bucks, which basically lasted the trip," Vlad remembered. "The first time we got intimate was near Bangor, Maine. Then we were a couple, and it was so nice." It's hard to imagine now, in the age of Tinder, that people could date for several months, and even travel together, before they consummated the relationship. Yet it was the normal pace of things then, when Meatloaf bellowed mournfully on the radio about hoping a girl would go all the way.

There was one unsettling night that took on a more haunting significance for Vlad the following year. "We had driven to Stowe, Vermont," he recalled, "and we were planning to find a place to camp. It was dark, and we saw a hill with a clearing. We began walking up the hill and I started getting a weird feeling. It's hard to describe. You didn't feel like your feet were planted on the ground. We finally stopped walking and set up the tent. Theresa kept saying, 'Something bad is going to happen.' I felt it too, and I thought it was something that would happen to me. I was ready for it. I had a knife." The sun came up and they folded away their sleeping bag and the tent, then returned to the car. "Theresa said, 'Oh my God, we're walking through a graveyard.' We had slept in a graveyard. I will never forget that. She wasn't the type to freak out. It was so strange."

But soon forgotten, at least for the time being. In Stowe, they milled through a mountaineering shop because they both wanted hiking boots. They were into "that John Denver Rocky Mountain High" look, which Theresa had picked up from a trip out West the previous summer: denim blouses and cowboy bandanas. For Vlad, it had to be window-shopping because he didn't have much money. He remembers admiring a pocket knife in that Vermont store, and what remains so vivid is that "the year after Theresa died, her mom sent me a pocket knife in the mail. In the note, she said she was keeping Theresa's hiking boots safe. I was like, 'How did she know I wanted a pocket knife?' It was too weird, and so poetic." With a sudden death, people intuitively try to keep the momentum of that life going, finishing all of the business, extending the loving gestures, pursuing the hobbies and passions, breathing for the ones who've lost breath.

The shy new couple eventually made it to Saint John, where Marilyn remembers having a conversation with them about the dangers of hitchhiking, and how she got Vlad on her side in trying to persuade Theresa that it wasn't safe. Like the knife and the boots, the conversation would probably be lost to memory if it hadn't taken on such fixating importance in the year that was about to unfold. "I remember talking to your mother about the hitchhiking," Marilyn told me in the fall of 2018. "When I was growing up, you simply didn't do that. And your mother said, 'You can tell them not to do it, but they all do it anyway.' You think, *Well, maybe I should have bought her a car*, but they're too young for the responsibility of a car." Marilyn was talking to herself, not to me, and it was a well-worn conversational track, I suspected. All of those presents bought over the innocent years, the Christmas and birthday gifts, the robots and dolls and bicycles, and none of it so well spent as a car might have been.

But how could you know?

"I remember driving her down the highway one day," Marilyn continued, tears beginning to shimmer in her eyes, "and she said, 'Is it alright with you if I go back to school?'" By now she'd been out for eighteen months or so. "Well, jeepers! I just about stepped on the accelerator and went through a red light. I said, 'Oh *yeah*, that's fine by me.' Because I'd been trying to explain to her, you're not going to get anywhere without an education. She came to realize that, and Andre was already at Champlain College. I hadn't heard anything wrong with it. We went to register, and the girl registering Theresa was very nice. So it didn't—no alarm bells were ringing." How could they have?

"When Theresa decided to go to Champlain," recalled her friend Debbie Ferdinand, "I couldn't understand her desire to spread her wings and fly. I was the youngest in our group of friends. I was upset. It was a big move. I remember feeling afraid when she went away."

It was a normal emotion for a teenager, devoted as they are to their friends. But it's also another memory of almost-loss and, in retrospect, a sense of foreboding.

Vlad last saw Theresa in the fall of 1978 at her Champlain College residence, where she'd tacked up her new David Bowie poster in a second-floor dorm room. Bowie was then on a world tour called Heroes, and Theresa had attended the concert at the Montreal Forum the previous spring. She was deeply enamoured of the British star. "Bowie wails with crazed soul about two doomed lovers finding a moment of redemption together—just for one day," *Rolling Stone* magazine noted in 1977 about the anthemic song "Heroes," which would later become a beloved song for me and John. I saw Bowie at Wembley Stadium outside of London, England, in 1982. Love itself, we all seemed to feel, was a heroic act in perilous times.

In late September, Vlad told Theresa he was setting off to hitchhike across the country. "I wanted to know who I was," he told me. "I figured she would always be there. We never had a breakup. It was like, 'I love you, and I'll see you soon.'" Instead, the next time he set foot in the Townships, it was to hear from a cop that Theresa Allore was missing because she was "probably a hooker." The promise of everything bright and good turned from flame to ashes in his hands.

TWO

VIOLENCE BOILS IN THE GARDEN

"Le mal qui est dans le monde vient presque toujours de l'ignorance."
—Albert Camus

TO GET TO CHAMPLAIN COLLEGE, STUDENTS TYPICALLY TOOK A train or a bus through the bucolic rolling countryside of Quebec's Eastern Townships, a region since popularized by the crime novelist Louise Penny and her serene fictional village of Three Pines. The Townships are a blend of farm and forest, seemingly untouched by urban industry. Many residents are summer cottagers nestling around small glacial lakes. Others raise dairy cows and tend apple orchards. A Benedictine monastery, Abbaye de Saint-Benoît-du-Lac, is famed for its blue cheese and cider. The area is dotted with old covered bridges and rounded barns, built that way, it's been said, so that devils couldn't hide in their corners.

A little less than two hours southeast of Montreal, students arrived in the pretty village of Lennoxville, downriver from the old stone mill city of Sherbrooke, with its topography of waterways and hills, a similar look to Pittsburgh and other nineteenth-century cities built around mills and mines. At the heart of the much smaller Lennoxville and its two-block main street is Bishop's University, founded in 1843 as one of only two English-language universities then in Quebec, the other being Montreal's McGill. With little competition, Bishop's effortlessly gained an outsized political and cultural influence over the Townships, acting as the intellectual locus of prestige, despite the population being largely French-speaking. As late as 1970, fewer than a third of Quebec's francophones were even graduating from high school. Quebec society had been run from birth to death by the Catholic Church for over three hundred years, with education run exclusively by clergy. By the 1960s, this was about to change. The province began shaking off its traditional distrust of secular education in order to expand opportunities for French students. The government introduced a slate of new colleges, called CEGEPs (*collèges d'enseignement général et professionnel*, or general and professional teaching colleges), which were meant to broaden educational avenues in the province and serve as stepping stones to Quebec's six universities.

For English-speaking students who had completed grade eleven, the new system required them to attend a college like Champlain, which borrowed some facilities from Bishop's, before they could apply to university. Locally, Champlain came to be known as the "country club" for its population of affluent anglophone teens flowing in from across the province. That spelled trouble in the late seventies, when these sixteen- and seventeen-year-olds were arriving in greater numbers than the campus could accommodate. Bishop's didn't have enough infrastructure, and funding applications were submitted to construct new dorms. Over fifteen kilometres south of Bishop's and Champlain, down a forested road leading to the tiny hamlet of Compton, stood an abandoned girls' boarding school known as King's Hall, which had run into financial trouble some years earlier and put its grounds up for lease. The property featured a rambling gabled brick residence in the Arts and Crafts style with adjacent sports fields and a tennis court, evoking its past life as a self-contained world shaded by maple and oak trees, where the strictly supervised girls would have slept, studied and played their games of soccer and ball hockey on-site, and from which they'd have been bused out, together, for chaperoned excursions.

Now, confronted with climbing enrolment for Champlain, over two hundred students as young as sisxten were hastily assigned to rooms either in the main school building of King's Hall or in a second dormitory called Gillard House, notwithstanding their remoteness from Champlain's actual classrooms in Lennoxville. The first director of residence, Gordon Glass, held a rather utopian view of affairs at King's Hall. He envisioned its dorms becoming a "totally student-run residence" within two years, where everyone took turns cooking. They could even become self-sufficient through farming. "I'm interested in having a hen master or mistress, raising chickens and providing us with the 65 dozen eggs per week we need," he enthused to the college paper.

Champlain arranged for shuttle buses to run ten times per day, ferrying the teens along the largely unpopulated road lined by stands of pine and fir for fifteen minutes to the Bishop's and Champlain campus. Getting students to class on time seemed important, but with only two shuttles scheduled after five p.m.—one at 6:15 and a last one at eleven—student safety seems not to have been factored in at all. Colleges are dynamic ecosystems where young people come and go spontaneously, to celebrate birthdays at bars, catch basketball games or attend their friends' plays. The system of shuttle transport was more suitable for a seniors' residence, where one might go to town for a Friday lunch or to visit the dentist, but would then invariably be home and tucked into bed after dinner. It was, in essence, a ludicrous solution for young, impulsive, inexperienced and disorganized kids, and disaster befell the experiment almost at once.

One attack, like many that weren't reported at the time, spun the trajectory of Champlain student Catherine Dawe's life into decades of shamed silence and difficult intimacies. Dawe, now in her sixties, is a photographer in Montreal who grew up in Europe, although her francophone mother hailed from Cowansville, Quebec, close to the Vermont border. When the family moved back to the Eastern Townships in the mid-seventies, Dawe was a slight teenager who had trained in gymnastics and looked young for her age, not yet fully developed. She finished grade eleven in Cowansville, but her mother was reluctant to send her off to the new CEGEP system, so she repeated grade eleven in French, not so much to improve her marks as to remain under her parents' wings. Finally, in the fall of 1976 they enrolled her at Champlain College. Her older sister had headed to Montreal, but for Catherine they felt "it was safer in the country." She was their baby; they couldn't abide her being in the city.

After a good autumn term, she went home for a two-week break to celebrate Christmas and her eighteenth birthday. Her boyfriend, whom she'd been dating since the summer of 1975, had asked her father's permission to marry her. It was a joyful, exciting holiday. The day she was due to return to her residence at King's Hall in Compton, the Townships were beset by a face-stinging blizzard. The roads were a slippery, snow-blinding mess, and Catherine's parents decided it would be safer for her to take the Voyageur bus from Cowansville to Sherbrooke than for her father to attempt to drive her. The bus would arrive in time for her to catch a local bus down to Lennoxville, from which she could grab the last student shuttle south to King's Hall at eleven p.m.

As it turned out, the Voyageur bus struggled to make progress in the heavy snowfall, and Catherine arrived at Sherbrooke's station almost ninety minutes late. "Everything was closed," she recalled. "The last local bus to Lennoxville had left, so I had also missed the last shuttle." Her only option, it gradually dawned on her as she stood in the empty station, was to hitch-hike. She'd done it a few times with her friends in Cowansville on summer afternoons when they wanted to shake off the heat and swim in a nearby lake. "The person who picked you up was usually someone you knew," she said. It was a small town. A mother or someone's brother would come along in their Chevy and give everyone a lift to the beach.

Now, in the freezing Sherbrooke night, Dawe dragged her small grey suitcase through the snow from the bus station to the road heading down to Lennoxville and stuck out her mittened thumb. Deep silence, flickering street lights, a southward route of twenty-five kilometres. At length, a car slowed and pulled over, its windshield wipers sweeping back and forth. An older man, tidily dressed, leaned toward the passenger window and beckoned her in. He explained that he could take her partway to Compton, although his turnoff to home was sooner, so he'd let her off there. It was so late, he explained, and his wife would be worried about him in the storm, but he wanted to help her get as far as she could because "I have daughters your age."

As events spin and spin in your mind ever after, she thinks today: *If he had daughters, why didn't he understand the risk of leaving me in the middle of nowhere?* She thinks: *Why didn't I tell him to drop me in Lennoxville, before his turnoff?* She had friends-of-friends renting a house near the main street of town. They would surely have taken her in for the night. Even if she'd met them only once or twice, they'd been welcoming. In hindsight, it was such an obvious option, given her predicament, but at the time, "I was too shy to knock on their door."

Instead, she allowed her impromptu chauffeur to drop her off south of Lennoxville on the unlit road. She stood facing a shadowy farmer's field, with her back to a towering line of evergreen trees, their boughs bending in the storm. The man drove away. "I remember his headlights going up a hill." It was one o'clock in the morning. The temperature was well below zero. "It was snowing so hard that I couldn't see across the road. I was hungry. I was cold. I waited, and waited, and waited. I don't know how much time passed. Snow was piling up on my suitcase."

She was so harrowed by her predicament that, when a car finally approached, perhaps half an hour later, she waved her arms in relief. But the sense of being rescued was short-lived. "When this guy pulled up, right away it was a different-feeling situation. The car was dirty inside. He was grubby. Not like a farmer who had been working, but skuzzy. When I opened the door, my heart skipped. But what was I going to do? Wait another hour? If I'd known there was a house behind the evergreen trees, maybe I would have made another choice." Her mind spinning and spinning in tormented retrospect. "It seemed like my only option."

Sliding onto the springy bench seat, she placed her damp suitcase between herself and the driver as a buffer, and avoided eye contact. "I said to myself, *This is not good, don't interact with him.*" Making her voice as cheerful as she could, she explained she was heading just a few kilometres down the road to King's Hall in Compton. Although that would be the first exit from where they now were, he made himself sound reluctant, she remembered: "It's a little out of my way, but I can take you there." Doing her a favour at one in the morning in a January blizzard. Magnanimous guy.

King's Hall sits a block or so to the east of Highway 147. When he turned off the highway and into the circling driveway of the residence, he kept driving, past the buildings to a small, forking service road that heads behind the hall.

"I said, 'It's here, turn here,'" but he ignored her and kept driving.

"I know where we're going," he said. "You need to pay me for my trouble."

"He parked beyond the residence and put his hand on my breast, groping me. I remember very clearly speaking to him in French: '*Monsieur, j'ai quinze ans! S'il vous plaît!*' The idea that I was underage didn't stop him for one second. He tried to go down my pants with his hands. I told him I had my period. He said, 'There's something else we can do.' He had his right hand around my neck, and he pushed me down, up and down, up and down. I can still smell him. I was half-gagging already. I said, 'I don't know how to do this.' He said, 'You'll learn.' I said, 'I know other girls who know how to do this. They can do it. Come back next Friday at nine p.m.!'"

Her desperate ploy was to no avail, and later she would feel terrible guilt for having set up future victims for his utterly indifferent greed. "I was gagging, I was crying. He ejaculated into my mouth."

Decades later, when she finally told a soul, she said it wasn't rape, but she came to see that "I was orally raped. Someone is using your body to sexually satisfy themselves: that is rape. This guy was doing it *in* my *face*. I would almost have preferred to be vaginally raped. He was literally in my face."

But, at the time, cold, hungry, exhausted and shocked, she complied. After reaching his climax, the man started driving forward, plowing further into the uncleared swath of snow. She wondered where he was going now, and if she was going to die. He lunged forward three times but couldn't break a path, so he returned to the King's Hall driveway behind them. "And he told me, 'If you tell anyone about this, I know where you live.'"

Then he got out and walked around the front of the car to open her door, which he had rigged, she realized, to be unopenable from the inside. "As he passed the headlights in front of the car, I saw that he was wearing jeans and a checkered or plaid green-and-blue parka." She hadn't looked at him otherwise, not at his face. She had observed his stubby, rough hands, his awful smell and his malice. "I was still looking at the ground when I got out of the car. He closed the door and he walked back in front of the car, and I went past and headed to the residence."

In her room, the newly adult Catherine, newly raped, put down her suitcase, threw off her coat and clothes, took a shower and didn't tell anyone for twenty-five years. "My mother thought I was safe at Champlain. She would have felt so guilty."

In the year 2000, as a single mother who hadn't dated for ten years, she decided to finally unburden herself of a secret that, she felt, had profoundly damaged her subsequent relations with men. Seated awkwardly on her kitchen counter, with the words tumbling out, she told a new lover what had happened to her. "The first thing he said was, 'It's not your fault.'" She was amazed to feel so liberated from the years-long burden of belief: that she'd fucked up, attracting the devil in the cold darkness by hitchhiking, justifying her hovering mother's worry, validating an older sister's sense that she was scattered and naive.

Although she increasingly sees herself as a survivor rather than a victim, for years she had nightmares about finding herself outside the dining hall at Champlain College, running across the unlit Reid Street bridge and through the arches toward the last departing shuttle, its red tail lights blinking, "crying and screaming: 'I'll have to hitchhike again!'"

It was in this period of the late seventies and early eighties that a male editorialist at one of the local papers warned about a young woman who'd narrowly escaped abduction from Queen Street, the main strip running a few short blocks through Lennoxville from the campus to the one-lane county road heading south toward Compton. "We may live in a small community," Robert Palmer wrote in January 1983, "but an incident early Tuesday morning shows we're not immune to the realities of city life."

In fact, darker realities had coursed through this small community for years, but there was likely a gender divide in awareness, as one supposes there ever has been. Boys in postwar North America played endless games in ample yards of Cops and Robbers, not Cops and Rapists. On January 23, 1980, the *Sherbrooke Record* ran an article headlined "It Was Busy Year for Coaticook QPF" [Quebec Police Force was the English name for the Sûreté du Québec]. The eighteen-man regional force, covering 2,500 square kilometres down to the US border, filed a year-end report describing robberies, break and enters, and acts of vandalism without mentioning a single sexual assault, either attempted or completed. That same year, the Lennoxville police were reported in the paper as having investigated "54 common thefts, six car thefts, three motorcycle thefts, four bicycle thefts and 10 cases of fraud." After all these, at least in the paper's listing, came six indecent assaults and two obscene phone calls. This was the year-end report for 1979, when Theresa's body was found, bruised and stripped nearly naked.

For men—for male reporters and male police officers—theft of property was long considered the main threat posed by criminals. The preferential focus on robbers stems back to the very origin of modern policing, which evolved in England and France in the eighteenth century as a response to the merchant class's need to protect wealth, goods and slaves without benefit of an aristocracy's liveried guard. There was never a human rights frame around police work. Safeguarding vulnerable people was the purview of religious orders, patriarchs and social justice crusaders.

An apt illustration of how Quebec police still leaned more toward securing property than sheltering lives could be found in the 1972 murder of a teenager named Ursula Schulze. It was early morning on July 13 in the Montreal suburb of Brossard. Schulze, an eighteen-year-old so shy that her parents had urged her to take a summer job to meet more people, was wending her way from home to collect her first paycheque when a man abducted her. Morning commuters watched the event—from their own vehicles, from the sidewalk—as if a surreal horror film was suddenly being projected into the placid summer street. A "dull red" car, perhaps a Datsun or Toyota, according to the witnesses, drove slowly behind the unaware girl, then parked haphazardly in the road behind her. Its driver, described by witnesses as stocky, dark-haired, middle-aged or a bit younger, got out and lunged for Schulze with all the power and abruptness of a crocodile attacking from a river.

"The girl just had time to turn her head," one witness told the press, "when the guy rushed and grabbed her with his right arm. The thing I remember most about the man," this witness continued, "was his large hand. He just gripped the girl by the arm and yanked her into the car." Once stashed inside, likely in dazed shock, Ursula was subdued somehow, perhaps by a heavy fist knocking her out. Witnesses saw the man's rear end jutting out from the back seat as he went about his implacable business of predation. Then he closed the door, with Ursula no longer visible, walked around to the driver's side and headed off. "He stayed on the service road as far as I know," someone said, "because I didn't see him take the entrance to the highway."

Did no Samaritan give chase? Did no one call the police? We know that a restaurant owner across the street from the Schulze home immediately phoned the family, having seen what happened, and by lunch hour, frantic father Otto Schulze and his other daughter arrived at the Brossard police station with tremblingly assembled pictures of his missing child. A duty officer "told me to place the pictures on [Assistant Director Paul Émile] Blain's desk," Otto later said. "He said Blain had no time for that right now because he had a more important job to do . . . that he had a tip on something."

For his part, the duty officer ordered no roadblocks or highway searches and failed to call the Sûreté du Québec. Blain and his colleagues spent the day chasing leads on a robbery. Someone finally got around to questioning the Schulzes at 11:30 p.m. that night, fifteen hours after Ursula had been grabbed in view of multiple witnesses. By then, she was dead.

Her body was found by a trucker the following afternoon, tossed like litter against the wall of an abandoned soap factory about twenty-five kilometres away. No arrest was made. Her brother Dan now recalls that, at some point, his parents heard that the police knew who the suspect was, but didn't pursue it because he was connected to "some politician or celebrity."

At an inquiry held a year later into the breathtaking magnitude of this collective act of policing negligence, the Brossard force director, Marcel Renault, stood accused by commissioners of "learning nothing" from what happened, even in its aftermath. No new procedures for cooperation between police forces (in this case Brossard and the SQ, who could have set up roadblocks for the suspected vehicle but weren't informed for nineteen hours) had been put into place. "The off-handed manner of force superiors, coupled with the ignorance of force members on procedures and how to use regional communications systems, severely hampered the investigation," the commission concluded. The Schulze family sued. But there is no evidence that Quebec law enforcement shifted its priorities. The cops still wanted to chase robbers.

Obviously, for girls and women, the daily menace arose from different quarters. They didn't need the police to keep their bicycles and briefcases from being stolen, although that would be nice. But they really did need them to ward off the prospect that they would be stolen themselves.

One week after a ten-year-old Sherbrooke girl disappeared off the street in January 1978—which was, in turn, one day after a Lennoxville woman sought medical attention for a beating and attempted abduction that the police chose to ignore—a female reporter from *The Touchstone*, the Champlain College student newspaper, raised the alarm:

> A Champlain student was the victim of an assault and attempted rape two weeks ago. The thing that makes matters worse is that the local police are doing almost nothing about the incidents. Other similar incidents have been known to occur over the past few weeks. The description the girls gave of the unidentified assailant was basically the same—young man wearing jeans and a green parka. One girl reported to *Touchstone* that she was accosted by a man standing about 5'4" with a beard and curly black hair. . . .

One Champlain student says that she used to walk to Lennoxville from campus, but now gets rides from friends. "I find that I look at every stranger as a potential attacker," states a girl who has been bothered by an unknown man in the vicinity of Lennoxville.

The women's anxiety was made worse by the forbidding darkness of the Champlain campus, where lights had either never been strung or had stopped working and lapsed into disrepair. The report continued: "From Reid Street to campus (across the bridge) it's completely dark. You couldn't see anyone even if they were there. 'I feel pretty scared and nervous crossing the bridge. Safety comes in numbers,' says one girl."

Contacted by the Bishop's student newspaper, *The Campus*, the Lennoxville police "indicated that there is no case and that everyone was making a mountain out of a molehill." Whatever they thought the molehill was, four days later, *The Campus* ran another story: "Police Ignore Assault Victim." The *Sherbrooke Record* ran a story too, on the front page: "Attempted Rape Unprobed."

On February 10, 1978, student journalist Carolyn Rowell penned a story about how a Champlain student, cited only as Jane Doe, was walking alone in late January at one thirty in the morning on Rue Bel-Horizon at Queen Street, across from the Lennoxville Post Office, when a young white man, about five foot four, in blue jeans and a green parka, leapt out from the shadows and grabbed her purse. When she resisted, he pinned her to the ground. Unable to free her hands, she bit him on the chin. He responded by smashing her in the head with a board and beginning to tear at her coat. A neighbour, woken by her protesting screams, turned on their porch light, and the man fled.

Jane Doe went to the hospital, where she received stitches for her gashed face. The doctor told her to report the attack to the Lennoxville police; he even phoned them to say the young woman would be coming in. When she arrived, however, at the nine-man detachment, no one was there. Later that day, when Bishop's University nurse Sue Turner checked Jane Doe's stitches, the nurse told her there had been another incident of sexual assault—perhaps referring to a woman she'd treated—and that she should go back to the police. Jane Doe called the station, and the officer she spoke to "seemed to have heard about the guy before. When I was giving the description, he was able to fill in pieces of information which I had not yet told him. For example, I told him he was wearing blue jeans, and the officer asked me, 'Was he wearing a green parka?' He was."

Jane Doe wasn't asked to write a statement. She was told she would be contacted if any leads developed. No one followed up. Two days later, when Carolyn Rowell phoned the Lennoxville police, they denied that Jane Doe had ever filed a complaint. A week after that, Jane Doe, according to Rowell, "gave another report to two officers whom she met in a local restaurant. These officers expressed surprise when she asked them if anything had been done in her case as they had never heard of the attack before. To further the woman's feelings that her story was being ignored, she found that in talking to a Lennoxville police sergeant a few days ago, this sergeant [also] knew nothing about the case, and in her opinion, didn't care to know about it."

The same day that Rowell wrote her article for *The Campus*, the *Sherbrooke Record* reported that "For more than a month, rumours of attempted rape, assault and indecent exposure have circulated throughout the town, but police spokesmen have refused to confirm or deny the reports." On February 14, coincidentally or not, Lennoxville's town council asked the town police chief, Kasimir Kryslak, to retire.

What were they thinking, this small squad of cops, like a gang out of *Fargo* with their insulated boots and muffling hats, blowing in and out of the office with steaming cups of coffee and cigarettes? Did they figure that women who described the same assailant—"a green parka"—had just gossiped at a slumber party and spooked themselves, like tweens whispering about the Candy Man? "Hey boss," I imagine the cop who took the January 26 assault complainant's call saying, "we got another one of those girls." Nervous, excitable girls!

"Ah, just ignore it. They'll calm down."

A female student wrote an editorial in *The Touchstone* on Thursday, February 8. "Will someone have to get raped before the police will stop shrugging off the problem and start trying to solve [it]? Maybe when they stop polishing their badges and start looking into these complaints then the situation wouldn't even develop into a problem."

Of course, the rapes had already happened by then. "There has been as many as eight rapes in Lennoxville in the past year," the *Record* reported, "a few involving hitchhikers." For the Lennoxville police, those would be examples of the mountain, submerged by women under waves of shame and pain, that they were making into molehills in the winter of 1978.

Rape culture is so often referred to now that we may forget what it looked like when it didn't have a moniker. It was in 1975 that the American journalist Susan Brownmiller published her land-mark book *Against Our Will: Men, Women and Rape,* spelling out on behalf of women everywhere that rape happened com-monly, that it was a commission of violence and that society needed to completely rethink how it treated its victims. Hers was only the first salvo in what would become a decades-long war of attrition against traditional views on sexual victimiza-tion. As she was working on the book, Brownmiller wrote:

> I was invited to address a seminar for police lieutenants training for promotion to captain at the New York Police Academy. I spoke about rape and was met with a chortle of hoots and laughter from the thirty assembled men. "Honey, you don't believe there is such a thing as rape, do you?" a lieutenant called out.
>
> "Don't you?"
>
> "Nooo" came the nearly unanimous response.

Brownmiller discovered a reassuring passage for cops in a police manual:

> "Forcible rape is one of the most falsely reported crimes," a California police manual, *Patrol Procedure,* begins its instruction. "The majority of 'second day reported' rapes are not legitimate." Chatty and chummy, *Patrol Procedure* warns the cop on the beat that rape calls often result when a husband leaves town on busi-ness and a wife takes the opportunity "to go out on the town," with later remorse. "These situations must be delicately handled," the manual advises.

Another "common scenario" officers-in-training learned about in the sixties and seventies was of a sex worker claiming rape because she didn't get paid. And that was pretty much it: wily wives and pissed-off sex workers. "From the 1970s onward," historian Joanna Bourke wrote more recently, "it was common for the police to profess that one in every five women reporting rape was making an unfounded claim." But the most comprehensive study, conducted in the United Kingdom by the Home Office in 2005, found that just under 3 percent of allegations could be categorized as false, which is precisely the same percentage as for other felony crimes.

Where did this vacuum of real knowledge about sexual violence arise from? Were men really that naive about the behaviour of other men? Or did they not want to know because it was too uncomfortable, too close to a home base the culture had built for them? Certainly, in law enforcement, the culture was completely skewed against female realities: "Because the police are accustomed to working in an innately violent context, many have a very different idea of what constitutes force or violence," a report on police attitudes toward rape noted in 1976. "Being accustomed to weapons, they are less intimidated by them. They are less susceptible to psychological aggression; less attuned to subtle intimidation. Many hold inherently violent attitudes to sexuality." It's hard to summon a more striking illustration of this than the back page cartoon published in Quebec tabloid *Photo Police* in the late seventies that depicted a woman with her back against a wall lifting up her skirt to reveal her naked crotch, which she was thrusting forward as a giddy cop rushed toward her, wielding his phallic baton.

In fairness to young police officers, though, one could argue that they were inheriting a male narrative about female sexuality that dated back centuries, if not millennia, and that got codified anew by medical authorities in the late nineteenth century. "In the 1890s," wrote cultural historian Bourke, "the authors of the text-book *Medical Jurisprudence, Forensic Medicine, and Toxicology* . . . noted that the 'Majority of writers' agreed that 'a fully matured woman, in full possession of her faculties, cannot be raped, contrary to her desire, by a single man.'" Why not? Well, according to a paper published by the respected journal *International Clinics* in 1913, the "mere crossing of the knees absolutely prevents penetration" because "taking into consideration the tremendous power of the pelvic and abductor thigh muscles . . . a man must struggle desperately to penetrate the vagina of a vigorous, virtue-protecting girl." This view was not considered archaic by the 1970s; on the contrary, it was supported in 1973 by the Lawyers Co-Operative Publishing Company in a book called *Crimes of Violence*. Rape, the male authors decreed, was almost literally impossible when women deployed their "hands, limbs and pelvic muscles."

With medical experts asserting this claim, it fell to further male experts to explain why it was, then, that women persisted in making false allegations about an apparently impossible crime. The influential forensic evidence expert John Henry Wigmore would have advised most young police officers who studied his texts at the academy that "Modern psychiatrists have amply studied the behaviour of errant young girls and women coming before the courts in all sorts of cases. Their psychic complexes are multifarious, distorted partly by inherent defects." Behold the tricky female specimen! Or, as the view of such experts was expressed in 1928, women who had the temerity to report rape, according to the president of the medical board and chief of the Department of Genito-Urinary Disease and Dermatology at Bronx Hospital, were "hysterical, psychopathic, notoriety-seeking or simply vicious."

If you claimed rape and no one could be convinced that you had the temperament of a honey badger, then a whole other set of male experts could be relied upon to concede that it might have happened after all, but it was your fault. The director of scientific research at Sing Sing Prison in New York noted in *The Psychology of Crime* (1960) that "the victim herself unconsciously also may tempt the offender. . . . Often a woman unconsciously wishes to be taken by force. . . . We sometimes find this seductive inclination even in young girls."

If you *didn't* secretly want to be raped by some random, malodorous felon, then another possibility was that you were stupid. The author of *Cry Rape: Anatomy of the Rapist* (1967) asserted that "many women who work in isolated areas and keep late hours are not more cautious in their goings and comings and will often shun public transportation in favour of walking along lonely, dark streets. If we may speak of the 'accident-prone' individual, we must surely regard such behaviours as 'rape-prone.'"

A mere two years after this view was so assuredly articulated, the 1969 US National Commission on the Causes and Prevention of Violence found that, while 22 percent of murders showed "discernible signs of victim precipitation," such as men piling into a gang fight that led to one of their deaths, only

4 percent of violent rapes did. In other words, 96 percent of women who were raped did nothing—took no risk—that significantly increased their exposure to the calamity that overtook them. And yet the myths persisted as long as men remained the experts. Rape is impossible, or it's rare, or it's invited, or women are too witless to look after themselves. In Catholic Quebec, this miasma of beliefs was likely solidified on some deeply unconscious level by the equation of female sexuality with sin. Just as some of Ireland's Catholic nuns behaved with stunning cruelty toward unwed mothers and their infants, arguably despising them for the inherent sinfulness of their association with sexual lust, so one gets the sense that Quebec in the 1960s and '70s was unable to perceive sexualized victims as any kind of victims at all.

As Joanna Bourke argued, in the era after the birth control pill became widely available, with "anxieties about permissiveness growing, the denigration of 'no-good girls' and the claim that rape victims had 'asked for it' became particularly shrill. Was it any surprise that the increasing candour, if not sensual abandonment, of young women might be construed as invitations to sexual intercourse, some people asked?" The idea persists even to this day that if women are sexual at all, they are, surely, willing to have sex with *anyone*. In the 1970s, all of these assumptions, prejudices and anxieties created a social atmosphere that was made all the more chaotic by an altered landscape of transportation and freedom of movement. Cars were a particular problem. Cars, bars, highways, hitchhiking.

"In recent years, rape and other crimes of violence have been reported with increasing frequency at formerly protected citadels like the college campus," Brownmiller noted in 1975, adding dorms to the geography of sexual assault. Thirty-five years later, Bourke would be able to look back at what Brownmiller was observing and concur: "The broad trend seems to be high levels of rape in the early-modern period, which dipped significantly in the period of the mid-nineteenth century. Rape rates then rose steadily from around the 1910s, with the exception of the 1930s and 1950s (where they stabilized and even dropped). From the mid-1960s, rape did not simply rise: it soared."

As young women saw and experienced this rise, they still contended with a masculine establishment—male cops and reporters—that didn't recognize what was threatening them at all.

On the morning of November 3, 1978, early in the day that Theresa disappeared, the Bishop's student newspaper published an edition featuring a poem written under a pseudonym. It was unusual for them. They were a newspaper, not a literary journal. The synchronicity of this poem appearing on that day is almost astounding, and yet it is also of a piece, at that time, in those years, with young women trying to give voice to their distress while the powers that be failed to listen:

> GRACE
> Understanding
> Or questioning,
> Looking up into ugliness,
> Looking straight across

At yourself.

I speak, hoping

Someone will answer.

I remember

That things happened because they happened

And never because

Of a reason.

Why we continue

Is beyond me,

Appearing at breakfast,

Appearing at dinner,

The light ascending,

At evening someone will take a stick

And destroy all life;

Someone will take a scarf

To strangle all sound.

Violence boils in the garden;

We pray for darkness

Going down on our knees

In wonder at our own passivity,

Calling for weakness

Of the old days,

Calling for strength.

THREE

WHISPER GAMES

"When mores are sufficient, laws are unnecessary;
when mores are insufficient, laws are unenforceable."
—Émile Durkheim

In the fall of 1978, with her parents settled into their new home in Saint John, New Brunswick, Theresa moved in at Champlain College. A new residence being built closer to campus than King's Hall had fallen behind schedule, and Champlain staff had announced that they would have to "run Compton again." Student editors at *The Touchstone* were aghast. "I was enraged," one wrote, "by the smug way in which the fates of two hundred more new students were so easily dispatched." For the fall term, the students would have two staff members on site: a twenty-five-year-old named Jeanne Eddisford and a former elementary school principal named Stewart Peacock. Both of them slept in King's Hall. Neither inhabited Gillard House, the squat brick coed dormitory next door, which was where Theresa was assigned. No one conducted room checks, although many of the kids were the same age as boarding school seniors. The students were encouraged to make their own meals and to be as independent as possible.

"For most boys and girls, it's their first time away from home," one Compton resident told *The Touchstone*. "There are no restrictions, no curfews, and especially no parents. They go wild." It's hard to know exactly what this meant, but there would have been plenty of beer and pot to go around. The youthful giddiness of her fellow students appears to have made Theresa uncomfortable. She was a little older, at an age when increments of years can seem like a chasm. She had already lived on her own, already travelled with her boyfriend. One of her best friends in Montreal, Haidi Muller, was a mother. Whooping it up at dorm parties wasn't her thing. "Do you still feel out of place social-wise at college?" Vlad asked her in a letter he mailed from the Rockies in late October. "If you do, don't let it get you down. It sometimes takes people a little extra time to get their shit together. Hell, look at me." He joked about how high he had gotten at a Halloween party.

Theresa focused on what interested her, which was her courses at Champlain and trips back to visit her close circle of friends in Montreal. One day in early October, a palm reader set up a table in the Golden Lion Pub, the students' favourite watering hole along Lennoxville's Queen Street. Ever curious, Theresa sat down with the man and offered her hand. Gazing at the whorls and seams of her palm, he said that she came from a very close family, but something was soon to happen that would rupture their sense of peace. Skeptical but slightly unsettled, Theresa relayed this prophesy to Andre. Then the pair of siblings flew from Montreal to Saint John to celebrate Thanksgiving and toast her nineteenth birthday.

On the day she and Andre were to return to school, a fog rolled in from the Bay of Fundy. Marilyn remembers their flight being cancelled. "So we said, 'Hooray! We can all have one more meal together.' It was a really happy time." But when the weather remained too inclement for airplanes, she and Bob eventually drove their kids to the train station. Both were anxious to get back to school for the mid-term exams.

"I remember there was a billboard in the train station advertising Mexico," Marilyn told me, "and I said to Theresa, 'Whatever you do, do not run off to Mexico. Because you can get arrested for drugs there and that kind of thing.' I remember that." She paused, reflecting. "And I remember that Theresa kept getting off the train. She must have come off that train five times, to hug us goodbye."

"Was that unusual for her?"

"Very." She chuckled. "I remember going home and feeling really happy, and yet thinking something wasn't right. It's hard to explain. I was standing at the kitchen sink, looking out the window, and I just had the feeling, that feeling of happiness, and the sense that something was about to change."

Of course she remembers those details: the fog, the billboard, the goodbyes, the fleetingness of joy—everything—because it was the last time she saw her daughter alive.

After the mid-terms, Theresa got her first report card on October 24. She had pulled off nineties in her science courses, with an overall average of eighty-three. On Sunday, October 29, she ate dinner at King's Hall, where she chatted with the young staffer Jeanne Eddisford about the hiking trip they'd both enjoyed the day before at Mont-Orford, a ski resort between the Laurentians and the Appalachians near the town of Magog. Between 7:00 and 7:30 p.m., as such things are meticulously timed in the aftermath of a disappearance, Theresa dropped into Compton's sole restaurant, Entre-Deux, and bought a pack of Player's Light cigarettes from the vending machine. She handed out a few to fellow students and then walked back toward King's Hall. She must then have hitchhiked in the dark to Montreal, because she arrived at her girlfriend Joey Nice's place at around ten p.m. that night.

(I find myself struck by the physical confidence and expansiveness of someone who could just decide to hitch two hours northwest on a dark fall evening. But little seems to have daunted Theresa. She had skydived. She had cycled for dozens of kilometres. Once, according to her friend Debbie, she turned down a lift from a driver who wanted to show her his penis. She deadpanned that she'd already seen one. Later, her friend Caroline would comment, "She had an intelligent attitude toward most things—very wise. Except when it became a question of her own independence. She didn't realize how dangerous hitchhiking was, obviously." When you grow up loved, you assume that you move through a loving world.)

In Montreal that night, Theresa told Joey about learning a meditation exercise in her psychology class, which she'd found fascinating. She slept over on her old friend's couch and returned to Lennoxville the next morning for a full week of classes.

On Wednesday, there was a birthday party for Andre at the Golden Lion. He was now eighteen, the legal drinking age in Quebec. Pint glasses of beer clinked. Onward into adulthood!

Friday, November 3, was gloriously mild for late autumn in the Eastern Townships. Theresa left her room on the second floor of Gillard House early that morning and walked across the lawn wearing a long beige sweater-coat, a pair of Chinese slippers with no socks, and a flowing green scarf that her mother had given her for her birthday. She joined a couple of friends she'd gotten to know at King's Hall, Jo-Anne Laurie and Caroline Greenwood, in the dorm's pretty dining room. Sun streamed through the French doors. She made herself toast, perhaps, or scrambled eggs. The girls rolled their eyes at the AM radio music being piped into the room: it was like eating breakfast in a mall. Caroline half-listened, but was cramming for a calculus test. The trio then caught the shuttle and disembarked near the Johnston Building at Champlain for their morning science classes. "I asked her what she was going to do for the weekend," Jo-Anne later told the police, "and she said she had to finish some work, mainly her humanities."

Jo-Anne saw Theresa at lunch, and the pair walked together to the edge of campus so that Jo-Anne could connect with a friend she was planning to hitchhike to Montreal with. "That's the last time I saw her—Friday, just before one p.m."

On that sunny afternoon on the college grounds, as the maple trees shed their last burnished leaves, it is possible that Theresa read the Bishop's University student paper while she waited for another class to begin. Perhaps she saw this editorial:

Last year when *The Campus* investigated the problem of sexual assault in Lennoxville it was suggested that we were making "a mountain out of a mole hill." The basic freedom to go about our lives without fearing every shadow and without having our dignities insulted is no mole hill. The incidents of sexual harassment that have occurred on this campus in the past few weeks are infuriating to say the least. . . . It can be argued that being smaller and "weaker" than men makes us easy targets. How does that explain the weirdo in the Union hallway Saturday morning who was much shorter than the woman that he tried to frighten? . . . No one has been physically hurt (as yet), but that does not mean no one will be.

Did Theresa read that? Or the poem "Grace"?

At six, as dusk fell, Theresa was finishing up supper in Dewhurst Dining Hall when she ran into another pair of dormitory acquaintances, Josie Stapenhorst and Suzanne DeRome. The young women agreed to meet up at Gillard House that night around nine p.m. to listen to new records. Genesis, maybe, or the Alan Parsons Project. "As I was sitting on the 6:15 bus, waiting for it to leave Dewhurst to go back to Compton," Josie later told the police, "I vaguely remember seeing Theresa leaving Dewhurst on foot, walking beside the bus. I never saw her again." Could she have been heading to the university library to spend a couple of hours working on her book report? The dust jacket of *Zen Mind, Beginner's Mind* was later found among her things, but not the book itself. A student named Sharon Buzzee was certain she had seen Theresa in King's Hall residence that night at around nine, heading up or down the main staircase. Buzzee asked her why she hadn't left town for the weekend, and Theresa told her she had too much homework.

Did Theresa descend once again, walk through the vestibule and go out onto the lawn? Did she return to her room in Gillard House? Or head the other way, walk down the circular driveway and set off along Highway 147 toward Compton village to buy a new pack of cigarettes? These questions bob up and down in the mind like horses on a carousel; they never still.

In 2002, Marilyn Allore walked from King's Hall along the gravelled side of the highway between canopies of maple and elm until she picked up the sidewalk in Compton, passing the faded clapboard houses, the handful of stores, walking along in silence, wordlessly retracing a possible route that her daughter took in her little Chinese slippers, sporting that long, flowing scarf like Isadora Duncan, before vanishing thereafter into darkness.

Champlain College, it appears, did not notice for over a week that one of its students was missing. Theresa's friends began to worry much sooner. They returned from their respective weekend adventures and knocked on her door to gossip, only to find her absent. None of them raised an alarm. "Theresa didn't need anyone to worry about her," Caroline Greenwood later stated. They didn't wish to seem nosy or neurotic.

"Monday," said Jo-Anne, "she wasn't around and I asked if anyone had seen her. No one had. I just assumed she had decided to go to Montreal and maybe slacked off a day. Tuesday morning, when she still didn't show up, we got worried." But they hesitated. On Wednesday, there was still no Terry, as they called her, in the halls of Gillard. Speculation arose that she'd gone to visit her boyfriend out West. They decided to check Theresa's room, where nothing seemed to be missing. If she had gone to Calgary to visit Vlad, would she not have packed her suitcase and taken her hiking boots, both of which were neatly stored in the dorm room? As teens tend to do, they kept the drama of their concern to themselves.

On Thursday, Jo-Anne checked the long row of orange metal lockers at Champlain to see what hints might be found. "I knew Theresa's combination," she explained. She and her boyfriend, Ian Catterill, found some course notebooks on the floor of the locker, a brush and some papers on the top shelf. Her purse, which she kept in the locker during the school day, was gone. There was nothing much to glean from this, although months later the fact that Jo-Anne and Ian had searched the locker would flare briefly into wild significance.

Aside from the obvious question of a missing student's whereabouts, the question nobody seems to have asked was why it would be up to this handful of kids to be searching on their own. On November 7, the campus newspaper ran a story headlined: "Compton Confusion." The article was a withering refutation of an interview that Stewart Peacock, head of resi-dence, had given, in which he talked about how much he enjoyed working with young people. "This statement did not go over too well with the students at Compton," the paper reported tartly. "Authorities at Compton have said that Peacock does not attend Residence Assistant meetings on a regular basis, had nothing to do with the gong show, and is very seldom seen at Gillard House, of which he is the newly appointed director." Students, the article said, "do not believe he is fulfilling his responsibilities as an administrator."

Certainly, Theresa's friends didn't seem to think they could reach out to the grown-ups around them for guidance. Without experienced adult judgment to aid them, they floundered for days with their rising sense of alarm. Finally, early on Friday, November 10, Caroline plucked up the nerve to phone Theresa's close friend from high school, Haidi Muller, in Montreal. Muller, who herself had started worrying about not hearing from Theresa, immediately impressed upon Caroline that their mutual friend, whom she'd known for years, was simply not the type of person to wander away without telling anyone. She was too responsible for that. Something must have happened. "Tell Andre to call his parents right away."

Vlad Kulich was working that fall at a ski resort on Fortress Mountain, about ninety minutes west of Calgary in the Rockies. On November 10, he got a call in the resort office.

"Hi, Vlad? It's Bob. Is Theresa with you?"

"The moment he said that, I got a chill," Vlad recalled some forty years later from his home in Los Angeles. "I was working with this boss named John West. He was a tough guy, a totally macho character. Pretty much John Wayne. I remember knocking on his door at five in the morning and telling him that I was going to drive down to Calgary. 'My girlfriend's disappeared.' And he just completely shifted—so much compassion. When I got on the plane in Calgary, I knew she was gone. I just knew she was dead. But you still act with hope."

After the crushing realization that Theresa hadn't gone out West to see Vlad, the Allores drove to the Saint John office of the RCMP. "The officer there was sort of ignoring me," Marilyn said, "until I lost my temper, at which point he took notice and began writing down what I had to say about my daughter being a good student, of good character, who wouldn't just 'go missing.' He said, 'I'm afraid you're heading for a lot of trouble in Quebec. You will get no help there.'"

From anyone, really, he might well have said.

One person remained in this constellation of loving souls who still thought the world stood on its axis. It was Remembrance Day weekend, and fourteen-year-old John had his part to play as the drummer in the cadet parade at his school, Rothesay Collegiate, outside Saint John, where I would meet him as a boarder the following autumn. "We all marched around the school square and went into the chapel for a service," he remembered. "My parents drove us back to Leinster Street in the late morning, and I was in my bedroom, hanging up my cadet uniform, when they told me Theresa was missing." By that evening, they were at Motel la Paysanne in Lennoxville, a ten-hour drive from Saint John.

The Allores would spend the ensuing days at the Paysanne on Queen Street, a small white motel with red doors and a faux–Swiss chalet dining room serving instant coffee and toast with plastic packets of jelly. It was a block or two down the forested road from the Golden Lion Pub, where Andre had recently celebrated his birthday. John either watched TV in the room or sat blankly in hallways outside tense meetings at Champlain College. Looking back, he cannot locate himself in all this. "I don't know where I was. The only thing I remember is coming out one night at dusk and looking into the Quebec interior, because the motel faced west toward a sea of evergreens and that purple light of autumn evening, and just this profound feeling of helplessness. *She's out there, and there is not a thing I can do.* I remember that colour of sky. It's curious, because I asked my dad recently about that week and how they felt. Wasn't it overwhelming? And he said, 'I just felt so confused. All I could focus on was the idea, *Theresa: she's out there.*'"

But where?

FOUR

THE DRUG THEORY

"A dreamer, I walked enchanted, and nothing held me back."
—Daphne du Maurier

WHEN THE ALLORES ARRIVED IN LENNOXVILLE, THEY WENT AT once to those in a position to help with their missing daughter: the college and the local police. Bob kept a diary of the encounters, to track any salient details that would help with the search.

Thursday, November 16
Office of Champlain College Director William Matson
3:30 p.m.

Dr. Matson gave me a theory that Theresa may have had lesbian tendencies. (No boyfriends on campus, friends with a 30-year-old woman with two children, etc.)

Was Matson referring to Haidi, who was Theresa's age, a young mother? Bob no longer recalls. But the insinuation was that their relationship was deviant. Matson then "said he would come to motel to talk to my wife and myself around 5:00 p.m. If we wanted to talk about it, I was to ask him to sit down. If not, he would just say hello and leave."

As if the matter were unseemly, and one had to use discretion when speaking of it.

Campus director William Matson, a nondescript middle-aged man with hair receding at his temples, arrived at the motel around five and repeated his theory. Further, he said Theresa, if found, would need psychiatric treatment, by court order if necessary. The Allores just stared at him, dumbfounded. Perhaps to break an awkward silence, Matson then asked if Theresa was an adopted child. They shook their heads. Theresa may have gone somewhere, he now advised them, "where disturbed people go, or worse, she may be dead in a ditch somewhere." But he was more optimistic about the former than the latter. He suggested they go back home, "get back to normal, and wait for something to happen."

This was Champlain College's response to the urgent crisis of their missing daughter?

Bob followed Matson into the motel parking lot. He asked the campus director to expand on what he'd said. Was this an actual place, this place "where disturbed people go," or some strange insinuation? Matson replied that his secretary had received an anonymous phone call "from someone who knows about troubled people and where they go, and this person had said that a person meeting the description of Theresa had gone to this place where disturbed or troubled people go in the area." The assertion was so maddeningly vague it was ridiculous. Matson offered nothing further and ducked into his car.

It is difficult enough to hold the terror, moment by moment, of your child's disappearance. To process such surreal indifference on top of that was almost more than the Allores could manage. "Our feeling," Bob noted down, keeping things terse and analytical, "was that 1) he was trying to get rid of us or send us home with hope or ease with this 'anonymous caller' theory, or 2) he was trying to put us on the defensive with the lesbian theory."

Stewart Peacock, the director of residence, never made himself known to the Allores at all, much less available to help. The college comptroller, Jean-Luc Grégoire, continued to bill them for tuition and board, with interest and penalties accruing. Theresa's disappearance wasn't reported in the student newspaper, *The Campus*—"informing Bishop's since 1944"—until November 24, nearly two weeks later, when Lennoxville police chief Leo Hamel called her vanishing "quite a puzzle." No search of the fields, no call-out for information.

"The school just didn't do . . . anything," Marilyn told me in a tone of quiet wonderment. "Our friends were shocked. She just disappeared. Just out of the blue; nobody seemed to know. Can you understand that, Patricia? A school not asking questions, why a student is not in her classroom, why is she not in her bed? How can you have dorms with no supervision, for people of that age? Bob went to Loyola College in Montreal when it was Jesuit-run. And the father used to sit at the front door and check everybody off as they came in. He was paying attention. If you're smoking, he's going to smell it; if you're drinking, he's going to smell it. There was an adult on every floor. I thought that when you went to school, that's what it was. Children are involved. I said, '*What the hell is going on?*'"

Meanwhile, as the young women of the area could have warned the Allore family, local law enforcement wasn't much interested in finding Theresa either, at least not at first blush. "We went to some police officer," said Vlad, who had arrived from Calgary, "and right away he was a standoffish prick. He suggested that Theresa was a prostitute. I didn't realize how much I was in love with her maybe until that moment. I remember saying to the cop, 'Do your fucking job.' Bob tried to settle me down, took me for a walk."

Adding to his disorientation, Vlad remembers walking into a common area at King's Hall on November 18 to find students gathered in stunned silence, watching the news about Jonestown, where more than nine hundred American followers of cult leader Jim Jones had murdered themselves with poisoned Kool-Aid in the Guyanese jungle. The world was going mad.

Where was the leadership? "We were sitting in the police station," Marilyn said, "and I got upset because I could see that they were bullshitting, and I didn't like it. I went out in the hall, I was leaving, and Bob followed me. I said, 'We're getting out of here, because they're not doing anything. I'm going to see [then prime minister] Pierre Trudeau.'" At this memory, she now laughs. But really, the impulse was to reach out to someone in authority who could be trusted to be guiding and sympathetic, not indifferent and derisive. It was a nightmare within a nightmare for this small-town Canadian family who'd always placed faith in the goodness of authority. They were at a loss. "Vlad said to Bob, 'We're on our own here.'" And he was right.

Andre, as it happened, was dating a student whose father was an affluent businessman in Montreal. Hearing of the Allores' predicament, he sent his head of security to help. The man helped Marilyn search through her daughter's dorm room. "He had me put my hand into all of her records to see if there was anything. There was nothing. Her bed was made, her closet was neat as a pin, and all her dirty clothes were in a bag, ready to take to laundry."

Bob went door to door to all of the area farms and homes, showing his daughter's picture. It was a photo booth snapshot he'd likely found in her dorm room, depicting her recent frizzy perm. Her expression is goofy; she was probably hamming it up with a friend. Cropped a certain way, as the newspaper tabloid *Le Journal de Montréal* would publish it several weeks later, the photo makes her look slightly crazed. ("My parents," John said, "were not happy with what they called the 'unfortunate tone' of the missing person circular that Chief Leo Hamel eventually distributed in late December.") How do you suddenly present this beloved person, this vivid, multi-faceted young woman to a world of bemused strangers in a flat, unflattering black-and-white shot? What do they perceive? What do they invest in or react to in what they see? Public relations and marketing experts have reaped billions over this question, but have likely never considered it in the context of missing person flyers.

Vlad, meanwhile, drove to some nunneries around Montreal on the faintest chance that she'd gotten pregnant and gone into seclusion. But she *had* been raised Catholic. There was a Buddhist temple in the area that the police had been surveilling as a possible cult. Could she have gone there? The possibilities were infinite. Bob wrote in his diary, "Moonies?" At another point he asked himself, "Did Theresa go to Vermont? Is she still there? She loved Vermont. Don't look for reason 'why' with this generation. Answer is 'to find myself.'" Chief Hamel took the picture of Theresa to show border guards in Vermont.

"Stories started to circulate," recalled Andre. A runaway turned up at a monastery: maybe it was Theresa. Someone saw a redhead with a scar under her right eye in such-and-such a bar. Someone swore they saw her on Halloween, saying that she was planning to leave, that she wouldn't tell anyone. Whether any of these narrative turns fit with what the family actually knew about Theresa didn't matter anymore. "There were these little moments of hope," Andre said. "You latch onto them."

Friday, November 17
4:30 p.m.

Went to see Leo Hamel with Vlad and Haidi. [A local man named] Les Picard and his wife arrived at Hamel's office and said someone meeting Theresa's description had been to his door in Birchton, a village some miles due east of Lennoxville, on November 7. The only thing that did not fit was the clothes she was wearing. The girl was looking for a priest to hear her prayers or take confessions. This is near Sawyerville, where there exists a community of hippy-type people—executives etc. living a health food life—[with] drug usage.

Bob didn't know what to make of these rumours. He was an engineer who'd never encountered hippies, or health food, or drugs. Vlad and Haidi went to check things out, but turned up nothing.

A brief article in the *Sherbrooke Record*, written when the Allores first arrived, led to a tip from hunters near the small town of Magog, about twenty minutes' drive southwest of Sherbrooke. On November 4, the hunters reported, they had seen a neatly folded pile of women's clothing on a tree stump in the forest. Could they belong to Theresa? They looked fresh, and cared-for, as though a woman had just gone skinny-dipping. Or forest-bathing, given that there was no pond nearby. The police chief and his deputies rounded up a sniffer dog and, as a cold rain dripped through the trees, tried to find the stump described by the hunters. Nothing. Just an echo of something else, a whispered taunt in a wide, dark wood.

"Hamel called the motel Friday morning," Bob duly noted in his diary, "to ask Marilyn if she remembered where Theresa was born." Forty years later, this still astonished her, this question. "How would I not know where she was born?" It may be that Hamel was following up on an insinuation of Matson's that Theresa was adopted, and had perhaps fled to her birth parents, but Hamel's health is now too frail for him to be interviewed. Time has softened Marilyn's perspective on the Lennoxville police chief, though: "Hamel was in way over his head." The father of two had only recently been hired by the town after a career in small-town policing. A few weeks into the search, he conceded to Bob, who wrote it down in his diary, that he had "never conducted an investigation on previous missing persons. He was visibly upset, unable to cope rather than hiding." Over the next six months, the chief's glossy black hair would turn almost entirely white.

"I do think that he felt bad, but I don't think he knew what to do," Marilyn says now, "and I think Bishop's ran the village. I don't have any proof of that. But they wanted us out of there. Because if there was an investigation at that school, that's a big deal; they could be closed right up, which they needed to be. It wasn't safe."

In late November, the Allores hired a private investigator whose name they had come across in Bob's McGill University alumni magazine. The issue had arrived in the mail when they returned briefly to their home on Leinster Street to board fourteen-year-old John at his school. (Of this time as a boarder he remembers virtually nothing, almost as if he'd blacked out from shock.) The young PI, Robert Beullac, would wind up working partly in tandem with Hamel, who needed the support. Beullac stood six foot five, wore pinstriped shirts, flashy ties and a bullet-studded gun belt. For the Allores, he must have felt like ammunition.

Bob talked to campus director William Matson and said, "I need a desk and a telephone for our private investigator." As Bob recalls, Matson thought this was too much, that the Allore family was being too intrusive and demanding. He said he couldn't be held responsible for every student on campus. Bob, a veritable role model for the global stereotype of the polite Canadian, slammed his palm against the wall. "You're responsible for absolutely everybody plus the mosquito on the *wall*! I've got 3,500 employees at a nuclear plant and I'm responsible for every damned one. So *don't give me that shit.*" He got the desk and the telephone for Robert Beullac.

As for themselves, as luck would have it, Bob's boss at the engineering firm Dominion Bridge had a farmhouse in the area, so Bob and Marilyn were able to unpack their suitcases and start a concerted search for their daughter. Their presence became a fixture in the streets: the quietly pleading parents who knocked politely on doors. "When we'd walk through the village," Marilyn told me in 2018, "there were a lot of people who lived there, in the farmhouses, who wanted to help us, but they just didn't know how."

Beullac arrived too late to organize a search of the surrounding fields, because fifty centimetres of snow had fallen since November 3. He interviewed more college students and several of Theresa's Montreal friends. He searched King's Hall and Gillard House, following Andre's logical question: What if she fell down a staircase, or a well? He questioned local residents and made enquiries at two Buddhist monasteries in Dorion and Magog, presumably on the basis that the last book Theresa had been reading for school was titled *Zen Mind, Beginner's Mind*. He also checked morgues around the province. This was a partial repetition, one assumes, of what Bob, Vlad and Leo Hamel had already done, everyone desperately trawling the Eastern Townships for elusive hints and clues.

The Sûreté du Québec, who were in a position to know and patrol this geography, were refusing to get involved without a body. (They were also immensely distracted, as we would later discover.) SQ Corporal Roch Gaudreault, who would eventually become the lead investigator in Theresa's case, wasn't anything like the novelist Louise Penny's philosophical investigator Armand Gamache. If you have that image of French-Canadian detectives in mind, toss it. This man, with his long seventies sideburns and tough, dismissive talk, was a study in machismo.

He was known to make up false witness statements to trick suspects into making confessions, and to engage in other underhanded cop-and-robber ploys (in 1980, Gaudreault would come under fire for producing false witness declarations in a 1977 Sherbrooke murder investigation). Before being assigned to the Townships, he'd worked with the Montreal SQ and handled one murder, of a woman named Carole Dupont who'd been killed in a village north of the city. Her body had been tucked behind a seniors' home, where it languished all winter. A witness predicted to Gaudreault that Dupont would be found when the snow "thawed out in the spring." Now Gaudreault told Bob there was little they could do, that the family should return to New Brunswick and wait for winter to end. Theresa's body would probably turn up when the snow melted. That comment, Bob said later, was like "a nail between the eyes."

Leafing through Bob's notebook from that time, I came upon a page where he'd jotted down what the student Sharon Buzzee had told his PI—how she had seen Theresa at King's Hall. Sharon was certain she'd run into Theresa in the hallway on the night of November 3 and talked about weekend plans. Bob's entry was dated December 4, 1978. The notation was terse: "Bottom of main stair case. One foot on bottom step. Going up." It isn't difficult, as a parent, to imagine the helpless desire to grab at that foot and pull your running child to safety. Beneath this, he added, with heart-sinking poignancy, "7:15 p.m.—Broke down."

Christmas of 1978—their first in the house on Leinster Street— was, of course, a traumatized walk-through of tree decorating and gift-wrapping, when there was only one gift they yearned for. John had never had a holiday like this; it was his first glimpse of how all the facets of life crack under the enormity of tragedy. "Emotionally, I remember trying to keep the party going," he says. "Theresa was always the gin in the juice, so I thought it was my job to keep everything elevated. I told jokes. I bought my father a shower massage gadget and forced him to dress up in a sheet with laurels like he was at a Roman toga party." (The movie *Animal House* had come out that summer, with frat boys in togas.) "I gave Andre the Rolling Stones LP *Some Girls*, and Springsteen's *Darkness on the Edge of Town* because Theresa had *Black and Blue* and *Born to Run*. I wanted to keep things moving." But it was too hard. On Christmas Eve, Bob was outside the house shovelling snow when he glanced toward the top of Leinster Street and saw a girl heading down the sidewalk toward him. She had wavy hair, wore a long sweater and carried a suitcase. He put down his shovel and strode toward her, his heart soaring. But as they drew near each other, he realized it wasn't Theresa. Later, he would say he'd never experienced so much joy and such crushing sorrow in so short a time.

Others who loved Theresa were having similar experiences, seeking her in lonely crowds. "I remember the moment I heard," her cousin Kathy told me. "I was getting a Coke out of the vending machine at the family business, and Mum came over to me and said, 'Theresa's missing.' From the beginning, I think Mum was thinking the worst, but I thought everything was going to be okay, because Theresa wasn't a troublemaker. I just couldn't believe that anything could happen to her, because she was smart." At home in Trenton, the town where she and Theresa had spent their childhoods, "Everywhere I went, I looked for her face," Kathy remembered. "I took the bus a couple of times to Toronto, and every face on the subway or the street I would look at. Sometimes, I'd see someone who resembled her, who had the same frame, and I'd get my hopes up. I kept hoping."

In late December, PI Beullac mailed an "interim report" to the Allores in Saint John. "We are also forwarding," he wrote, "a copy of an article which appeared last week in the *Journal de Montréal*. Director Hamel states that the article is pure fabrication and that he was never even contacted by the reporter who wrote the story. We do however hope that it may stir interest in the affair and might make someone come forward with pertinent information." *Le Journal de Montréal* was a rough city tabloid that had shown no previous interest in the disappearance of a college student in Sherbrooke. Now, out of nowhere, it announced to readers who had no prior knowledge of Theresa Allore that she was caught up in drugs. It quoted Hamel, who claimed not to have been interviewed. It featured the close-cropped picture of Theresa from the photo booth, with her frizzed-out hair and wild look. A druggie!

It remains a total mystery why the *Journal* ran this article, for it never mentioned her case again. Was the story planted, in effect, by someone in law enforcement who wanted to shame the family into quietly retreating? Bob's employer in New Brunswick was paying for Beullac. Would it continue footing the bill if Theresa was just an AWOL junkie? We have no way to know, but it seems clear—ironically—that Beullac himself began to be swayed by the drug theory. In his report to Bob, he noted that "during the night [of November 3rd], two students purchased LSD in Lennoxville which they later consumed in Compton: one was found unconscious outside on campus and suffered a serious case of exposure from which he later recovered. The seller has not been identified." (In fact, it was quite warm that night, and the student in question had also been drinking; he had passed out on the lawn.)

"Theresa does not appear to have a serious drug habit," Beullac continued, "but she did try on occasion in the past: cocaine, amphetamines, Marijuana, Hashish and Mescaline. She is known to have smoked Marijuana on campus with classmates and friends." It isn't clear where Beullac got this information about coke, speed and mescaline, since none of Theresa's friends make statements to that effect. Andre, himself, remembers being extremely surprised, and assuming that he didn't know his sister as well as he thought he had. Later, Haidi Muller would write to John that the friends, Theresa included, had all made a pact to never try hard drugs unless they were together. Beullac's assertion seems baffling now.

In his report, the investigator then veered into other speculations, pondering small, tantalizing mysteries:

What is the significance of the inscription in her handwriting: "McGreer 110 afternoon"? (The room is used by the Counselling Service.)

Was the young woman who went to Les Picard's residence in Birchtown (sic) on November 7, 1978, in fact Theresa?

Who is the girl with the red hair and the scar under her right eye who asked Jane Finlay if she had seen Theresa after her disappearance?

71

If Jo-Anne Laurie and Ian Catterill really did first see that there were no textbooks on the top shelf of Theresa's locker when they went through it after her disappearance was noted, how did those textbooks get there later before the locker was reopened?

Why did Theresa go down to Montreal on the evening of Sunday, October 29? Did she head for or return to Montreal for the same reason on the evening of November 3rd?

It was like he was playing the game Clue with himself, since there was no one to answer the questions. He concluded:

Based on the information available to us at this time, we feel that the events surrounding the disappearance of Theresa probably occurred in the following manner:

Theresa left Compton that night and headed for Montreal in the same manner—and for the same reason—as she had the previous Sunday night.

She may not have made it to Montreal, having encountered someone on her way there who has forced or persuaded her to remain with him/her or has caused her death.

She may have reached Montreal and contacted Joey Nice who is covering up because of something which happened after she arrived. (Such as drugs?)

. . .

By late January, the earnest and committed PI Beullac was going down a different rabbit hole altogether. He spent some time surveilling a thirty-one-year-old Montreal man named Norman Drakes, whom he decided to suspect because Drakes happened to know someone in the apartment where Theresa had lived before she went to college, and had once given Theresa a lift to the Montreal airport. In 1978, Drakes had been convicted of stealing merchandise from his retail employer. The man, Beullac told Bob, was "unstable and violent," had to be "approached with caution" and had "no visible means of support" yet drove "a Cadillac."

The official surveillance report Beullac filed now reads like satire. He noted that at 6:15 p.m. on January 25, at the R-Mart Plaza, he "observed male, black NEGRO, mid-20s, 5'10", short black curly hair. Wearing canary yellow ski jacket, blue 'wrangler' jeans. Wearing large gold ring on left ring finger. . . . Moustache evident, not prominent."

He was joined by a woman, minutely described in the notes, and together they bought some groceries, with Beullac in furtive pursuit. "Subjects leave shopping centre and go immediately across street to Chalet Bar-B-Q," he jotted down. At 9:25 p.m., they "arrived at 125 Sommervale [sic] Gardens. Observed subjects unloading bags of groceries from car." Twenty minutes later: "Intercepted pizza delivery man who confirmed that a black male was indeed in Apartment 4 of 125 Sommervale Gardens as they had ordered pizza." Tiptoeing around and eavesdropping at the door of apartment 4, Beullac was able to

report that he "heard female speaking loudly and asking com-
panion, 'Fix me a drink, will you?' 'What kind?' 'Oh, a rum will
do just fine honey.'"

Beneath this faithful report of humdrum domestic dialogue,
Beullac drew a detailed map of the apartment building, in case,
who knows? Maybe a SWAT team would need to burst in.

Police chief Leo Hamel took a statement from Drakes five
days later, after which suspicion of his involvement was dropped.

"I remember staying in some farmhouse," said Vlad of this
period of searching. "I remember walking, the snow crunching,
and Bob asked, about the PI he had hired, 'Should I keep with
this guy?' I thought, *No*. The guy was just pretending to know
shit. He didn't know what he was doing."

In mid-February 1979, a six-man team from the Alcohol and
Morality section of the Sûreté du Québec raided King's Hall,
following a tip from college administrators. One hundred grams
apiece of hash and marijuana were found in the rooms of a
couple of students. "We're not very pleased about the situation"
campus director William Matson told the student paper, "but
we can't close our eyes to an obvious infraction of the law."

Although Hamel publicly repudiated the theory that
Theresa's fate was mixed up with drugs in an interview he gave
to Sherbrooke's French-language newspaper, *La Tribune*, it
appeared that Beullac still wanted to gnaw on that bone for a
spell. Theresa's high school friend Deborah Ferdinand doesn't
now remember the names or titles of two men who interviewed
her that winter, but she recalls the direction of their questions.
"I made it very clear to the police officers that Theresa wasn't

into partying or drugs," she says about the afternoon they came to her parents' house in Montreal. "We all just smoked a little pot. I knew . . . that was illegal, and my parents were listening upstairs, but it was important. If anyone was wild, I told them, it was me. Theresa wasn't like that. They stood there, in their dark navy suits, talking to this five-foot-three black girl that they thought they could bully and steer. But I stood my ground. I remember being adamant: 'She only smoked pot.' I'm accustomed to being made to go with the story that's being presented, and I wasn't going to do it."

On February 21, Beullac disclosed to Bob that he was helping an attorney with a double-murder investigation in Sherbrooke, and that the slaughter had been gang-related. Was that why he could be persuaded by the implausible prospect that Theresa had been swept into some sort of nefarious drug-fuelled trouble?

What *was* going on with crime in the Eastern Townships around the time of Theresa's disappearance? Perhaps we should widen the scope of our lens.

FIVE

THE GREEN AND THE BLUE

"Sherbrooke in those days was wild."
—unidentified law-enforcement official

IN THE 1976 PROVINCIAL ELECTION, THE PARTI QUÉBÉCOIS WAS elected in a landslide victory, defeating the incumbent Liberal Party, which had dominated politics in the province since the early 1960s. Quebec separatists were elated, while much of the business community began transferring operations to English-speaking Canada for fear that the province would secede. North America was already in the midst of a deep recession. In Quebec, it could now only get worse. In Lachute, a town of fifteen thousand about a half-hour drive northwest of Montreal and a stark example of the economic decline, unemployment doubled in one year to 20 percent. The province began roiling with labour unrest and cultural turmoil, and saw a spike in armed robberies and hostage-takings.

Most remarkable, given everything else going on that *needed policing*, were the wildcat strikes by the police. One comes away from researching the period with an almost comical sense of the entitlement that these men—and they were, indeed, exclusively men—felt about serving and protecting themselves. In January 1977, facing wage rollbacks for all small police forces, the Quebec Federation of Policemen threatened a province-wide walkout. Union president André Nadon reminded the newly appointed justice minister that "It was an election promise that public servants would not have their settlements rolled back." But public wages were under pressure as the economy staggered. "I'm afraid if the government doesn't take on their responsibilities the worst will happen," Nadon warned. Was that a threat to the safety of citizens? It could certainly be seen that way, given that an earlier police strike in Montreal had led to the Murray-Hill riots of 1969, also known as Montreal's Night of Terror.

The province's mayors questioned why the Montreal Urban Community police service—the force that failed to pursue young Ursula Schulze's murderer—showed $15 million of unjustifiable and "irregular" expenses in its budget. The mayors pointed to higher-than-normal costs for pension fund contributions, injury leave and overtime, citing seventy-eight officers who earned more than $8,000 each in overtime pay during the previous year, some of it for figuring out where to put 100,000 confiscated copies of *Penthouse* magazines seized from Montreal businesses. The Toronto police force, by comparison, served a slightly larger population and employed 156 more officers than the MUC, but cost $21 million less. Did the extra resources lead to better policing? No. The proportion of major crimes solved by the force in the year 1976, when the city hosted the Summer

Olympics, stood at 13 percent. A Quebec government study on law enforcement found that the Toronto police force had a consistently better crime-solving record than their Montreal counterparts and fewer crimes to cope with. By the end of February 1977, the Montreal police were already investigating their twenty-third and twenty-fourth murders of the year: twenty-three-year-old Francine Binette, shot several times in the head in her apartment on Chabot Street, and twenty-nine-year-old Suzanne Grégoire, found stabbed in a parking lot on rue Saint-Denis. Neither case was ever solved.

The situation in Quebec was symptomatic of a malaise in the province's law enforcement system: "the criminal in Quebec," it was reported in *The Gazette*, "enjoys greater freedom of action and maneuver than in other comparable areas." It likely didn't help that, according to the Quebec Police Commission study, "a high percentage" of law enforcement officers in the province could not shoot properly and needed new revolvers.

Nevertheless, rather than address their operational challenges, the Montreal police union ordered a work slowdown for its members to put pressure on pension-fund negotiations. Starting on a Monday, the union declared that police would respond only to emergency calls. Small businesses such as corner stores were urged by the local merchants' association to close before dark. By Wednesday, the city had seen nineteen bank robberies and sixty-five holdups, including one that involved the shooting death of a store clerk. The Sûreté du Québec stood at the ready, with six hundred officers prepared to intervene, should the slowdown continue and the violence escalate.

"Since Monday, police tactics of suspending patrols and answering only emergency calls have been an invitation to lawlessness," *The Gazette* observed on Thursday. "They have given rise to anguish, danger to life and limb and a sharp upsurge in violent crime. No government can bow to this kind of pressure from essential public servants." When the slowdown ended on Friday, *The Gazette* fumed that a police overhaul was urgent. "The slowdown has given Montrealers a glimpse of the rat's nest of incompetence, disorganization, irresponsibility, dereliction of duty, and ill will that exists—top to bottom—in the Montreal Urban Community force."

The newspaper could have added flagrant corruption to that list. MUC officers during this time were convicted of selling confiscated goods like firearms, running their own marijuana grow-ops, accepting bribes and providing kickbacks to politicians. A 1982 inquiry into corruption in the hundred-man Trois-Rivières police force heard accusations of perjury, intimidation of witnesses, false reports, armed robbery, attempted murder, fabrication of evidence and conflicts of interest—in short, everything to suggest that the police force wasn't protecting residents, but actually posing a threat to them.

Who could police the police? *Gazette* reporter Steve Kowch ran a series of articles, "Dissension in the Top Ranks, Profiling Dysfunction in the Montreal Police," revealing that the root problem appeared to be that no one knew, for sure, who even ran the 5,200-man operation. But it seems to have been the cops themselves. By way of startling example, that year the Montreal police brotherhood introduced a plan to set up a four-day workweek. Newly appointed police chief Henri-Paul Vignola countered,

"It will cost a lot of money to implement the plan and it will take more men than we have available." Undeterred, the brotherhood simply implemented their four-day schedule without the chief's approval. At a news conference, fighting back tears, Vignola begged the officers under his command not to go through with this act of insubordination. A court ordered officers to stick with the official work schedule set by the department, but the cops just defied the injunction. Mayor Edwin Briggs of suburban Beaconsfield said, "Those guys are . . . hired to enforce the law. Who the hell do they think they are?"

Meh. These guys were used to getting their way, and they did. On January 9, 1977, the Montreal police resumed a five-day schedule after the Superior Court of Quebec weighed in, but many men called in sick with what they described as the "Vignola flu." Then they staged another spate of work slowdowns. They were granted their four-day week about a month later.

In the midst of all this, Quebec Premier René Lévesque accidentally ran over a homeless man lying in the middle of a downtown Montreal road. (Lévesque had been cautioned by staff on many occasions to use a chauffeur, for his own security.) The metaphor for political and policing chaos couldn't have been more apt. The disruption began to spread beyond Montreal and its suburbs. Throughout the province, small municipalities started abolishing their police forces to balance budgets. On March 10, the Sherbrooke police force went on a full-scale (and illegal) four-day strike to protest the city's refusal to pay previously agreed wages. The Quebec government appealed to local municipalities to pay their officers, but the Union of Quebec Municipalities refused. Police slowdowns took place all over the province. About forty municipalities decided to dismantle their police departments and turn security duties over to the Sûreté du Québec. Colloquially, this expanding provincial force became known as the Greens, while all local cops were the Blues. The Greens and the Blues did not tend to cooperate.

Quebec is geographically immense. The SQ's new mandate quickly exceeded its grasp. In the early-morning hours of Wednesday, March 30, 1977, for example, twenty-three-year-old SQ Constable Robert Brabant was taking part in a police operation near a town well north of Montreal. Driving alone, Brabant caught up with a red Oldsmobile Cutlass whose three occupants were suspected in a string of assaults and robberies earlier that night. Brabant radioed for instructions and was told to "follow the car at a distance and to wait for reinforcements." Brabant radioed that the fog was providing him good cover. It wasn't. At a curve in the road, the suspects set up a roadblock and ambushed him. Brabant was able to shoot two rounds but was quickly overwhelmed. "They're going to shoot me. I'm finished," he radioed. The men circled his car and showered it with bullets.

The murder caused a storm of anger and protest among the four thousand officers of the SQ. Brabant was already the third officer in 1977 to be killed while riding alone in a patrol car. In a rare display of police unity in the province, fifteen hundred officers attended his funeral. Some things simply could not stand.

On March 23, 1977, twenty-year-old Louise Camirand disappeared near her apartment in Sherbrooke, Quebec. Her body was found two days later in the snow near Magog. Her case was never solved.

On April 14, Jocelyne Houle, twenty-four, disappeared from the streets of Montreal while walking with friends from a pub called the Vieux Munich to La Calèche du Sexe on Saint Catherine Street. Her beaten and raped body was found on the weekend in Saint-Calixte, an hour north of Montreal. Her case was never solved.

On June 29, thirty-eight-year-old Louise Bédard was found strangled in her home on Saint Denis Street. Her case was never solved.

On July 30, Joanne Dorion, seventeen, went missing after getting off a bus in Fabreville, north of Montreal. That same day, sixteen-year-old Chantal Tremblay disappeared after last being seen at Montreal's Henri-Bourassa metro station. Dorion's body was found eleven days later near Fabreville. Tremblay's bones were recovered almost two years later near her home in Rosemère. Neither case was solved.

You might find yourself wondering, given the organizational chaos and shrinking resources, how the SQ chose to spend its time and money. Well, one case that caught their avid attention was a hostage-taking in the Eastern Townships that distracted the whole force for about eighteen months. On Saturday, August 6, 1977, a middle-aged loan officer with the caisse populaire bank in Sherbrooke was kidnapped from his chalet-cottage in Stoke, just north of the city. At the time of the kidnapping, the victim, fifty-seven-year-old Charles Marion, was in the company of a fellow bank employee with whom he was having an affair. The kidnappers tied forty-one-year-old Aline Yargeau to a toilet and left her in the chalet to be found the next day by Marion's wife—which is surely one of the oddest variations in recent history on the theme of discovering that your husband is cheating. Denise Marion immediately reported her husband missing. His van was later recovered at a small regional airport.

The abduction was similar to one that had been carried out a couple of years earlier, in June 1975, when sixty-five-year-old Lena Blanchette, the wife of a wealthy margarine manufacturer in the Townships, was held for a $1 million ransom for five days before being released. Bank extortions involving hostages had become a popular criminal pastime in Quebec in the mid-seventies, with nearly fifty taking place between 1974 and 1975 alone. Charles Marion's kidnapping would prove to be the longest in Canada's history.

After hearing from Madame Marion, a special team of SQ investigators snapped into action and scoured the countryside. On Monday, August 8, a note was found in the night deposit box of the caisse populaire, demanding that specific messages be broadcast on local radio stations. During the Padres–Expos baseball game on Tuesday, radio announcers uncomfortably cleared their throats and read, "Mr. Nebets wants to talk to Mr. Noiram." The names were those of the kidnapped man and the manager of the bank—spelled backwards. In an ensuing conversation, the kidnappers demanded a ransom of $1 million for the safe release of Mr. Marion.

The police announced that they had a photo of the kidnapped Marion, showing the credit manager with a revolver pressed to his head. A copy of the Sunday, August 7, edition of a local newspaper had been held up to his chest to prove the date. On Saturday, August 13, the police confirmed that they had received a letter from Charles Marion himself. "I know my life isn't worth a million but I want to live," he pled. "I presently am suffering martyrdom. If you were in my place you would know that, to be detained, I am certain—I am convinced—that if the demands are not accepted they will kill me." His wife received a colour photo of her husband with what appeared to be blood on his face, although some speculated that the red matter looked more like ketchup.

On Wednesday, August 17, the SQ reported that the "group" holding Charles Marion had designed its own logo: "It has all the signs of a terrorist or politically-motivated kidnapping, what with the use of the communiques and their own logo . . . we are obviously dealing with pros," they told the press. It was described as a hand-drawn picture of several snakes. One police source said it looked like "a poor imitation of the logo used by the Symbionese Liberation Army," the terrorist group that had kidnapped Patty Hearst in California in 1974. The Marion kidnappers branded themselves "Les Septs Serpents."

In a coded message broadcast over a local Sherbrooke radio station, caisse populaire officials informed the kidnappers that, upon reflection, they were willing to pay only $300,000 for the return of their employee. "The ball is in their court now," an official said.

Marion family members grew distraught when the kidnappers made no further response. But on August 19, the hostage wrote to the *Journal de Montréal* and complained that his bank valued its assets more than his life. "I am writing without restraint from my jailers . . . [the SQ] have done everything to have me killed." At this point, some reporters began speculating that the kidnapping was a hoax arranged by Marion himself. His son, Pierre, denied the charge: "It is not within my father's character to do something like that, to put his family through what can only be described as a nightmare."

By September, caisse populaire officials had dropped their offer to $200,000 and demanded proof that Marion was alive. They wanted his signature written seven times. After a stretch of silence, the kidnappers furnished the signatures. Sherbrooke television reporter Normand Maltais read a new communiqué on the local evening news. The kidnappers had decided that Maltais, a local celebrity, should make the ransom drop. They also requested a dry run, as a sort of dress rehearsal.

On September 10, on her eighteenth birthday, Hélène Monast was found murdered in Chambly, Quebec, between Sherbrooke and Montreal, naked and strangled in a parkette. Her case was never solved.

By early autumn, 450 police officers had become actively engaged in the hunt for Charles Marion. It was a larger force than had been deployed to search for British Trade Commissioner James Cross during the Front de libération du Québec (FLQ) crisis in 1970, a nation-rattling act of separatist terrorism that had led Prime Minister Pierre Trudeau to declare a state of martial law. So intent was the SQ on apprehending Marion's kidnappers that they were now keeping a helicopter and a province-owned

DC-3 airplane on standby at a nearby airport. The elite investigative team included members of the Montreal police's special tactical squad. Sherbrooke television reporter Normand Maltais, waiting to act as the go-between, remained under police guard at a local motel.

On Monday, September 19, a six-page, handwritten communiqué was found outside the north-end offices of the *Journal de Montréal*. If the ransom wasn't paid within forty-eight hours, the note warned, the credit union would "receive only Marion's head and only that. The rest will never be found." Police and caisse populaire officials prepared the final details for the cash drop.

On September 20, thirty-three-year-old Katherine Hawkes was found murdered in the bushes near a commuter train station in the suburbs of Montreal. The assailant, overcome with remorse, had called from a payphone after the attack to say that his victim was still alive, and even explained where to find her. The police didn't arrive for hours, by which time Hawkes had succumbed to her injuries and died. The case was never solved.

On Friday, September 23, Normand Maltais and popular Montreal reporter Claude Poirier awaited contact from the kidnappers, acting as the two appointed intermediaries who would offer the ransom. They received a communiqué that evening instructing them to drive to the nearby town of Weedon. From there, Maltais and Poirier were to head farther east to a dead-end road where the drop-off could finally be made. After an hour's wait, the two celebrities got spooked when a truck driven by men dressed as game wardens from the Quebec Department of Lands and Forests roared onto the scene. The journalists pegged them for cops and called off the drop. It was later admitted that the "game wardens" were actually investigators "in disguise." At the same time, a reporter and photographer from *Photo Police* had wandered into the secret drop-off location. *The Gazette* characterized the now fifty-one-day hostage-taking as "a complicated chess game," but the SQ appeared to be playing KerPlunk.

Tempers flared. *Gazette* photographer Jean-Pierre Rivest was threatened by SQ Sergeant Jean-Guy Charland for attempting to photograph two suitcases in the back seat of a police vehicle. "If you print that picture in your paper, I'll come looking for you and settle the matter when we're alone," he reportedly said. The SQ conducted raids at two Sherbrooke motels where reporters were staying; two of them were slapped with criminal charges for being in possession of police-radio monitoring devices. Meanwhile, SQ spokesmen vented frustration with their superiors about stonewalling them. Nobody knew what was going on.

On September 26, the skeletal remains of two women described by the French language newspaper La Presse *as go-go dancers were found in the woods near Saint-Calixte, an isolated hamlet between Montreal and the ski resort of Mont-Tremblant. Investigators quickly deemed the deaths of Suzanne Morrow and Francine Loiselle a "suicide pact," even though they lay in the middle of nowhere with no vehicle parked nearby. The cases were never solved.*

On Thursday, September 29, authorities and their journalist intermediaries tried a second ransom drop. Maltais and Poirier left the offices of the caisse populaire around seven p.m. with two suitcases. They were instructed to leave the money at a location between Sherbrooke and Lennoxville at eleven p.m. Before midnight, two unidentified men, assumed to be the kidnappers, grabbed the suitcases, but hidden officers opened fire, prompting the ransom collectors to flee into the evergreen forest. The SQ thundered into action. Their DC-3 aircraft circled the treetops and dropped illuminating flares. Two helicopters hovered and swooped. Trained dogs ran barking through the woods. At length, the police found a panel truck believed to belong to the kidnappers. Empty. "I don't know how come," spokesman Pierre Lemarbre later said, "but it was a total failure; the suspects managed to get away." A Lennoxville local snorted to the press, "You don't need 200 guys and a DC-3 to catch two men. It would probably have been better if it was just me and my neighbour with shotguns."

Humiliated, police waited several days for further contact from the kidnappers, which duly arrived at the offices of the *Journal de Montréal*. This time, they complained that they had cut open the suitcases and found nothing but pieces of cardboard and an electronic tracking device. "We won't have to liquidate Marion if this keeps up, he will pass on by himself..."

Poirier and Maltais, incensed by the potential damage to their reputations, released a statement claiming they were unaware that the luggage had held no ransom. If another drop were to be done, the men huffed, the police would have to allow them to verify the contents of the suitcases and not interfere in the operation. "If they say no to our conditions then we won't go," Poirier said. "I have been in this business for 17 years and have delivered 80 people wanted by police to the authorities," he added, revealing a hitherto unknown sideline gig for crime reporters. "The police have asked me eight times to help them and this is the first time they double-crossed me. Why? I don't know."

Finally, a week later, a local reporter for *La Tribune* found a communiqué slipped under the carpet in the lobby of his apartment building. The kidnappers now requested only $50,000 in ransom—one-twentieth of the original amount—just enough to cover the costs of the kidnapping. In the letter, Charles Marion instructed his family to sell all of his property to raise the cash. "Sell everything I have and do it as fast as you can because I am suffering horribly . . . and if you don't, they'll kill me." His son Pierre Marion agreed to make this new drop-off along with his friend Jean-Paul Fouquet, with one officer acting as a bodyguard. Before midnight on October 25, Pierre delivered money in a clear plastic bag to an undisclosed location forty kilometres southeast of Sherbrooke, and two days later, Charles Marion walked out of the woods near the East Angus airport. He was taken to Sherbrooke's St. Vincent de Paul Hospital, where he was pronounced in good health. "He looked like he needed a bath," a nurse told reporters.

In a Halloween interview with *The Gazette*, local politician Fernand Grenier called on Quebec Justice Minister Marc-André Bédard to provide an explanation for police conduct during the kidnapping, "because I am tired, like most people in the area, of picking up the [tab] from the Quebec Police Force without knowing if they did a good job or not." *The Gazette* reported that the vast police operation had cost citizens $1.2 million dollars, with the police hampered either "by bad luck, or their own incompetence."

> *On Monday, October 24th, a truck driver found the naked body of twenty-three-year-old Denise Bazinet abandoned in a ditch along Route 35 near Saint-Jean-sur-Richelieu, about half an hour west of Sherbrooke. She had been strangled. The case was never solved.*

Seven months after Marion's release, the SQ arrested a motley crew of misfits for his kidnapping. The case had gone cold and might not have been solved, or so the press reported at the time, but for a fluke encounter by an off-duty police officer in a Sherbrooke disco. The fellow was having a drink at the Disco René when he thought he recognized thirty-eight-year-old fugitive Michel de Varennes from his days as a guard at the Saint-Hyacinthe jail. The officer went back to SQ headquarters to review old wanted posters. Sure enough, there was the mug of the two-bit thief who had escaped prison in Cowansville the previous year. He had gone on to win disco dancing contests in Sherbrooke, often imitating John Travolta in the same establishments where cops looking for Charles Marion were blowing off steam. The officer went back to Disco René and arrested him.

A connection was made to the kidnapping when the freshly arrested de Varennes was found in possession of a $20 bill linked to the ransom money. He, in turn, reportedly ratted out a man named Claude Valence. SQ officer Roch Gaudreault (the man accused of forging documents in a murder investigation, the man who told Bob and Marilyn to go back to New Brunswick and wait for the snow to melt) searched Valence's home and found two newspaper articles—one about the kidnapping of Italian Prime Minister Aldo Moro in March 1978, and the other about Pierre Laporte, kidnapped and murdered by the FLQ in 1970—hidden under a mattress. Gaudreault also discovered, he would later tell the court, a revolver, a leather case, an electronic dart gun and a knapsack containing a compass, rope, gloves and a whistle hidden in a closet.

The SQ clearly had much to gain from solving a case that had riveted the Townships and cost over a million dollars in policing resources. In early July 1978, they took curious citizens, or lookie-loos, on an escorted tour of the property where Marion said he had been held during his kidnapping. It was like "an overnight tourist attraction," a reporter for *The Gazette* commented. There was a photo of *Gazette* crime reporter Steve Kowch, who had been covering the case quite seriously for almost a year, goofing it up in the entrance of the "prison" as if it were a carnival house of horrors.

On October 2, 1978, a month before Theresa vanished, the trial proceedings began against Claude Valence—he of the hidden newspaper clippings. Crown prosecutor Pierre Sauvé had subpoenaed 450 witnesses, which prompted a sessions court judge to raise his eyebrow: "That's one heck of a lot of witnesses." The Montreal-based trial, moved from Sherbrooke due to publicity, involved Valence and his wife, Jeanne, who stood accused of acting as a part-time accomplice, allegedly having penned the notes for the kidnappers' demands, which is an oddly supportive yet peripheral role, like a wife whose involvement in watching the Stanley Cup playoffs is to lay out the chips and beer.

Under cross-examination, Marion admitted that—contrary to earlier testimony that he had been held captive with chains around his neck and waist—he was, in fact, untethered many times and could possibly have escaped quite easily.

Claude Valance testified that he had agreed to take part in the kidnapping only after being told that Marion had consented to his own abduction. He identified the middleman who brokered the plan as Michel de Varennes, the disco dancer. Valence claimed that he'd received only $6,000 for his participation in the scheme. But he also testified under cross-examination that he had been beaten and tortured by two SQ officers who questioned him soon after his arrest. He was, he said, punched repeatedly in the stomach, hit hard with a stick against a telephone book placed against his head and threatened with death like a "dirty dog" by an officer holding a pistol against his temple. Valence said he signed a false confession only after being threatened that his wife would be tied naked to a floor—however that worked—and kicked.

On December 19, in his closing statements, defense attorney Jean-Pierre Rancourt argued there was simply too much evidence pointing to the prospect that Marion was involved in his own kidnapping. The jury appeared to agree. Valence was cleared on four of five counts against him, being found guilty only of attempted extortion. It was a major blow to the Crown prosecution and the SQ.

In 1989, Valence was shot and killed in an incident over

barking dogs. A decade later, Charles Marion took his own life at his chalet in Stoke, the location where everything started.

The second case preoccupying Townships law enforcement around the time of Theresa's disappearance offers glimpses of dubious and distracted police work as well. It had to do with some of the bottom feeders in the Sherbrooke underworld— petty thieves and drug dealers who were often recruited by the SQ to act as informants on higher-ups in Quebec's rampant biker gangs. On July 6, 1978, the bodies of Raymond Grimard and Manon Bergeron were found in a field south of Lennoxville. Grimard had been shot several times in the back of the head. Bergeron, a young mother of three small children, had a nylon cord wound around her neck. (She'd also been beaten or knocked out with the butt of a rifle.) A resident near the crime scene said she'd heard a car cruising rapidly in both directions and blowing its horn twice around four o'clock that Thursday morning.

There was no further mention of this case in any local newspaper until the trial began in April 1979, around the time that Theresa's body was found. A local man named Fernand Laplante, unemployed and in his twenties, had been arrested and now stood trial for two counts of murder. SQ officer Réal Châteauneuf, one of the men assigned to Theresa's case, testified that he had been keeping the accused, Laplante, under surveillance the previous summer, after receiving a tip that the aspiring thief was planning to rob a bank. Châteauneuf— accompanied by Noël Bolduc and Roch Gaudreault—had arrived at the scene of the murders and found a piece of paper on Grimard's body with the phone number of the Sherbrooke

SQ office written on it. The assertion at trial, then, was that Grimard was a suspected stooge, and that Laplante had grown paranoid and whacked him.

The star witness for the prosecution was twenty-two-year-old Jean Charland, who claimed to be Laplante's accomplice. The two men, he said, had been planning to rob a bank with Grimard, but they began suspecting him of tipping off the cops. On the night of the crime, Charland said, he waited in a car while the accused escorted Grimard and Manon Bergeron into a field, shot Grimard, then strangled Bergeron. Charland honked the car horn at Laplante's request, to cover the sound of the gunshots. They then threw the rifle into a nearby river, abandoned their car at the Lennoxville golf course and took a taxi back to Sherbrooke.

Fernand Laplante was defended by Jean-Pierre Rancourt, the same attorney who had collapsed the Marion prosecution. Rancourt told the jury that Charland worked in drug trafficking with the Gitans motorcycle gang, carrying out contract robberies and arsons. He was hardly a credible witness. Further, during cross-examination, the lawyer got Officer Châteauneuf to concede that when the SQ brought their potential star witness into custody on November 11, 1978, they lied to him by pretending that Laplante had incriminated him in the summer murder of a young woman named Carole Fecteau, who had been found naked by a stream near the village of East Hereford. (The young thugs all pointed fingers in the case, gossiping at one point over a game of snooker in a Wellington Street bar about how she'd been given a "good go"—or gang raped—before being shot.) Fecteau, the cops knew, had been friends with Charland's brother. So they lied, and pretended that Laplante had something on him. Was the message here "frame or be framed"?

Asked if this type of deception was a normal practice for the SQ, Châteauneuf replied, "Yes, it's one of the tricks usually used." Another witness, who was serving time for robbery, testified that Châteauneuf and a second SQ officer had urged him to testify against Laplante, warning him that if he instead testified for the defense, his parole could "go badly." Three more convicts alleged that they, too, had been intimidated by the investigating officers. One of the witnesses said, "I really don't have anything against [the cops]. They are only doing their job, but sometimes I have to admit doing their job includes some kicks and punches."

Remarkably, no one in the media covering this trial seems to have raised an obvious question: Why was Carole Fecteau killed, and then why was Manon Bergeron killed? Why murder this young single mother, who seemed to have a purely social affiliation with the gang, in addition to the supposed informant Grimard? What did *she* do? For that matter, why strangle her, which is a much more intimate kind of attack, not to mention one that takes a great deal longer to complete than shots with a rifle? Bergeron was almost never mentioned in the daily reporting, and Fecteau's death barely registered. No one was ever convicted for her murder. The erasure, in retrospect, is astounding.

Finally, taxi driver William Pettigrew told the court that he drove Charland and an unidentified man back to the south Sherbrooke intersection of Short and Belvedere Streets at around dawn on the day of the crime (it's curious to note that Carole Fecteau lived in an apartment in this area). The second man on the ride, the driver recalled, had tattoos on both arms. Fernand Laplante rose to show the jury that he had no such markings.

Attorney Rancourt speculated in closing arguments that Charland was protecting someone by agreeing to testify and spin the story the way he had. (Indeed, he later successfully appealed his conviction and said he'd heard in a bar about what happened.) For reasons lost now to the decades, however, the jury figured that young Fernand Laplante committed the murders. He was sentenced to life in prison without parole, although to this day he maintains his innocence. John tried to talk to him once he was released, to get some background on the criminal world in Sherbrooke in the late 1970s, but Laplante wanted to put it all behind him.

After this second high-profile trial, it's worth noting that private investigator Robert Beullac decided he'd seen enough of shady Townships police work. The following summer, he filed a complaint with the Quebec Police Commission alleging that provincial police officers had beaten suspects, intimidated witnesses and fabricated evidence during investigations of crimes in and around the city of Sherbrooke. He accused them of using threats against witnesses in the kidnapping trial of Claude Valence. (Years later, Beullac would tell John that both Valence and Laplante had suffered the "phone book trick.")

"The problem is that provincial police in the Sherbrooke area cannot solve cases by the normal methods," Beullac told the press at the time, "so they have started using shortcuts." That seems like a bit of an understatement. Finally, Beullac demanded that Justice Minister Marc-André Bédard probe what he called gross misconduct in the handling of the Fernand Laplante case. Beullac's demand was ignored.

"Sherbrooke in those days was wild," a local law enforcement official would tell us. "I always called it my China Town. The SQ were dirty cops. They were very sloppy. These are people who don't want to be challenged. They were a special group, let's put it that way."

If only Bob and Marilyn had known this at the time. They might not have bristled with upset and confused anger when Theresa's grieving friends came to her funeral—these young, loving friends who served distracted cops as convenient suspects for an unimportant crime.

SIX

WHEN THE SNOW MELTED

" . . . and into this bizarrerie . . . I quietly fell."
—Edgar Allan Poe

ON SATURDAY, APRIL 14, 1979, THE ALLORES WERE IN THEIR hometown of Trenton, on a bay of Lake Ontario, having supper with the clan—the aunts and uncles and cousins who all appear, smiling and waving, in Bob's Christmas home movies from the sixties. The phone rang. John's Aunt Linda beckoned his father to take the receiver. "My brother and I were whisked to the basement. I remember standing down there, discussing what the call might mean," John said. "Then we were told to go with our cousin Paul, who was a bit older." The teens wound up lighting a bonfire at another cousin's house, listening to Van Halen and drinking beer. They stayed up all night, "and the next morning I woke up and watched some sci-fi movie on TV, like *Earth vs. the Spider.*" Eventually they all climbed into Paul's ragtop MG and drove around listening to Steely Dan and Max Webster. Around three p.m., John and Andre were dropped off at their grandparents' house. It was like a surreal interlude, a dance on the edge of knowing. "We walked in the door, past the laundry room, and my grandparents were sitting on the sofa, crying. I'd never seen them cry. We went into the back bedroom where my parents stay, and they were on the bed, crying." Theresa had been found. She was dead.

"I walked outside. There were patches of cloud in the sky. For some reason I had an Instamatic camera, and I started taking pictures of the sky. I wanted to capture the moment I knew she had died. My younger cousin Christine was fooling around in our grandfather's Pontiac convertible. She didn't know what had happened, so she started laughing at me for photographing the sky. 'What are you doing, are you crazy?' I just felt embarrassed. I wasn't about to tell her."

On an impulse, John began running. He left the yard and ran—for probably fifteen kilometres, the longest run he's ever done in his life, "before or since. You gotta get some distance between you and the grief, or the grief will eat you up." He understands that now. At the time, he was fourteen; it was primal. Run from the walls that are about to fall in, run from the roof collapsing, and then further from the shattering sky.

Within twenty-four hours the family was in Montreal because Bob had to identify his daughter's body. "The four of us drove, but I don't remember talking. What I remember is arriving at the lab, and the corridor was green." They were at the Laboratoire de médecine légale de Montréal, in the main headquarters of the Sûreté du Québec on Parthenais Street in the east end of the city. Theresa's former roommate from Pointe-Claire, Joey Nice, had been summoned to the lab earlier to see if she could make a positive ID. She couldn't. Corporal Gaudreault showed Nice the clothing found in a green garbage bag at the entrance to the Gagnon farm in Compton where the trapper had encountered his "mannequin." These clothes did not, she said, belong to her friend. A pink fluffy sweater? The clothes were wrong, but so was the body. None of it belonged. Bodies don't just immediately transform from Sleeping Beauty to Halloween skeleton. There are deeply disconcerting and disorienting visual transformations along the way that add an indefinable element of horror to the emotional devastation felt by families whose loved ones are found as remains.

John said, "My father walked down that corridor to see the body. He came back out, and he was a completely different man. I remember him saying to my mom, 'Theresa had a scar on her eyebrow, right?' And she said, 'Yes.'" But he couldn't recognize his child. He had to authorize them to remove her jaw to try for a dental match. "After that, we went to pick up her Bottecchia racing bike. It was green. I still own it. She had it in the shop for repairs. Then we went to this Italian restaurant that we used to all go to, along Décarie." No one knew what to do with their forks and knives. "We came out into the parking lot afterward and I just lost it, sobbing in my mom's arms."

Later that afternoon, Corporal Gaudreault, Coroner Michel Durand and Bob Allore convened at the SQ headquarters. Everyone agreed that the body was almost certainly Theresa's. Gaudreault told Bob that, despite the decomposition, the autopsy would reveal Theresa's fate. For now, Gaudreault was leaning toward a possible suicide, or perhaps a drowning or a drug overdose. "He assured me that the whole matter may be resolved quickly," Bob wrote in his diary, "[that she] may have been intoxicated by liquor or drugs." Durand mentioned observing bruises under the armpits. What was the explanation for that? Gaudreault didn't know, but he doubted that Theresa was the victim of a sexual predator. He pointed out the underwear: if she had been raped, her underwear would have been torn, he explained. The underwear on the body was in pristine condition. You cannot rape a woman without tearing her underwear! You cannot rape a woman using her mouth or her hands! The three men sat around in silent agreement, resting in their ignorance of women's experience.

Before the men went their separate ways, they inventoried the belongings found on the body. Gaudreault produced the earrings from the autopsy, and the ring and watch. A favourite necklace of Theresa's was missing, found neither with the body nor in her dorm room. Bob released the objects back to Gaudreault as evidence. The transfer was witnessed and attested to by Durand.

Back at the lab, pathologist Teresa Sourour observed the body of a young Caucasian woman, five foot seven, weighing 115 pounds, with auburn hair. The body was in an accelerated state of adipocere, making the skin thick and soapy. The fingers and toes were missing nails. The hair disengaged easily. Sourour noted several old scars on the arms and forehead. She authorized the removal of the upper and lower maxillaries for dental identification by odontology expert Dr. Robert Dorion.

There were no visible traces of external traumatic lesions on the body. Sourour examined the head. There was no trauma to the scalp, no fractures to the skull. There were signs of mucus in the trachea and bronchia. The gullet contained "a little vomiting matter." The lungs showed no signs of trauma. The stomach contained a small mass of solid food, digested or decomposed. The intestines were void of matter. The uterus, ovaries, vagina and external genital organs were "without noticeable particularity." Before concluding the autopsy, Sourour authorized the transportation of the liver, spleen, kidneys and lungs to the chemical laboratory for toxicological analysis.

On Saturday evening, Bob had placed a call to Robert Beullac, who was already aware of the discovery of Theresa's body. They discussed how the body was found, face down in the water near Compton, the state of decomposition, the absence of signs of physical trauma. Beullac assured Bob that the autopsy would determine the cause of death, and that the worst was over.

"The pathologist, because of the state of decomposition, was unable to determine the cause of death," Gaudreault told Sherbrooke's *La Tribune* on April 17. (This was the day that the trial of Fernand Laplante began, for the murders of Raymond Grimard and Manon Bergeron.) "On first glance, there was no sign of bullet holes or physical violence. But more analysis will permit us to make a complete and detailed connection."

It would be decades before *Gazette* journalist Paul Cherry filed a Freedom of Information request for the coroner's original report and discovered that he'd noted, "She had the marks of strangulation." Why Gaudreault made no mention of this to the press or the Allores remains a mystery. By the time Andre

Allore talked to him about his sister, in the mid-nineties, he would claim to have scant memory of the case.

Gaudreault and Constable Guy Lessard began their investigation by canvassing homes in the village of Compton. Repeating what Hamel, Beullac and the Allores had already done, they went door to door asking people if they remembered seeing anything suspicious on the night of November 3. No one did. The investigators tracked down the bus driver who had been on duty that night to show him Theresa's picture. If this student had ridden the bus from Lennoxville to Compton that evening, he didn't recall her.

Gaudreault and Lessard reviewed statements by Andre, Josie Stapenhorst, Jo-Anne Laurie and Caroline Greenwood, provided to Hamel five months earlier. They decided to re-interview Laurie and Greenwood, bringing them in to the Lennoxville police station on April 17. Greenwood was first. She repeated the same information she had given to Hamel: Theresa was her friend; she'd last seen her on Friday, November 3, at noon; Theresa had declined an invitation to join Caroline for the weekend in Hemmingford. Gaudreault asked about Theresa's drug use. "Theresa had smoked up (taken marijuana or hashish) a couple of times," Greenwood wrote in her statement. "She never told me that she had ever done cocaine, however I've the impression that it could be a possibility. She's lived on her own and worked and had more experience than most girls her own age."

Jo-Anne Laurie came in next, and repeated much of the same information. When asked about Theresa's drug use, she had little to offer. (These were kids who had known one another for only ten weeks or so.) "She wasn't into drugs, she got high on life and liked reality better than being stoned. She was easygoing and got along well with most people. She had taken a year off school and worked and now she appreciated going to school."

The following day, the SQ questioned Jeanne Eddisford, the young acting director of residence for King's Hall who had gone hiking with Theresa the week before she disappeared. She told them Theresa was a good student, always happy, very intelligent. She said students would sometimes come to her with confidential concerns, but no one had asked to discuss Theresa's fate. She dismissed the idea that there was a drug problem at the dorm.

The investigators weren't gleaning much from their line of questioning. "I know for a fact that Theresa wanted to live and was very happy in life. For no reason would she want to commit suicide," her friend Suzanne DeRome stated. "She was not afraid to hitchhike alone, day or night. Occasionally she would smoke drugs but was by no means addicted, nor did she use any chemicals."

At the very least, Gaudreault and Lessard felt they could place Theresa at King's Hall that Friday night, thanks to a new statement from her acquaintance Sharon Buzzee: "I knew Theresa Allore quite well although we were not best friends," Buzzee stated. "I was walking through King's Hall on Friday evening November 3rd. The time was approximately 9 pm. I saw Teresa standing or walking on the stairs (the main staircase) and we both stopped and talked. That weekend Teresa was supposed to be staying at a friend's house Caroline Greenwood, and because of this I said to Teresa something to this effect, 'why didn't you go to Caroline's this weekend? and she replied with, 'I couldn't, I have too much home work to do.' I asked her what she was doing that night and she said she was going to do her homework. We departed and I think that she went up the stairs, but I did not really notice. I can't really remember what clothes she was wearing."

Theresa's friends Josie and Suzanne couldn't make sense of this scenario when the police told them of it. If Theresa had come back to Compton, Suzanne said, "the first thing she would do is go to her room" in the second residence of Gillard House, which was directly opposite theirs, and they had their door open. "There is no reason why she would omit to tell us" that she had changed her mind about listening to records. "I do not believe that Theresa was ever in Compton that night."

On April 20, a farmer was riding through his fields on a tractor in the early morning when he noticed an object by the side of the road, about 120 metres from his house. Curious, he climbed down from and walked over to get a better look. In amidst some withered brambles was a wallet. He bent down to collect it and peered inside. "When I saw the first piece of ID, I saw the name, Theresa Allore," he wrote in a statement. "I got on my tractor and returned to my house." Remembering the recent news, he immediately phoned the police.

Theresa's cherry-red Buxton wallet, a Christmas present from her parents, was found on the shoulder of chemin Macdonald, a back road on the outskirts of Sherbrooke, approximately twenty kilometres from the field where her body was found. At this point, Gaudreault rejected the suicide hypothesis. Between April 23 and 26, he and Lessard interviewed more than ninety students living at King's Hall. The interrogations led nowhere. No one confessed. No one seemed suspicious or wilted under the heat. The statements were a litany of rumours and mundane recollections:

"I went to her room to see if her chemistry homework was done. She wasn't there."

"I was her roommate. I saw her smoke pot once."

"She usually worked in the library until late."

"I heard it said that she had gone to the States."

"I own a grey 1978 Omni."

"I own a car, a Ford Torino."

"I never heard a story about students on drugs that Friday night."

"I heard that she went out West to meet her boyfriend."

"I heard she was in Florida."

"I hitchhiked. I had no problems."

"To my knowledge, she didn't use dope."

"I met her at the Halloween dance."

"I own a green 1974 Ford Thunderbird."

"I remember two boys said to me that they wouldn't be surprised, when the snow went away, if she was in the bushes somewhere."

On April 25, a King's Hall resident named Glenn Kelly told the officers that he remembered a student named "Vick" being on drugs the night that Theresa disappeared. A lead? On the first Tuesday of May, police tracked down and took a statement from

David Vick, a Champlain student who had swallowed a hit of LSD and drunk beer with friends at Gillard House, having bought the drug from, according to Vick, "some guy in Lennoxville." This was the acid trip that PI Beullac had written to Bob Allore about at Christmas. It hadn't been a fun experience for Vick. "As I left the room late I walked over to King's Hall and passed out on the lawn being sick," he wrote. "Two people brought me to my room and then Allan, a Residence Assistant, helped me into a station wagon and brought me to the hospital. Next morning, the doctor gave me a lift to Lennoxville and I crashed out for a while at a friend's room on campus."

On May 9, the investigators took a statement from the former night watchman at the student dorm: "I recall that at the beginning of November I drove a kid that had an overdose [to] the hospital in Sherbrooke. It was the morning of the 4 of November. When I came back I had an argument about drug problems with Mr. Peacock. He didn't want to do nothing about it so I quit working there. I knew Theresa Allore to have seen her. I don't recall when I saw her last."

Clearly, these post-mortem interviews were an attempt to implicate drugs in Theresa's death, though it required an event sequence that defied even rudimentary logic. Theresa would have had to abandon her plans to study, or to visit her friends Suzanne and Josie in their room, in favour of suddenly consuming drugs powerful enough to kill her, which is virtually unheard of with LSD or THC. And there is no evidence that anything stronger, like heroin, was circulating. She would have done the drugs with acquaintances who were never identified at a time when her expressed intention to several people was to finish a psychology essay. She had made a pact, moreover, with her Montreal girlfriends never to try a drug stronger than weed without them all being together. Nevertheless, these unknown persons, who presumably also consumed doses of some very potent drug, then took off Theresa's clothes and shoes, drove her northwest of Compton, dragged her across a field, made off with her purse, dumped her wallet twenty kilometres north as a diversion and destroyed her T-shirt, sweater, pants and shoes, leaving no trace. And they did all of this unwitnessed. After that, these perpetrators would have resumed their lives without aches of conscience throughout all the months Theresa's family spent searching in terror for their missing daughter.

All of that had to be accepted, first, as entirely plausible by police investigators before they even homed in on this line of questioning about drug use with Theresa's friends.

The young women who knew Theresa suspected a far more probable explanation for their friend's disappearance and death: she had been killed. "When they described how she was found, I knew she was raped and dumped. I could envision it right away. I knew it in my gut," Deborah Ferdinand told me. Years later, one of Andre's friends wrote in an e-mail to John: "Your dad once asked me if I truly thought Theresa died from drugs. I can't remember what I answered, but I remember the dilemma of wanting to tell him that I thought she had died at the hands of someone bad, but not wanting to see the anguish in his face."

Not even Leo Hamel, as inexperienced as he was, bought the panicking-drug-associates narrative. At the time, either he or someone in his squad speculated to the private security man lent to the Allores by Andre's girlfriend's family that Theresa had been "frightened to death." Whatever that meant. Maybe this "frightened to death" concept had to do with someone sexually assaulting her, causing a heart attack. Even police at this time had little to no understanding of forensics, or autopsies if they were working in small jurisdictions. There were no TV shows like *CSI*. We were all watching *The Bionic Woman*. It would be another decade before crime novelist Patricia Cornwell began her series about the pathologist Kay Scarpetta, helping the public understand what sort of knowledge could be gleaned from a crime scene and a corpse. The fact that strangulation can leave no visible marks six months post-mortem would scarcely have been considered by citizens. If Theresa's autopsy unearthed no clues about violence, then many took that to mean there had been no violence inflicted.

On June 16, Corporal Gaudreault typed up a report on his findings, although he didn't provide a copy to the Allores. It just went in the police file:

> *Before we can make a conclusion of this information, we need to look deeper. In our investigation we discovered a surrounding problem of drugs in the environment [that the victim] frequented. Unfortunately, the autopsy could not give an exact cause of death, and I expect that this will be the same with the lab results. Notwithstanding these difficulties, there are still other people to interview, in the family, among friends, and the community. We will therefore continue this investigation, and in a new report we will record anything worth mentioning.*

There was no new report. The SQ mailed Theresa's personal effects, including her wallet, to her family.

On the evening of Friday, April 20, campus director William Matson met with the board of governors of Champlain College. Dr. Matson thanked the membership for welcoming him back after a spleen operation. In his report, he notified the board that he was pleased to announce the appointment of Miss Jeanne Eddisford to the professional staff as coordinator of student housing services. He also informed the board that the construction of the new 315-bed residence in Lennoxville was proceeding well, and that the buildings would be ready for occupancy well before the start of classes the next fall. Matson pointed out that the demand for rooms was high, with over 750 applications received to occupy the 315 spaces. Shortly after ten p.m., the meeting adjourned. According to Suzanne DeRome, a student representative in attendance, Theresa Allore's death was never mentioned.

No one from Champlain ever sent the Allores a note of condolence.

SEVEN

REMEMBER A DAY

"Is there no way out of the mind?"
—Sylvia Plath, "Apprehensions"

IN 1975, WHEN THERESA STILL LIVED AT HOME IN MONTREAL, her father was driving back from a business trip to Ontario. Near the town of Cornwall, on the side of Highway 401, he saw a young woman of about his daughter's age standing with her arm raised and her thumb up, calm and hopeful for a ride. He slowed his Chrysler to a stop and invited her to get in. The hour was late, and when they reached the West Island suburbs of Montreal, Bob didn't relish the idea of this teenager continuing to hitch rides. Her destination, she told him, was Atlantic Canada. He invited her to spend the night with the Allore family at their home in Pierrefonds. John remembers how intrigued he and his siblings were, ready for bed in their PJs, by this free-spirited American girl with her knapsack.

When Sarah Priestman finally made it to the Maritimes, she sent a postcard to the Allores to say she was fine and to thank them. Years later, she would write about her hitchhiking adventures, in which she covered 34,000 miles of North America. The piece, titled "Starlight" was included in the 1992 edition of the annual anthology *Best American Essays*. Roaming the highways, Priestman wrote, she envisioned her friends "waiting for a class to end, a job to get to, a boyfriend to make the phone jangle. I imagined them waiting for opportunities, anticipating changes, hoping for recognition, expecting something to be over or something to begin. I watched for automobiles and trucks, satisfied that the immediacy of my isolation was more invigorating than the dull suspension of their lives."

Did Theresa feel this way too? Restless with her Champlain College social life among teenagers two years her junior, relishing her freedom to hitch back to Montreal? Neither young woman, it seems, was fully aware of how limited her freedom truly was. In "Starlight," Priestman mused about this, how she came across the groundbreaking seventies reference book by and for women, *Our Bodies, Ourselves*, from which women could finally learn and talk to one another about their sexuality and their bodily functions, their periods, their menopause, instead of hearing prim and ridiculous proclamations from men. She spent time with some feminists "kneading massive piles of whole-wheat dough in pursuit of kinship . . . I listened to the women debate about things I'd assumed were mine until they disclosed to me that they were not: freedom, choice, independence." She hitchhiked to her best friend's college dorm with the book in her knapsack. Was it possible that men weren't just powerful figures to giggle and swoon over, but oppressors? They needed to think it over. Her friend "winced at the gynecological drawings in my book. She said she'd never heard of what I was talking about, and, no, she didn't understand."

If Priestman and many millions of other North American women had time to digest and reflect on these changing ideas about their real status as women, Theresa's friends and family had the revelation hit them shatteringly hard and head-spinningly fast. "For years," Debbie Ferdinand told me, "every time I drove down Highway 401 and passed Trenton," where Theresa is buried, "I would start bawling. She was the first, for all of us. Theresa's murder was a defining moment, an impact that reached well into the future. I was racked with guilt about the fact that hitchhiking for us had been a no-brainer. I felt guilt that I didn't go to her funeral. I felt guilt about not seeing her before she died. No one counselled us. We didn't know how to reach out to her parents. It made us all stop and think about how we were treating one another."

In Trenton, Theresa's cousin Kathy grieved, but she also grew fearful. "When my sons went out as teenagers, I waited up each time. I don't go to church anymore, but I'd say a Catholic prayer: 'Please put them in the palm of Mary's hand.'" Theresa, another friend wrote to John, "is the reason I still watch [my children] get on the school bus every morning even though the oldest is fourteen. She is the reason that I panic if my youngest disappears from my eye at the arena even though everyone tells me that X is such a small town you don't have to worry about things like that. I want to tell them, 'Compton was a small town too.'"

Vlad, Theresa's boyfriend, could find no compass. "She was such a good person," he told me. "When I lost her, I just didn't trust society anymore. I was out of my fucking mind after that."

He returned to Alberta at the end of November, operating a ski lift, then drifted to the Pacific coast to work on a prawn fishing boat. After that, he bought a truck and drove to Florida. When Bob contacted him about the discovery of Theresa's body, he returned briefly to Montreal, but eventually headed west again and founded a rafting company, where he worked for ten years before moving to Los Angeles. "It made me unable to fall in love. I was afraid to commit; I didn't want to lose a relationship." From November 3, 1978, until 2007 he avoided heartbreak by making bad, doomed-to-fail romantic choices.

The Allore family suffered the greatest damage, of course, although I didn't understand that when I met John in the autumn of 1979. People continue to function, don't they? They still make dinner and turn on the TV—at that time, it was *Brideshead Revisited* on PBS, which I watched on Sundays with Marilyn in their upstairs den. The Allores struggled to remain kind. I remember standing in the kitchen as Bob sliced onions, which he advised me were good for heart health. I don't know why I recall that small moment; perhaps because he was fathering me and my parents were far away. In his Buick, he used to keep cassettes of Pink Floyd's *Dark Side of the Moon* and *Animals*. I didn't know it then, but these had been his daughter's favourites. She had gone to the Animals Tour in 1977 when the band played in Montreal.

In the summer of 1896, the American author Mark Twain lost his twenty-four-year-old daughter Susy to a sudden case of spinal meningitis. He and his wife, Olivia, were devastated—all the more so because they were in England when Susy, about to set sail to join them, died in Connecticut. "It is one of the mysteries of our nature," Twain later wrote, "that a man, all

unprepared, can receive a thunderstroke like that and live. . . .
The mind has a dumb sense of vast loss—that is all. . . . It will
be years before the tale of lost essentials is complete, and not till
then can he truly know the magnitude of his disaster." About
seventy years later, what Twain described came to be known in
the grief literature as the "latency period." The grief can be
deferred. In traumatic loss it can also go unresolved, or, as the
psychologist Shelly Rambo has written, "Suffering is what, in
time, can be integrated into one's understanding of the world.
Trauma is what is not integrated in time; it is the difference
between a closed and an open wound."

If you wanted to clear the room at the Allore house, all you had
to do was mention Compton, John has told people. "At the dinner
table we always had to be careful. You were pretty safe if you just
kept to mentioning how good the meal was. Whatever you did,
you did not want to talk about education. It was like talking about
Sodom and Gomorrah. Someone would say the word *Compton*,
and that would be it. My mother would turn into a harpy, my
father would make a beeline to the kitchen, and anyone with
any sense would run to their rooms and lock the doors. *Compton,
Champlain, drugs*; these words were like daisy cutters. They could
rip across a room and cause total devastation."

Bob wanted to sue the school, but Marilyn said no. "We'd
never survive it," she warned. Even her family doctor had told
her not to pick a fight with a well-respected university like
Bishop's. "They'd drag our names through the mud. Think of
the boys. Andre is still at the CEGEP."

As John sees it looking back now, his parents had lost their
confidence. He sensed it, and on some level felt abandoned.

"Car rides home [from school] were horrible," he told me one evening when we sat before the fire in my farmhouse living room. It was the weekend of American Thanksgiving, but in rural Ontario, all was quiet and very, very dark. "They'd do the usual thing," and here he slipped into a chipper falsetto voice: "'How was your day?' They were just idiots to me. Unconsciously I blamed them. And I never got answers or advice from either after that. The attitude was, 'Well, don't ask me. I killed my daughter.'" He looked into the flames and rubbed his chin. "On some level, that's what I was being told, because they both kind of gave up. They felt it was their fault, that they hadn't sufficiently deterred her from drugs. Even Andre was standing with me, once, at the site where Theresa was found, and he said, 'I just think of her lying there face down in that amount of water . . .' It was clear to me what he meant: 'Had I just been there to pick her up, to lift her.' We all do it. I'm the least guilty person. I had no control over this; I was fourteen years old. So where does my guilt come in? *If only I'd been older. I could have done something.*"

Bob sought counsel from his own father about how to survive the death of a child. John told me, "My uncle died in his father's arms when he was twenty, of influenza. He was looking up at my grandfather, saying, 'Take me home, Dad,' and then he died. After Theresa, my father said, 'I don't know how to do this.' And my grandfather's advice was, 'You have to close the book and move on.' He had already lost a brother at Vimy Ridge during World War One. Then he lost his son, then his granddaughter. Charlie moved on very, very well."

Bob tried to follow his father's lead, and still does. Let life flow forward. Brace for the shocks. It was easier intended than done. "I don't mean to say that my family became like the family in the movie *Ordinary People*," John said, referring to the Oscar-winning film we both saw in 1980 at the mall in Saint John, in which a family staggers under the weight of one son's drowning. "But holidays were not fun. They would end in a fight, tears, too much drinking, heading upstairs and shutting the door." Every holiday meal would end that way until he and Andre started hosting gatherings at their own homes, with happy grandkids underfoot to temper the grief.

John experienced grief as an erosion of trust. "At this point I knew," he told me, "that, regardless of the drug theory, all of the people in authority had let my parents down. If I listened to anyone, it was to people who were anti-establishment, like my grade twelve teacher Ned Dickens, who showed us the film trilogy *O Lucky Man!* He would take me out for beer beside the school racetrack. This was playing to exactly what I wanted: a rebellious authority figure. That was right up my alley."

John was still young, and there was yet to be any vocabulary around a concept like grief triggers. But one year, when the school Remembrance Day parade came around, just as it had on the day he'd learned that Theresa was missing, he served as the drum major, a key figure in the procession getting under way at Rothesay Collegiate School in the spent and leafless autumn. "I just didn't want to get out of bed," he said. Then, a dry bark of a laugh. "I drove up to school, forty-five minutes late, and the teacher was furious. I made up some bullshit that I had a flat tire. Because you could do that; there were no cellphones. But I just didn't care."

At university, he became obsessed with the films of David Cronenberg and wrote violent comic skits. One featured animal vivisection; another, him being beaten to death with a bat. Later in New York, he would walk through Central Park alone late into the night, and once visited the body dump site of murder victim Jennifer Levin near the Metropolitan Museum of Art.

When we fell in love in 1980, John pulled me into a kind of folie à deux of mild lawlessness. This was when we went back to my cottage at Stony Lake and broke into neighbouring cottages for booze, leaving notes that said "sorry." We drove boats recklessly, and caught and coaxed crayfish to fight while covered with shaving cream, easily the most bizarrely sociopathic thing I have ever done. John took on his big sister's charisma, but in a bent direction. Before she died, he told me recently, "I was this dumpy-frumpy kid. This sounds horrible, but it's true. With all of them in the way—Andre, the older male; Theresa, this dynamo; my parents—I was never going to be anything but this stupid loaf of a kid. It wasn't until Theresa died, and the other three all just stopped . . . they just stopped living . . . that I began to assert myself in a position of dominance. The year we met, I was a red-hot guy: chasing skirt, *Rocky Horror Picture Show*, new wave." It wouldn't have crossed his mind that he was traumatized.

And he was, this broken young man, romantically attractive to me because he was edgy, and reckless, and beautiful, and dominant, and he took me to interesting brinks. As with Sarah Priestman and her hitchhiking, I was beguiled by the *Where now?* immediacy, the daring forays.

"I remember walking you to the train station in Saint John," he told me, "because you were going back to Halifax." I had gone on ahead of him to Dalhousie University in 1981. And he got on the train with me without a ticket. "What a shitty thing to do to my parents. For five hours they had no idea what happened to me. But I didn't care about their feelings. I didn't even think of their feelings."

Neither did I.

I went along on John's wild ride for three years, and then I broke up with him when we were at the University of Toronto. I was almost nineteen when I wrote in my diary:

April 22nd

There comes a point when everything that we felt and desired wearies and is lost. I despise that point. It is the heartless, tired phone call that ends with abrupt indifference: "We don't have anything in common, goodbye John.". . . He's in a phone booth at bleakest night in the endless droning rain in the middle of some damned city, and nobody in the world gives the damn necessary to alleviate that powerful loneliness. When [family friend] John Moore's wife died, who was capable of truly feeling his pain? It isn't that people are callous, they are not. But their empathy falls short. The depth of feeling that gave T.S. Eliot the power to write "The Waste Land" isolates him entirely from his peers. Because there exists a certain profundity beyond which one stands entirely alone, and there stands John. Uncomforted in his own unique misery because nobody can share it with him. There stands my own anguish because I could, by some superhuman effort, console him, but I draw away. Forgive me. My heart lies with you from this

impenetrable distance that, because of its very existence,
severs us always.

So, I knew, and yet I didn't know. I don't remember writing in this diary. I found it when I was moving houses in the summer of 2018, and then I fell silent, contemplating.

"Without a doubt," he told me, "when you broke up with me, that was huge. It felt like someone had died. I dropped down to a half-course at U of T, and I was planning to go live with my grandfather at his farmhouse. I remember riding the Toronto subway back and forth until it closed. I went to Montreal to visit my brother. I remember listening to the Clash and then leaving to go back to the train station. Andre ran out after me. It was snowing. He was panicked, and he just grabbed me and asked, 'Are you okay?' It was almost like he felt it was going to happen again."

Years later, a woman John fell in love with broke it off to go to graduate school. "I remember her saying on the phone, 'John, I'm not dying.' And I thought, *You're clueless. It* is *like a death. It* does feel like she died."

There was another entry in my diary that was dreamlike, free-associative, with references to my childhood in India when my father was posted there, and to John, himself, being childlike:

> I could not fight this hollow, bitter impulse to leave him behind,
> and I have visions of childhood like flashes of cold sunlight.
> The innocence and wonder of life that is life and not pain. The
> scent of burning leaves, summer sinking into the wood of the
> front porch, the crickets and cicadas, the silent, magical winter.

The smell of his skin, the look in his eyes, the feel of his silky, dark hair.

Sex dampening the sheets, the hot, exotic swirl of the market in India, fresh rain between my lashes, warm kitchen smells. He once made ice cream in the garden, patiently churning, his new project. He'd have stayed outside 'til the moon rose and a chill pricked at the skin of his bare feet on the grass, if it had taken that long. In the hotel room, he was up, cross-legged in front of our TV. "Bugs Bunny," he shouted. I murmured and slept on, my breast exposed in the sunlight, his eyes alive on the cartoon.

At the zoo, he wondered at the tiger, pacing with fierce anger in the Man-world. John shook and cursed, his brows knit deeply together. I used to be afraid of the elephants in Delhi. Their trunks swinging back and forth in the red dust. I was so tiny, shivering. They couldn't see me. I told my mother they'd surely crush me, and then she'd be sorry.

Freud would have had a field day. But it was like that, in the seventies, as we rushed headlong into our sexual freedom. We were dealing with forces we didn't understand and couldn't contain.

John eventually finished his degree and moved to New York, where he bartended and studied acting. Our paths would cross from time to time when I attended Columbia's School of Journalism and drank bourbon at the place he was working in Chelsea. A couple of years later, I took over a room he'd been renting on Grand Street in SoHo, but he mostly remained wary of me. In fact, he was alternately wary and defiant where much of his life was concerned. "Looking back," he says, "at that time, I felt guilty about Theresa, so I retreated, but then I felt resentful for having to retreat and acted out. Fuck *you*, guilt! I went through a kleptomaniac phase in my mid-twenties. It was all about whether I could pull one over on society. I didn't steal anything I needed, just boxes and boxes of hockey cards. Ridiculous stuff, not a winter coat because I'm freezing. Stupid shit that I could easily afford. It was all about 'Society fucked me, so I'm going to fuck society.'" A continuation of our minor crime spree at Stony Lake.

In the early nineties, he wound up in Los Angeles, where he commiserated one evening with the crime novelist James Ellroy, whose mother was murdered, an unsolved mystery that became the focus of Ellroy's 1996 book *My Dark Places*. It was around then, in 1995, that I reconnected with John. Having spent several years by then as a crime journalist, I was researching a book about how and why women could be violent. I needed to investigate a couple of female serial killers, and John accompanied me one day to the shabby apartment block that once housed a woman named Carol Bundy, partner to Doug Clark. Together, they were known as the Sunset Strip Killers.

We didn't talk about Theresa at the time, and John didn't tell me that Andre, having become a father to a daughter, had decided to reinvestigate her death. Their parents cautioned Andre against it, urging him to move on, to focus on his wife and child. But, Andre wrote in a journal, "I've decided to pursue this on a more personal level. I need to find out more about what happened. I need to talk to my old friends. Find out what they think. It still really bothers me that we essentially know nothing." (As a reader, you know more at this stage about Theresa's case than the Allore family did then.)

Andre still accepted the overdose theory as a given. He assumed that the Sûreté du Québec knew what they were doing, and although it had surprised him to think that his sister was capable of lethal recklessness in terms of drugs, he didn't consciously question it. Instead, he found himself needing to know *who* could be so horribly callous as to strip and dump his sister rather than take her to hospital, and all these years later still let the family suffer in not knowing her last moments.

Once Bob conceded that Andre needed to do this, he gave him another question to think over: "The police file must be in Sherbrooke. What was done after? After the body was found— what was done?"

Andre, like his father before him, bought a fresh notebook and began jotting things down. First, he compiled a list of key questions:

Where was [Theresa's] purse and scarf found?
Location/contents.
[Jo-Anne Laurie's boyfriend] was absent from campus for
 a few weeks that November. [He had checked Theresa's
 locker with Laurie when she went missing.] Where did
 he go? Why?
Who owned a car?

Andre arranged to meet with private investigator Robert Beullac, who apparently had forgotten that he'd stalked a "large negro" around Montreal on suspicion of involvement in Theresa's death. Noted Andre later, with neat blue penmanship in his diary, "He agrees that Theresa's death was most probably accidental and more than likely drug-related. Only a small group know what occurred. As I do, he has a difficult time with the theory that the body was taken from a room in Gillard House, and put in a car, and then taken to the Coaticook River without being seen. It would have been much easier to just put her back in her room, and close the door. He thinks they may have been in a car when this occurred, or they may have been near the area."

This suddenly gave Andre an idea: "They're out driving around," he wrote, "completely wasted on acid. They approach the bridge area and Theresa decides that she wants to get out of the car. She's sick. Or for some reason she decides she wants to go swimming. (In November?)" He briefly doubted himself. "She removes her clothes except for bra and panties, jumps in [water] and drowns. Cover-up."

Beullac encouraged Andre to "shake the tree" with Theresa's friends, to see what he could knock loose. Maybe one would confess something. "He cautioned my approach to contacting Caroline, Jo-Anne or anyone else that may have been close to Theresa. Take a very general approach, 'Someone has come forward. There's been new evidence. It was accidental. I don't have a lot of details yet.' You want them to react."

At the end of their meeting, Beullac warned Andre to be prepared for the truth. Emotionally, it could be difficult. "Expect nothing. Time is on your side." (This echoed what Gaudreault had told Bob: "Just wait, and someone will talk." But seventeen years had gone by.)

A good friend of Andre's reassured him, according to the diary. "If people are willing to talk now they may talk to you because you're quiet and not threatening."

Andre is a gentle, soft-spoken, charming man with cornflower-blue eyes, but that probably wouldn't cause people covering up a Dostoyevskyan atrocity of conscience to say anything new.

In Andre's second meeting with Beullac, the PI pointed out that Theresa was found to have vomit in her gullet. In the late seventies, rock stars choking on vomit in their sleep seemed to be all the rage, but in reality, vomit in the gullet can occur in death as a release of bodily fluid from all orifices. It signifies nothing in particular about a drug overdose. This was no longer the late seventies. It was the mid-nineties. But ideas are pervasive, and Andre was an IT guy, not a forensics expert. He had no way of knowing that vomit is also symptomatic of strangulation.

One November morning, Andre left his home in Montreal and drove down into the Townships. On rue Belvédère, the main road connecting south Sherbrooke to the town of Lennoxville, he made a wrong turn and wound up near the train station from which he and Theresa had departed to Saint John for their last Thanksgiving together. She had gazed out the window and he'd slept, and now he rued the fact that he hadn't done more on that train with her, engaged more. How precious our relationships are; how we chase them backward through time.

From there, he made his way to Sherbrooke College, where former SQ investigator Roch Gaudreault, who had retired in 1988, was teaching a course in policing. They met in his college office. Gaudreault was cordial, but made it clear that this was a long-ago case, far from his mind, difficult to summon to memory. He was sympathetic, but puzzled that Andre was visiting him, "He said, 'I guess it's difficult for the family, not knowing what happened.' I got the feeling he was trying to figure out why Theresa's death was still bothering me. This case just was not that interesting. No bullets, etc. I think they just wanted to bury it from the beginning, with the school being involved. As I filled in most of the details he kept saying, 'Yes, it's starting to come back to me . . .'"

Andre continued, "He believes that Theresa probably died accidentally at Compton and either one or two students got scared and dumped (or brought) her to the river. No violence. I asked if anyone had seen her at Compton on November 3. He said, 'Oh! She was there quite positively.'" This was an interesting remark. For a man who claimed to remember very little about the case, he was certain on this one detail supporting the idea that she had overdosed on drugs at her dorm. "He thinks I should try contacting people who were there at the time. They may talk now."

Gaudreault wrote down the names of two contacts at the SQ. He told Andre to contact them in case they had the file. Later that day, Andre met with Sergeant Guy Desmarais at SQ headquarters in Sherbrooke. Desmarais first called Gaudreault to "verify he could talk to me or something." When the police officer returned, he carried two large brown files. He read aloud to Andre the statements of Caroline Greenwood, Josie Stapenhorst, Jo-Anne Laurie and Sharon Buzzee—the one witness to place Theresa at King's Hall that night. He further read the statement by Dave Vick, who had been found high on acid on the campus lawn and was taken to hospital for observation. (None of the police seemed to have walked themselves through the logic of how the only kids known to have done LSD on November 3 at King's Hall wound up in medical care while Theresa was somehow, of necessity, stripped and hidden in a cornfield. Nor did they think through *who* drove her body there, if Vick was found passed out on the lawn while another acid-tripper snored in his room. Somehow, the mere fact that two guys had been tripping in their college dorm was enough to explain the death of a young woman who didn't even socialize with them. It was death by association—what Gaudreault described in Theresa's case file as a "surrounding problem of drugs.") How Desmarais managed to zero in on these statements out of more than a hundred in the file on the same day that Andre first brought his interest to the SQ's attention is a mystery.

Sergeant Desmarais went on, unexpectedly, to express disregard for PI Robert Beullac, according to Andre's diary. "He mentioned that Beullac caused a lot of problems for the investigation. I asked for an explanation, and he said that R.B. just wanted money. He wanted the investigation to go on and on." Andre took the officer's concerns with a grain of salt, writing, "Well maybe that's the difference between a P.I. and an SQ officer. The P.I. gets paid to get results, whereas the officers get paid to file away the case."

Andre's diary continued:

I asked, "Where was her purse and scarf found?"

"On Macdonald Road." He didn't know where that is, but I later found out from a local in a bar in Compton.

I asked about the clothing. "Items of clothing were found in the same area as her body," Desmarais said, checking the file, "but these clothes were not thought to be hers." [Was he referring to the torn scarf?] No description. A plastic bag with clothes was found in the area, again they concluded these were not hers.

Desmarais asked for more time to review the file, and Andre left, feeling none the wiser. He began mulling over the fact that Laurie's boyfriend had left Champlain for a couple of weeks after Theresa had vanished. Hadn't he been known to deal drugs on campus? What were the implications?

Andre stopped for lunch in Compton to ask locals where Macdonald Road was, wanting to track down the place where Theresa's red wallet and scarf had been located. He'd now learned that it wasn't her purse, which, in fact, had never been located. He was also told, incorrectly, that her scarf was found there. "According to the police both items were found by a local in his ditch, together. Question is how did the items get here?" He later asked Gaudreault, who speculated that a wild animal carried them. (As wild animals, fulfilling secret fantasies of being couriers to nowhere, are wont to do.) Andre found the explanation absurd.

"By this time, it was getting late," he continued, "meaning 4:00 p.m. I headed back to Lennoxville and on to Sherbrooke, then home to Montreal. I thought about Theresa hitchhiking along this same highway at about the same time of day 16 years ago. I remembered a story Rose [his girlfriend] told me about Theresa. Rose had asked her if anything weird had happened to her while hitchhiking. Theresa replied by mentioning that one time a guy asked her if she wanted to see his cock and she'd said, 'No, I've seen one already.'"

Could his clever, confident, charismatic older sister have been wrong about how vulnerable she was? Andre didn't allow himself to grasp this, it seems, even as it arose in his mind. He did, however, pull over onto the side of the highway back to Montreal because, he found, he couldn't stop weeping.

For a few weeks, Andre doubled down on the cop-given theory of friends who'd betrayed his sister. "I remember hearing Jo-Anne Laurie on the phone upstairs in Gillard," he noted. "She was saying, 'You have to come back.' This would have been around the 10th, 11th, or 12th. I'm sure she was talking to Ian." In a diner in Toronto a little while later, Andre met with Marty, an old friend from Champlain, and confided his thoughts. It bothered Andre that when he had decided to call his parents about Theresa being missing, her friends had said to wait until they checked with other friends in Montreal, as if stalling for time. "Marty [agreed that] this was strange. He said, 'How did they know who to call? How did they know the phone numbers?' I never thought about it. How did they get Theresa's phone book?" His mind spiralled.

Andre resolved to call Jo-Anne Laurie, who had, over the years, been under a vague cloud of suspicion due to inconsistencies in her memory of what had been in Theresa's locker. But it was a suspicion that led nowhere. Like most of Theresa's female friends, her response, even after all this time, was straightforward. "She may have been hitchhiking from the Bishop's campus to Compton and never made it." Indeed, all of the young women, as far as we can tell, intuited foul play at the time.

Laurie conceded that it was *possible* something had happened at Compton and Theresa was taken to the field by peers because "people were scared." But she doubted it. They kicked around some ideas. "She kept referring back to the hitchhiking theory. I told her that there was no sign of violence or rape. Then I said that Theresa was seen at Compton Friday, November 3, at 9:00 p.m. Dead air." By which he meant that Laurie made no reply. He told her that it had been Sharon Buzzee who'd seen Theresa then. "Jo-Anne replied, 'I don't remember who that was.'"

A few days later, Andre jotted down another theory. "Theresa died somewhere off campus. Maybe at Caroline's place in Hemmingford. Then they decided they had to get rid of the body. Not in Hemmingford area, because that might implicate Caroline. Actually, they were all from Hemmingford, they went to high school together. So, they decided to bring her back to the Compton area in a location that they thought would look like a hitchhiking mishap."

Allowing himself to be guided by the police theory, Andre grasped at ways to connect the smallest of inconsistencies, to make sense of pauses and hesitations in phone calls, to track any and all curious behaviours lest they shed light on his sister's death. The Allore family had always loved puzzles. (The last picture puzzle they did together depicted NHL icon Tony Esposito; what a perfect Montreal family pastime.) Puzzles could be solved—this could be solved—by examining the edges of each tiny piece.

Reading his diary in 2018, I found myself wondering if, on some level, it had simply been more bearable for Andre to consider Theresa's death accidental. When I asked him, he said he had no context in the late seventies or even in the nineties for doubting police authority. He figured they had some basis for their overdose theory, even if it didn't square with his sense of Theresa. "I thought I hadn't known her as well as I'd assumed." Andre's only frame of reference, in this era before the Internet, were the words of investigators and the slew of old onion-paper documents he had inherited from his father. These were the puzzle pieces that came in the box.

With considerable effort in that pre-Facebook time, he managed to track down the second man who had taken LSD in November 1978, to press him for details. "Mark thought the fact they had taken acid was insignificant" in terms of David Vick winding up on his back on crackling leaves on the lawn. "The same thing could have happened if he had only been drinking." People who drop acid may do strange things, like marvel at kitty litter or stroke lampshades for three hours, but they rarely get physically ill in any serious way. "He said Theresa wasn't with them and he really didn't socialize with her. He didn't know of anyone else trying acid that night." Andre then noted in the diary that "Mark M. specifically said that his room was in Gillard Hall and Dave Vick's was in King's Hall." But the Champlain College student directory for that year "has them both listed in the same room . . . Either, honest mistake. Forgot. He switched rooms during the semester. [Or] He's hiding something." Andre's questions could only free-float.

As it happened, Theresa's girlfriends had struggled with suspicions too. Deborah Ferdinand remembers a day when a guy named Terry (the girls used to hang out with him in Montreal "because he had awesome stereo speakers"), marshalled a group of them "to drive to where Theresa died." Deborah felt uncomfortable. "It didn't feel right. Why was he doing this? Did he want to see what we knew? Then *Terry* became our suspect." And on it went, with all of those who loved Theresa left to their own devices and whirling upon one another. "I would get so confused with all the theories flying around," Deborah said. "We lived off of rumour, suspicion and finger-pointing."

At length, with a career to tend to and children to raise, having poked around only when he could on the weekends, Andre began to give up. "I started to think that after sixteen years, why should anyone say anything to me?" he wrote. "I'm dealing with people who feel they have covered all their tracks. No one has ever questioned them."

He was right, but he may have been wrong about which people, precisely, had made those tracks.

EIGHT

BAD DREAM HOUSE

"What's past is prologue"
—William Shakespeare, *The Tempest*

JOHN LIVED UNEASILY, IF LARGELY UNCONSCIOUSLY, WITH THE police story of his sister's death until the late nineties, when, as fate would have it, his turn came to sleep in the house of a dead girl.

He had just started working as an accountant for the city of Durham, North Carolina, after moving to his wife's hometown from Los Angeles. They didn't have much money, but Elisabeth found an affordable house for sale on a cul-de-sac called Robin Road in the nearby community of Carrboro. From the outside it looked quite charming, with a wood stove visible through the window. But when they opened the realtor's lock and peered in, they saw a sea of debris. Coke and Cheerwine and Mello Yello cans all over the floor. Pizza boxes everywhere. It looked like the members of a rock band had lived there. The messy kitchen had a seventies feel, with orange countertops and bright-yellow walls. The main room, where the wood stove was, featured a collection of VHS porn tapes. More alarmingly, the wall was covered in pornographic anime cartoon drawings. There was a fully decorated Christmas tree (it was the week before Easter). A Japanese warrior figure stood in one corner, and here and there were Star Wars figurines. Dog urine stained the floorboards. In one bedroom, the floor was so rotted that they could see through to the basement. According to the realtor, a mother and son were selling the place after the father had died here of terminal cancer. Everything had clearly just gone to seed.

John heard music coming from down the hall and thought, *Holy shit, somebody's here.* He walked toward a door that had bullet holes and knife slashes on it. Poking it open a little, he saw someone on the bed. "This guy just rolls over toward me, staring blankly, and then rolls back. He looked goth, like a heavier Trent Reznor. I was like, *Holy fuck!* This was the fixer-upper from that *Simpsons* Halloween episode "Bad Dream House." Elisabeth was thinking, *It just needs a little love. We will cure this house.*"

The master bedroom had potential, but it, too, was a total mess. On the wall next to the closet hung, of all things, a Christopher Pratt print. John and I had gone to boarding school in New Brunswick with this Canadian artist's children Barbara and Ned. Seeing a Pratt in Carrboro, North Carolina, was surreal. It was also strangely nostalgic, perhaps a sign that things could be made right.

John took Saturday morning clinics at Home Depot and learned how to rip things out and grout and DIY renovate. He found and removed a bizarre assortment of weapons strewn around the backyard: big knives, swords, spears. For two months, Elisabeth and baby Amelia stayed with Elisabeth's parents while he worked evenings and weekends to clean up. Almost immediately after moving his family in, John received an urgent message at work from Elisabeth. There'd been a call from the police. Apparently, the former owner's son, the man they'd seen spaced out in the bed, was the lead suspect in a missing person's case. In fact, the police wanted to come to the house and look for a body.

John drove home to find on the front porch Chief of Police Carolyn Hutchison, whom everybody called Hutch, investigator John Lau and the town attorney. They explained the circumstances. Andrew Dalzell, the sleeping son, had gone to a pool hall in Carrboro called Sticks and Stones the previous year. He was seen sitting in the corner, drawing anime on his sketchpad and drinking a Coke. A thirty-something local named Debbie Key showed up, a little tipsy, and was seen giving Dalzell a shoulder massage before leaving with him. The next day, her car was found abandoned in the parking lot of the Bank of America next door to the bar. Her purse remained in the unlocked car, but Debbie Key had vanished.

It took the police almost a year to trace Debbie's disappearance back to Dalzell. They eventually connected the guy witnesses had seen drawing anime in the bar to the man who was living at 500 Robin Road. They couldn't prove his involvement, so they would drive by the house periodically. Recently, on one of Hutch's drive-bys, she'd noticed that all the junk in the yard had been cleaned away and replaced with children's playthings. Her first thought was, "Holy crap, somebody bought this place?" Then she called Elisabeth.

"By the time the police told us about this, Sticks and Stones no longer existed," John later told me. "Instead, it had become a children's consignment store called Chicken Noodle Soup— owned and run by Elisabeth after we got a town loan. So, just to be clear about the complete absurdity here, we had acquired and renovated the abduction site, and then we had acquired and renovated the suspected murder site."

Hutch and her colleagues wanted to bring a cadaver-sniffing dog to the house, and the couple agreed. What else could they do? "We were scared shitless. Our imaginations ran wild. We thought Dalzell was going to come back in the middle of the night and slaughter us. I remember them saying, 'The dog can't come this week, he's really busy.' Apparently, he'd just done a site in Atlanta and was tired. We had to wait, so we fled to the Outer Banks. There was no way we were staying there."

Eventually, a whole crowd of investigators showed up at the house: the FBI, the cadaver dog, everybody from Carrboro, many of them in their SWAT gear. The State Bureau of Investigation brought two forensic experts with luminol bottles, for detecting bodily fluids. There was a man from Pee Wee's Pump Service to clear out the septic tanks. "I remember that tank level going down and down and down. We were expecting at the end to see the crest of a skull or something. There was nothing. They went through the house with the luminol: nothing. I'd ripped everything out."

Finally, they decided to send the sniffer dog into the crawl space under the house. Almost immediately the dog "lighted," which is to say he started scratching at the ground. This was Carolina clay. It would be hard to dig a six-foot hole in that earth. The team had brought shovels, but they couldn't get far down, so they determined that the dog was lighting on where Debbie Key had been stashed temporarily—hidden under the house, possibly for three weeks, while Dalzell decided where to dispose of her.

Years later, he confessed that he took the body to a Dumpster in Wilmington, North Carolina, a couple of hours away. She became landfill. The confession was thrown out for legal reasons, but there's no reason to think it wasn't true, and Dalzell was eventually caught in a sting operation trying to have sex with an underage girl who was actually a police officer. In 2010, he received the maximum sentence.

In the meantime, after that day with the investigators, John kept feeling apprehensive that he would find Debbie Key somewhere on the property, which edged down to a stream. The anxiety dogged him every time Amelia and then his second daughter, Grace, wanted to play at the back of the garden. Then Amelia began having a recurring dream. "We overheard her in the hallway one morning as she walked in her nightie and bathrobe to the bathroom, saying to herself, "Nope, nope. Not gonna have that dream again. Not gonna have that dream where Mom and Dad turn into skeletons."

John and Elisabeth organized a smudging ceremony for the house. Somebody advised them to put a crystal in the southwest corner. "We put a crystal in every fucking room." It wasn't that the house felt haunted to John; it was more that "it just felt dead. The wind didn't blow there. Our wind chimes never stirred."

One night, the family was asleep near dawn when the front door went *boom, boom, boom.* A man's voice called, "Is everybody alright in there?" *Boom, boom, boom.* "Is everybody alright in there?" They got up and walked down the hallway from the master bedroom, Elisabeth behind John. "We could see the cherry top light of a cop car. Adjacent to the front door was a rectangular window, and I could just glimpse the hat of a state trooper." John opened the door, and the trooper repeated his question: "Is everything alright in here?"

"Yeah, we're fine. It's fine."

The officer looked past John to Elisabeth. "Ma'am, are you alright?"

She nodded, mystified. "What's going on?"

"We got an emergency 911 call from this house," he said.

They sold Robin Road after living there for less than three years.

NINE

SENSE OF DOUBT

"In the beginner's mind there are many possibilities,
in the expert's mind there are few."
—Shunryū Suzuki, *Zen Mind, Beginner's Mind*

In the spring of 2001, John called me from North Carolina. I was, at the time, a columnist at Canada's *National Post* newspaper, and we hadn't seen in each other in some years. The whole business with Debbie Key had been unsettling him, making him think about what happened to Theresa. But he wasn't sure what to do. He wondered if I might write something about her story, an article, say, that might encourage those kids—the mysterious adolescent conspirators—to break a silence they had apparently held since 1978 and come forward with an account of Theresa's last night. I thought about this, but from a different perspective than I had at the age of fifteen, when everything grown-ups said was either irrelevant or incontestably true. Unlike Andre, I had been professionally trained, now, to doubt such things.

"I don't buy the theory, John. It doesn't make sense to me. Why would they take off her clothes?" He didn't know, and he'd grown skeptical too.

"Why heave her body into a creek, when it wasn't their fault that she died?" I persisted. "I can see trying to distance themselves from her death, but why hide her? Why not take her to the hospital and leave her on the lawn, or at least leave her at the residence somewhere?"

These questions had, of course, churned around in John and Andre's minds.

"Her wallet was found several miles away from her body," he offered, based on what his brother had discovered.

"So they stripped her of clothes and ID?" This seemed crazy to me. Some students took a friend who had died accidentally, and coolly, systematically, turned her into a Jane Doe?

After Andre's look into the matter, he'd passed along his notes to his younger brother. John, who has an incisive, almost lawyerly curiosity, now started expanding the file. He'd requested a copy of their sister's coroner's report, studied newspaper clippings and tracked down climate data from Environment Canada for November 3, 1978, an unusually mild day reaching twelve degrees. (This is how we know that no one could have taken LSD and then been hospitalized "for exposure," as Beullac told Bob Allore had happened that night.) John sent me photocopies of what he'd gathered. When the package arrived, I sat down at my dining room table in downtown Toronto with a cup of coffee. I looked at the report from the coroner and noted its inconclusive conclusion: "violent death of undetermined means." The results of a toxicology workup on Theresa's body had been negative: no evidence of either prescription or illicit drugs were found in her liver, lungs or other tissues. Why was the police hypothesis a drug overdose? All of this was brand new to me. I sat back in my chair, intrigued.

John and I met up in Sherbrooke—a seven-hour drive for me and a two-stop plane trip for him—when our schedules finally aligned. Andre, who still lived in Montreal where he worked in IT, would join us the following evening for dinner; his son had a hockey tournament that weekend in nearby East Angus. I was expecting John to be tense, given what we confronted, but he was quite the opposite. He had been running around all day without a coat in spite of the cold March weather, wearing only a light-blue cotton sweater. There was a jauntiness about him, as if he felt huge relief that he was finally staring down the demons of grief. His hotel room was littered with papers, news clippings, notebooks, the lights of his laptop winking beside the coffee machine. He had written out the tale of the last two days, describing a city he had not been to since he was fourteen:

From the hotel window, Sherbrooke looked cold and grey. Looking south, I saw King Street, the main drag, bisecting the city east-west. Beyond King was the Magog River, separating the northern part of Sherbrooke from the south shore. The south shore crept up from the banks of the Magog, cresting at the top at mont Bellevue, which was marked with a large white cross. Over mont Bellevue, to the east, lay Lennoxville and Champlain College. Farther south was Compton—where she died. At the foot of my hotel, I could see rue Don-Bosco and the offices of the Sûreté du Québec. The police were expecting me at 8:00 a.m.

I sat in the hotel dining room and drank coffee. I was nervous about meeting with them. They said I could look at my sister's crime file. What if they showed me photos? What if I were allowed to see photos of the body or the autopsy? What would that be like? Would there be a full shot from the front? One of the back? The head, the chest, the legs? The face? The face in profile? Before leaving North Carolina, my doctor had given me a prescription for Xanax. I told her it was for my fear of flying. It was really for this. I clutched my bag and checked the side compartment. The bottle of pills was still there.

After I booked my flight, I called the Sûreté du Québec to confirm our appointment. They had said I could see all of the contents of my sister's file. They had nothing to hide. Now, they had changed their minds; Caporal Théorêt had discussed the matter with his supervisor. I could only see certain portions of the file.

"What parts can I see?"

"When you come, you can see the parts that you can see."

It was like talking to the fucking Delphic oracle.

I arrived punctually at eight for my appointment. The offices of the Sûreté du Québec reminded me of a mental hospital. There was Nurse Ratchet sitting behind the Plexiglas. I introduced myself to her, explaining that I had an appointment with Robert Théorêt. She pushed a button and told me to be seated, and after about two minutes, Théorêt appeared and let me in through the secured door. We walked up the stairwell while I tried to exchange pleasantries.

"Do you like hockey, Caporal Théorêt?"

"No, I do not."

I was led across the squad floor to a small interrogation room in the corner. The room was pretty stark—a folding table, two chairs, a telephone. *Great*, I thought, *a set-up. This is when they sit me down and slap me around with a phone book. "This will teach you to come to Sherbrooke, pushy American!"* On the table was a stack of papers about four inches thick. It contained some notes from the original investigation conducted by the Lennoxville police, some reports from the coroner and some of the statements from the witnesses. Barred to me were the final report, the statements from suspects and some photos of the crime scene.

He left me alone, and I leafed through the papers. Mostly they were statements—photocopies—some in French, some in English. I glanced at a page. *I first met Theresa Allore around August 28th at a Champlain pub.* Strange. I was looking back in time. I skimmed another statement. *She seemed hyper. Her boyfriend moved out West. Theresa was friendly with other boys, but they weren't boyfriends.* It was like opening and closing a book.

You could enter it, then shut it off. *She was wearing a white t-shirt, blue cord slacks, a long beige sweater and Chinese slippers. She went to dinner. She hasn't been seen since November 3rd.* I got out my French dictionary and notebook. I would just copy it all down, like taking dictation. If I concentrated on making my notes, then I couldn't be affected by it. I copied all the statements. Reading the information was eerie. This wasn't some made-up story. My parents had lived through this. Theresa had really died.

For me, much of the story of Theresa's death had been like hearing people talk about a foreign country—a place that you longed to visit yourself, but you were at the mercy of the information of others. I had these impressions, these postcards in my mind about how it all looked. When I finally got to see these places for real—the towns, the roads, the buildings— it wasn't that it was so different than what I expected, it just seemed too normal. There was nothing that would tell you something bad had happened here. And now I was in the landscape. I was trying to be an impassive observer. After copying the statements, I drove down to Compton, and realized that I had unwittingly become part of her story.

King's Hall was now a "resort" hotel. In advertisements it referred to itself as a "Four Seasons Resort." Not a "Four Seasons *Hotel*," as in the world leader in luxury hotels and resorts. *Four seasons*, as in, this hotel is open all four seasons of the year. After the lease was up in 1979, the owners tried to unload the school on the Canadian government for $1.1 million, but the government took a pass. I pulled into the parking lot. There was one car in the drive.

One car, and over one hundred rooms. This place wouldn't last through the summer. I entered the lobby. There was a suit of armour propped up in the corner. In any other situation, I suppose I would have called it beautiful—mahogany panelling, a tea service, a harpsichord. In the Townships, it just seemed weird. A bed and breakfast, maybe, something country-quaint to go along with the cows and the gristmills—but this place? It was a gothic anomaly in the middle of dairy country, like Hill House. I recalled my brother telling me he had visited this place during his investigation. Upon entering the lobby, he was faced with two middle-aged women sitting on a mahogany bench, sobbing, "She's gone, she's gone!" It felt surreal.

I introduced myself to the receptionist and asked to speak with the owner, if possible. Soon after, the manager appeared—a very chipper British gentleman. I told him who I was and why I had come. Rather than turfing me out, he was very coopera-tive and invited me to look around. There were many things that caught my eye, but it was difficult not to stop gawking at the main staircase in the middle of the reception area. This was the place where, one student claimed, Theresa was last seen. And there it was. Curved handrails. Sculpted balusters. Beautiful, and strangely familiar. Like those pictures of the *Titanic* at the bottom of the North Atlantic.

I walked up the stairs to the second floor, where my brother had lived. You could tell that the building had recently been restored, but just to the way it had looked in the late seventies. I came outside and checked the grounds. You could almost see the shadows of the students. People sitting on the grass, drinking. Boys playing touch football and Frisbee. Students walking with books in their arms. I walked around the corner of King's Hall to where Gillard House had been. I was expecting to find it levelled, but there it stood, as if it hadn't been touched in decades. The place was still painted with its original colours—orange and brown—it looked like the A&W Root Bear. I entered the building and climbed the stairs to the second floor. Gillard had been built much later than King's Hall; it was your typical sixties-style college dormitory. The rooms were laid out next to each other in corridors. I looked at the doors and tried to imagine which room would have been hers. I thought about the statements I had read that afternoon. This room might have been where the two students were listening to records that night, waiting for her to return. But she never did. Spooky. All the people are gone. Now I am here.

It was getting late. I wanted to visit chemin de la Station—the place where her body was found—before it got dark. Pulling out of the King's Hall parking lot, you couldn't help but feel like you were recreating that last drive, and that she was there riding alongside you. I turned right and coasted down the hill into Compton village. I drove past Entre-Deux on my right—then a student bar, now a vacant property. Just past the post office, I turned left on chemin de la Station and drove the half mile down the hill into the Coaticook valley. At the crest you get a beautiful view of the land—farms and rolling hills, a grain silo on the other side of the ridge. At the bottom I could see this little oasis of trees; this little spot tucked around a small pond. My heart just dropped into the seat of my stomach, because I knew that spot. I had never seen it before, but I knew. I got out of the car and walked to the bridge. To the north of me stood the farmer's house. I could see the cornfields, now crushed, brown and damp. I could see the melting snow. I could see the trees that lined the banks of the pond. The water looked stagnant and brown. In the reeds, a family of ducks was nesting. I stood and I stared. The wind blew cold. I hoped that some new idea or thought would come along and rescue me. Nothing came. I looked for an answer; all I got was the wind and the ducks and the cornfield.

What does it mean to stand in the place where your sister died? I don't know. It's a special place. It's special to me. But I can't say why. It feels like a big, sucking magnet. You're drawn there. You get there. You say, "Okay. Here I am"—and nothing. I could go home right now, I told myself. When my wife asks, "What did you find?" I could say, "Nothing. Let's get on with our lives."

I drove back to the hotel with a spiking migraine. It was so bad that by the time I reached the room my vision began to tunnel. I went to bed thinking I had made a mistake, coming here. In the morning I stiffened my resolve. Over breakfast, I thought about the previous day, and the information the police had allowed me to see: 115 statements—most of them from students—and the Lennoxville police chief's notes. That was it. The chief's notes were a mess. There were only about seven pages, and his reports mainly consisted of his attempts to establish Theresa as a runaway. Now the Lennoxville police were defunct. The Sûreté du Québec had taken over their jurisdiction years ago. So there was no risk in showing me Chief Hamel's notes; if I found fault with his police work, the unit was no longer around to be criticized. This left the statements from students, the thoughts of a group of teenagers, their speculation on what had happened. Where were the documents concerning the *investigation*?

On Friday afternoon, I had some spare time, so I decided to go back to Champlain College to see if I could talk to someone with the school. I turned right on Belvédère and headed out to Lennoxville. I hated Champlain College the way a Hatfield hates a McCoy. It was inherited hatred. I knew nothing about the place. But my parents hated the school, so I did too. Champlain College officials were snakes, they were cowards, they were arrogant, self-interested bastards who never cared that my sister went missing, and cared even less after her body was found. Champlain's interest was self-preservation, and nothing—least of all the life of some drug-addled student—was going to tarnish their academic position, their sterling status in the community. My father had one word for Champlain's former campus director, Bill Matson: *asshole.* He called him "the master of the cover-up." My mother's opinions were equally vitriolic. "That school killed my daughter!" Or "The teachers were as high on drugs as the students were!" Or "One of the teachers was arrested for diddling himself in public!"

I didn't know if my parents' opinions were valid or not. What I did know was that the school had caused my parents untold suffering. In turn, I had suffered. So I hated the place. I had known the names of all the players it seemed my entire life. Bill

Matson had died years earlier, but his name still wielded power. Say the name William Matson and you might as well be uttering the word *Voldemort*, the man was so despised in our home.

As I entered the administration building, I tried to suppress the bile that was bubbling up at the back of my throat. I walked around—unannounced—snooping through the hallways, sticking my head into offices where I clearly had no business. *Fuckers. Bastards. Disrespecting shits.* Eventually—and quite by chance—I stumbled upon the offices of the director general of Champlain College, Gerald Cutting, and his ex-wife, Melanie Cutting, the director of student services for the school. Both Cuttings had been at Champlain back in 1978–79. Melanie Cutting was then in charge of student housing services, while Gerry was a recently appointed director of student services. I introduced myself as the brother of Theresa Allore—the younger brother, not the one who had attended Champlain. Talk about your conversation stopper. You'd have thought all the air had been sucked out of the room—although Gerry kept his composure. He invited me to sit down, and asked what they could do.

I told them I was interested in obtaining copies of any old records concerning the event—files, a list of students, any correspondence between my father and Bill Matson, a yearbook, a directory for the rooms in Gillard House and King's Hall—these kinds of things. Gerry Cutting stated that he didn't know if this information existed, but they would check through the archives and, if anything turned up, they would certainly share the information with me. I asked Gerry what he thought had happened to Theresa. He looked confused. *Hasn't anyone told you?* Then, without hesitation, he stated matter-of-factly, "Well, your sister was murdered."

"Is that your opinion?"

No, he clarified, he had known the lead investigator, Roch Gaudreault. They went to high school together—in fact, so did Leo Hamel, the former Lennoxville police chief. He went to the same high school. According to Cutting, when the Sûreté du Québec took over the investigation from Hamel, Gaudreault quickly developed a theory that it was a murder. Gaudreault believed that the crime had taken place in residence, and that there had been accomplices. He reportedly told Cutting that he thought she had been put in the water on chemin de la Station to make it look like she had died while hitchhiking.

"Did Gaudreault ever tell you how he thought Theresa was murdered?" I asked.

"Strangulation."

Now it was my turn to feel shock. I had entertained a lot of wild-ass visions of my sister's death. Overdoses, drowning, suicide—maybe even murder. But in my head all those years it had been a generic murder; it didn't have a name. It wasn't stabbing or bludgeoning or bullet wound. It was a sanitized version of a death. Now someone had given it a name. This was out of the blue. Strangulation had never once entered my mind.

. . .

This was the John I found at the hotel early that evening: ener-gized because he was beginning to feel vindicated. The drug theory *was* a red herring. His charismatic, loving big sister was *not* complicit in her own demise. He could relieve his brother and parents of that burden. He could say something different to his daughters. We talked about this in the hotel bar, where Andre joined us. I hadn't seen Andre since John and I slept on the floor of his Montreal apartment in the summer of 1981 after seeing the Police at the Forum. I was struck again by what a lovely, soft-spoken man he is, lighter in both colouration and temper than his brother, blue eyes to dark, elven archer to combative soldier. I could see why Marilyn saw them as balancing one another.

As we scraped peanuts out of the bottom of a bowl, John began thinking over the fact that Gerry Cutting had been so unexpectedly forthcoming compared to anyone else. It didn't make sense to him. "Why would he tell me these things?" he asked, sitting with his legs crossed and one arm jutting straight up from the armrest at his elbow. "Why would he risk the school's reputation by telling me a bunch of idle gossip?"

"Maybe he was confused," suggested Andre.

"He didn't look confused. He wasn't struggling to remember things; it all rolled off his tongue effortlessly, like knowledge he had always possessed." Both he and Andre found themselves wondering why Roch Gaudreault would have been so evasive with the family, but so forthright with someone he only knew socially, just an old schoolmate. If anyone was left feeling con-fused, it was them. Later, John called Bob to ask him about this.

"Dad, did Roch Gaudreault or Leo Hamel ever suggest to you the possibility that Theresa was murdered, that she had been strangled?"

"No," his father said.

John circled back to Corporal Robert Théorêt to ask if he would reinvestigate, given the revelation from Cutting that Theresa was thought to have been murdered. Théorêt was affable but evinced little interest, pointing out that he was short-staffed. "I have lots of cases," he said. "Why should I investigate this one?"

"Alright," John said. "I want to investigate it myself, then. What was Roch Gaudreault's final conclusion?"

"That information is privileged," Théorêt replied.

"Okay. What about forensic evidence? Where are Theresa's bra and underwear, which we could test for DNA?"

"We threw them out," Théorêt said.

What? "You threw them out?"

"Yes."

"When would you have thrown them out?"

"Not long after the coroner's verdict." (That's the "violent death of undetermined means" he was referring to.)

"After five years, you threw them out?" (The coroner's final report was issued in 1983.)

"Yes."

"Who would have authorized that?"

"Whoever was in charge at that time."

"Is there some sort of paper or document authorizing this?" John asked.

"If it's not in the file, then maybe it got destroyed."

Maybe, but John didn't have access to all the documents in the file, so how could he even begin to know? He felt like the world was upside down. It seemed to him as if, to Théorêt, the destruction of evidence was business as usual, no big deal. John had been raised on *The Rockford Files, McMillan & Wife, Quincy*. He thought, *Murder evidence doesn't get destroyed.*

"Do you have Gaudreault's number?" John asked.

"He doesn't want to talk to you," Théorêt answered.

To say that John felt stymied is an understatement. Who owns the secrets to a young woman's death? The cops and the robbers, it seems. Without access to key parts of Theresa's file, John didn't know where to begin. He was just a guy—an accountant—who lived hundreds of kilometres away. Eventually, after consulting a lawyer, he filed a Freedom of Information request. The response would sluggishly wend its way back from provincial officials over several months, where-upon a fax arrived in John's office in North Carolina: in addition to what had already been made available, he could see his brother Andre's statement from 1978. That was all.

The next morning, John took me to King's Hall, which I had never seen, although my mother had once resided there as a boarding-school student in the 1940s. Gazing at the staircase, just as John had done the day before, I pictured Mum as an ado-lescent with her chestnut braids and plaid skirts, skipping up these same steps three decades before Theresa. It was such a strange coincidence, but it wasn't haunting for me the way it was for John. In a way, that set the tone for our shared quest: he would be navigating landscapes of memory and emotion, constantly trying to calibrate his reactions, while I followed along like Scully behind Mulder, furrowing my brow and asking clinical questions.

Was the student Sharon Buzzee correct in her memory, I wondered (for instance), that she'd run into Theresa that night on this staircase? What was Theresa doing? If she was there, she may have hitchhiked back from Bishop's University library at around eight p.m. Perhaps she was on her way up to the second floor to visit Andre, who remembers a knock on his dorm room door that he didn't answer. He was otherwise (romantically) engaged. Did she descend that central staircase once again, walking through the vestibule and out onto the lawn? Did she return to her room in Gillard House (which her friends doubted, because they would have seen her)? Or did she turn the other way, walk down the circular driveway under the maple trees and set off toward Compton village?

At chemin de la Station, we stepped into the mud and matted cornstalks, and followed the creek away from the car. John stopped where the shallow, meandering water curved. He pointed. "You could drive to this point in November, no problem. There are no street lights, no houses around. Nothing. You could leave her right here." He was gesturing calmly toward the ground. "The farmer who owned this land told the police that the water rose eight to ten feet that spring. She got caught in the spring runoff and floated toward the bridge." John stood there in his cheerful blue cotton sweater, musing. Had his big sister come here, to this shadowy field, in her bra and underwear? Walking barefoot through the corn? Or was she hauled out of a car that had turned off the road and juddered across the clodded earth, driven by someone who knew exactly where he was, how invisible he would be?

Where were her clothes? Where were those Chinese slippers? Where was her favourite necklace? Why had the police found women's clothing in a garbage bag ninety metres from the body, clothes that didn't belong to Theresa? If she died here, why weren't her clothes here? We stood there staring for the longest time, as if the earth itself would reveal a memory, as if we could will ourselves to see what had happened on this quiet stretch of land.

For a time, we chased the ghosts of whispered suspects, pondering the teachers at Champlain (a possible affair?), considering the students just as Andre and Bob had done. We were committing the classic mistake of novice investigators. "Work from the evidence," a homicide detective I knew advised me. "Never work from the suspects."

I phoned an acquaintance in Washington, DC, a criminologist named Kim Rossmo, who was directing research at a think tank called the Police Foundation. Originally from Vancouver, Rossmo had been a beat cop who earned his doctorate from Simon Fraser University by pioneering a technique called geo-profiling, which maps the local pathways of serial offenders. His technique—and the software he developed—are used by the RCMP, the FBI and Scotland Yard. Rossmo was the first Vancouver investigator to propose that a serial killer was plaguing that city's red-light district in the gritty Downtown Eastside, where dozens of sex-trade workers went missing between 1995 and 2002. At first, the city brass dismissed his concerns, with

Mayor Philip Owen refusing to offer an award for leads from the public, saying he wouldn't finance a "location service" for "hookers." This proved memorable because he'd just posted a $100,000 reward for help with a sequence of garage robberies in one of Vancouver's tonier neighbourhoods, and further because Rossmo turned out to be right. The cost of excavating serial killer Robert Pickton's fourteen-acre pig farm for human remains would ultimately exceed $70 million. DNA traces of thirty-one women were found. A "location service" for missing sex workers—also known as a proper police investigation with a tip line—would have been a bargain.

When I called Rossmo, a few months after Pickton's arrest, I described what had happened to Theresa, how she had been found and the theory the police had favoured about how she'd died—the overdose and the panicking friends. He questioned me carefully and then said, "The theory doesn't fit."

"Why not?"

"Because she was found in her bra and panties. What you've described appears to be a sex murder."

"But the pathologist didn't find any evidence of rape."

"That doesn't mean anything. He could have used a condom. He could have had a deviance that didn't include intercourse."

Scholars who specialize in this dark subject define a sexual murderer as one "whose crime is accompanied by sexual assault or mutilation of sexual organs or who left his victim naked or in a sexually explicit position." (In conservative Catholic Quebec in the 1970s, being stripped to bra and underwear fell well within the rubric of being left in a sexually explicit position). "The murder is not necessarily sexually gratifying in itself," criminologists Jean Proulx, Eric Beauregard, et al., noted in their definitive book on the subject, *Sexual Murderers: A Comparative Analysis and New Perspectives*, "and in fact is usually motivated by rage. Sexual gratification typically is provided by a sexual assault concomitant with or subsequent to the murder. In some cases, the murderer's initial intention is sexual assault, and the murder is committed to eliminate a witness, whereas in others, it occurs accidentally during the struggle between the sexual murderer and his victim . . . more often than not, the murder is a reaction to a rebuff, offence or quarrel."

Perhaps the assailant had forced Theresa into masturbating him, or demanded oral sex while she vehemently resisted. I thought about something I'd read in the autopsy report: how Theresa still had a fulsome amount of "stomach contents" when she died, suggesting that she had not thrown up. Yet traces of vomit had been found in her throat. Had she gagged? On what? On the man who was assaulting her, or because of the way she was dying?

John sent Theresa's autopsy report to a pathologist and had it reanalyzed. Was it possible that she had been strangled?

"Yes," he said, "it is possible." This was the kind of case, he added, where police work was vital to solving the crime.

If Theresa was murdered, the question that John and I asked ourselves now was: Where? How, we wondered, could she have been killed at her student residence without anybody noticing? This was a problem with all of the scenarios. How could she have died in some manner related to drugs and been carted away without witnesses? There were students milling about everywhere that evening. There was a night watchman outside. How could someone have laboriously stuffed a body into a car and driven off? We re-examined the buildings, and then we reread the original statements. Theresa had bummed a smoke from Josie Stapenhorst, a fellow student, at six p.m. on the evening of November 3. The week before, according to private investigator Beullac, she had turned up at the Entre-Deux restaurant in Compton to buy Player's Light cigarettes from the vending machine. I phoned Andre to ask if Theresa was a regular smoker. She was, he said.

Entre-Deux was four hundred metres down Highway 147 from King's Hall, a quick walk on a dry autumn night. Maybe she left to buy cigarettes before meeting up with her friends at Gillard House to listen to records. She went out onto the unlit road with a quick errand in mind, and on the stretch before the sidewalks of Compton village begin, someone barrelled toward her. That someone had a car. And with Theresa in the vehicle, he doubled back or whisked past her residence and turned left onto the concession road at Compton Station, where he strangled and dumped her. The coroner had noted that there were bruises under her armpits, we learned later by reviewing Bob's diary.

Once we had established the possibility that Theresa was out on the highway, we could think about the assailant's route. Panicking students, for instance, would have returned to their residence after abandoning her body—all the more so if they were high or drunk. Not much executive function. But Theresa's wallet was found much farther north than King's Hall on a road that leads directly into Sherbrooke. Chemin

Macdonald, as it is called, is a concession road that locals use to bypass Lennoxville if they are heading north from the villages in Compton and Stanstead counties. Chemin Macdonald forks off Highway 143 and runs steeply uphill past a few houses and farms before changing its name to rue Belvédère, a boulevard that takes you straight into the southern section of the city. Whoever left Theresa on the side of chemin de la Station did not return to Compton or head into Lennoxville. They drove up to Sherbrooke.

Why?

This first foray into the Townships left us reeling with new information and questions. I drove back to Toronto, while John spent some time with Andre at his son's hockey tournament, then headed to the airport in Montreal. He e-mailed me as soon as he landed in Raleigh because of something he'd found. "I got to Dorval Airport totally burned out," he wrote. "I checked in, cleared customs and went to my gate. I was paged. I went to the ticket counter and the flight attendant handed me a note. It was from my brother: 'You forgot your cellphone. I tried to catch you before you cleared customs, but I was too late. I'll send it along to you next week. Good luck.' I started to cry. It was a rough week. I hate leaving Andre. I never say it, but I hate it." He got on the plane and started flipping through some photocopies he had made of the newspapers in Sherbrooke from dates around Theresa's disappearance and discovery. In an article written in *La Tribune* on Saturday, April 14, 1979, he noticed the following paragraph:

With the discovery of the body of the young girl on Good Friday yesterday, this marks the second consecutive experience that SQ agents have had to deal with. On March 24, 1978—Good Friday—children found the body of Manon Dubé of Sherbrooke. The cause of her death is still unknown and the case is still open. Another coincidence: both victims, as it is evident with Theresa Allore, went missing on a Friday night, and they were both found partially submerged in water.

TEN

HEROES FOR GHOSTS (A TRIO OF MYSTERIES)

" . . . memory, the warder of the brain."
—Shakespeare, *Macbeth*

IF YOU FOLLOW RUE BELVÉDÈRE NORTH INTO THE CITY OF Sherbrooke from Lennoxville, you come within a couple of blocks of the intersection of two streets in a populous working-class neighbourhood: rue de l'Union and rue Craig. It was near this intersection, John learned, that a tall, brown-haired ten-year-old girl named Manon Dubé had disappeared on a Friday evening in January 1978. Her disappearance took place one day after the failed attack on the young woman in Lennoxville whose screams caught the attention of neighbours—who had reported it to the police, who hadn't followed up. It was the assault for which the duty cop had remarked on the victim's description of the assailant: "Was he wearing a green parka?"

Manon Dubé was last seen a six-minute drive away, up rue Belvédère, from that failed ambush. She had been walking with her eight-year-old sister, Chantal, to the family's first-floor apartment on nearby rue Bienville after playing in the snow that had banked up in a parking lot. Chantal ran ahead along the sidewalk because she was cold. She last saw Manon in a salmon-pink toque and blue snowsuit walking behind her beside the icy yard of the local elementary school, but when she turned around at the corner of Bienville, some moments later, her sister wasn't there. "Manon!" the girl called three times, before scurrying home.

The Sherbrooke Municipal Police put out an all-points bulletin to be on the lookout for a girl with long brown hair who stood four foot nine and weighed seventy pounds. They combed a nearby wooded area with tracking dogs and went house by house on rue Bienville, but there was no trace of Manon. The police widened their parameters, entering the surrounding Eastern Townships countryside. More than 1,500 people on snowmobiles volunteered to search the area's farmlands. Manon's sister, Chantal, told police that for days they had been followed by a man driving a car that, from her rough description, seemed to police to be a Buick. Clairvoyants from the region were consulted, to no avail. Finally, on the evening of Friday, March 24, two young boys found Manon's body face down in an icy brook near the village of Ayer's Cliff, southwest of where Theresa's body would be found near Compton Station. To get to the brook from where Manon was last seen, you would drive down rue Belvédère and chemin Macdonald, then south on Highway 143—the exact route that someone took, presumably, in the other direction when he, she or they disposed of Theresa's wallet.

Investigators from both the Sherbrooke Municipal Police and the Sûreté du Québec's Coaticook detachment—including Corporal Roch Gaudreault—arrived on the scene shortly after dark. The body was embedded in five centimetres of ice and had to be carefully extracted by the officers, using a hatchet. On first view, there were no signs of violence or molestation. The only thing missing was one red mitten. Manon Dubé's autopsy, like Theresa's, revealed no determinate cause of death: no bone fractures or bullet wounds. Except for a superficial gash on her forehead, which may have occurred post-mortem as she was transported in the trunk of a car or rolled into the brook, her partially decomposed corpse bore no injuries. Her death remained a mystery. Investigators wondered if she had been struck by a car, causing the forehead cut, and the panicked driver had whisked her body to the brook. The case was never solved.

I explained the hit-and-run—or hit-and-hide—theory of Manon Dubé's death to Rossmo, who found it bizarre. He told me about his criminological theory: the "least-effort principle." In his research, those who commit crimes will minimize their effort. If they hit, they run. They do not stop, gather up the body, hoist it into their vehicle, drive it over thirty kilometres, drag it through the woods in deep snow and tumble it into a brook. That would be what you call "most effort." Their immediate preoccupation would be simply to distance themselves from the crime. But the opposite happened in this case.

At some point (it's not clear when), the police added to the Dubé file a proposition that her uncle had committed the hit and hide. He took his niece to a property his brother owned, unbeknownst to their sister, Manon's mother. This uncle, however, was never arrested or charged, or accused by the family themselves, and died some years later. If you walk the whole scenario through in your mind, it requires you to believe that:

- Manon's uncle was coincidentally driving down the street in the three to five minutes she was alone.
- He was driving fast enough along a very short block to hit her fatally.
- He drove onto the sidewalk, as she was last seen on the correct side of the street to turn right up ahead and walk home.
- There was no physical damage found at autopsy, yet this was a lethal car collision.
- No one on the crowded block heard squealing tires or saw a man reacting to the horror of having killed his own niece, then deciding to haul her into the car.
- Chantal turned around with her breath misting to look from the corner of rue Bienville, but saw no crestfallen uncle kneeling beside a wounded sister.
- An uncle would put his extended family through the agony of a missing child rather than admit to an accident and take her to hospital.

The police later claimed to have found Dubé's mitten in this uncle's truck—nine weeks after her disappearance, when her body was found. (An earlier version offered by police was that they found the mitten in his garage.) Either way, he'd have to have carefully, effortfully disposed of his niece but not the evidence linking her to *him*, leaving her out in the open on his brother's property and keeping her mitten. And, having found this mitten, the police nevertheless made no arrest, nor was the mitten logged as evidence. So, were we to believe he'd tried to cover up the accident, but not that hard, and police had given him a pass?

Another theory bandied about at the time was that, since her mother had recently received a small insurance payout, a relative had kidnapped Manon for ransom but the extortion attempt went awry. (Charles Marion's kidnapping had taken place the previous fall). Or, some officers wondered, could Manon have frozen to death?

In all of their conjecturing, investigators never appear to have seriously considered the possibility that Manon Dubé had been abducted for the purposes of sexual molestation. In 1978, the Quebec crime magazine *Allô Police* ran the headline "*Manon, 10 ans, a-t-elle été Victime d'un Maniaque?*" (Is she the victim of a maniac?) Another headline read, "*Victime d'un Pédophile?*" The original reporters at the tabloids *Allô Police* and its sister publication *Photo Police* generally worked in tandem with the Sûreté du Québec, whose headquarters were across the street in Montreal; the journalists had a lot of access to crime scenes. In many cases, there were also photos of the funeral, because at that time, due to the routines of the infamous Boston Strangler, journalists would take photos of the funeral in case the suspect came back.

The question of sexual murder was actually raised by the coroner on the day Manon was found. In his preliminary report of March 24, 1978, Coroner Jean-Pierre Rivard noted, "possibility of a sexual murder." In his final report of May 17, 1978, Rivard determined that "the death of Manon Dubé is violent and the

verdict concluded is VIOLENT DEATH with criminal negligence." These details were never relayed by police to the press.
And there is nothing to indicate that this line of inquiry was
even nominally pursued by investigators.

In 2001, Chantal Dubé requested that her sister's case be
properly investigated. The detective who took on the job,
Patrick Vuillemin with the Sherbrooke Municipal Police, was
disconcerted to discover that evidence had been tossed out.
(He is the one who told John, after reviewing the case file, about
the uncle and the mitten.) There was little he could do to help
Chantal, beyond using more modern forensic analysis to determine that some particulate matter found in the gash in her sister's forehead was metal. If it came from the fender of a car, she
would have to have been crawling in the road when she was
struck. More likely, it came from a weapon or some sharp edge
in the interior of a car's trunk.

Long after Andre's visit to Robert Beullac in 1995, the PI had,
apparently, remained bothered by his inability to solve the mystery of Theresa's death. Now, rather than advise John that the
guilty drug-takers would eventually talk, Beullac sent him a
news clipping about the case of Louise Camirand—a third
unsolved death of a petite, dark-haired female in or near south
Sherbrooke. Camirand was twenty years old in 1977 and worked
part-time at a hospital on Portland Boulevard. She was shy,
the type who "would blush at nothing," as a friend of hers told
John. Louise was also a military cadet. Most evenings were
spent at the downtown army barracks, home to the Canadian
volunteer armoured regiment, the Sherbrooke Hussars.

Camirand spent the afternoon of Wednesday, March 23, at her apartment with her fiancé, Daniel Braun, an accounting student. The two discussed their impending wedding day, which was scheduled for May 21. Shortly after three p.m., Braun left, promising to meet her later that night at the armoury, and Louise spent the remainder of the afternoon with Diane Lajeunesse, a close friend who lived in the same apartment building. At about nine thirty, Louise left her apartment to buy some cigarettes. She walked south on Bryant to King Street, then proceeded two blocks west to the Provi-soir at the corner of King and Jacques-Cartier. The storekeeper noticed that she lingered for a time at the newspaper rack, flipping through magazines, after buying cigarettes and milk. Then she left. He was the last witness to see her alive.

When Louise failed to show up at the armoury, Daniel Braun became worried. He called her at 10:30 p.m., and again at 1:15 a.m., but there was no answer. Braun had a friend drive him to her apartment. He found the place much as he'd left it that afternoon, except that her purse and boots were missing. Had she headed out to meet him? But then where did she go?

He and her family didn't have to wait long to find out. On Friday, March 25, Camirand's nude body was discovered in a snowdrift in a forest glade near the village of Magog, a twenty-minute drive southwest of Sherbrooke. This time, because the body was found quickly, the pathologist was easily able to determine the cause of death. Louise Camirand had been strangled. It was obvious anyway, because a bootlace had been cinched around her neck. She had internal injuries, as if she'd been stomped on. This fierce violence, as well as rape, seemed to have happened somewhere else, according to the coroner. Like Manon Dubé, stripped of one mitten, Camirand wore only one glove. Could the assailant's first demand in the cold interior of his car have been for a hand job? Her pants and suede jacket were left beside her body, but there was no sign of the other glove, her blouse or her undergarments. Her purse was never recovered.

Camirand lay in the forest above the shore of Lake Memphremagog, where a road runs along through a perfect unlit darkness, flanked by towering old-growth oak and birch trees on one side and a scattering of cottages and summer houses on the other. The road then banks down to the cool, deep lake shared by tourists in both Quebec and Vermont. If you were to turn off of Highway 112 East on a March evening and drive along this road for several kilometres, you would have to know where you were going. You would be seeking, without visible markers, a right-hand turn along a gravel side road cut and bulldozed into the forest some years earlier. Finding that and turning right on a slight incline in drifts of late-spring snow, you would again be seeking a shadow in the darkness, another right turn up some snowmobile tracks for about fifteen metres to an informal local dump amidst the trees. Here, there'd be bottles of beer and rusting paint cans, some rotting two-by-fours, perhaps old roof tiles: an assortment of junk easily concealed and reclaimed by Quebec's boreal woods. This was the seventies, when people tossed soda cans from the windows of their cars. No recycling, no need to visit the formally allotted garbage dump for the area.

It is a place, like the road leading to it, that you simply could not know about unless you had been directed there for some previous reason, by someone in the immediate area. Perhaps you were doing a roof repair job and the homeowner told you, "Take a right up the road there and you'll come across a clearing where you can leave the old tiles." Maybe you were with the Sherbrooke Hussars, who ran training exercises in the woods, and they pointed out the dump or took you past it. Certainly, a chance discovery of this spot seems unlikely, given how invisible your destination is at night. If you have a murdered woman in your car, you might need some certainty about where you could unload her body, unseen.

In any event, you find your way, and pull off the gravel road onto the snowy trail. Quickly, you drag Louise Camirand from your vehicle and lay her amidst the debris. There she lies in her nudity, white on white in the snow, face to the earth. Her clothes you also discard in the silent glade, but not next to her, and not all of them. You set them down some ways away, as if she must never don them again, mustn't have easy access to these items you feel identify her, or dignify her. There is no sign of her boots at this site. She would have had to ease them off in order to be stripped of her pants and socks, and that probably happened elsewhere. You have forgotten them by now, after this furtive ferrying through darkness.

When you abduct a woman, how do you keep her quiet? Where do you take her, to strip and assault her before you set off on a twenty-seven kilometre drive? Maybe these were questions that investigating officer Roch Gaudreault asked when he was assigned to the case. Or maybe they weren't. We don't know. Over a six-month period, detectives interviewed more than 250 people who might be associated with the crime. They found nothing. From tracks made in the snow where the body was, investigators were able to determine the type of vehicle that had transported Louise. They searched for a car with a forty-four-inch separation between the tires, something like a Renault 5 or an Austin Mini or a Toyota Celica. No one came forward with information. Gradually, the case lost momentum. By the end of 1977, Louise Camirand had become a statistic: one of 197 murders committed in the province of Quebec that year. (In Statistics Canada's 2005 report on homicide, Quebec had the highest number of homicides in 1977 of any province. Over the course of the seventies, Quebec had the worst clearance rate for homicide cases in the country.)

In the spring of 2002, after receiving the news clipping from PI Beullac, John tracked down Bernard Camirand, Louise's brother. Although her murder remained unsolved, his family had grown resigned. They preferred to leave the matter in the past and move on. At first, Bernard said, some attention had been focused on the boyfriend, Daniel Braun. A rumour spread in the Townships that Braun later hanged himself in grief over the crime he supposedly committed. It wasn't true. Braun was alive and— as far as the family was concerned—innocent. In fact, the two men remained close after Louise's death, with Bernard attending Braun's wedding. A second theory gnawed over by detectives, according to Bernard, was that Camirand's death was related to her association with the Sherbrooke armoury. What if she had been picked up that night by a member of the regiment, someone who knew her and might have been jealous of her relationship with Braun? The detectives pointed to the "military-style" bootlace around her neck. What they seemingly failed to consider was that Camirand herself wore military boots. Her footwear was missing from the dump site. In all likelihood, she was strangled with her own lace.

The day after Theresa disappeared in 1978, two hunters came across some women's pants and a shirt draped carefully across a log, as we've said. Although Lennoxville Police Chief Leo Hamel, who went over to investigate with a sniffer dog, could find nothing, he forged a link in his mind between the women. He said as much to the crime magazine *Photo Police*. "A plausible hypothesis and one held by the investigators," the magazine reported on December 2, 1978, is that "Theresa agreed to get into the car of an unscrupulous individual who attacked her. In fact, the police fear that the girl suffered the same fate as Louise Camirand of Sherbrooke." Had Hamel suggested this to Gerry Cutting too? The police chief never mentioned it to Bob and Marilyn, who didn't read *Photo Police*.

Shortly after that article was published, the *Journal de Montréal*, which had collaborated with the Sherbrooke SQ in the Charles Marion affair, ran their one and only story on Theresa Allore, placing her frizzy-haired and goofy face from the photo booth alongside a story connecting her disappearance to drugs. It comes across now as a rejoinder to the first article in *Photo Police*, or a containment of damage. There are many different ways to consider this. In 2017, the American journalist Bill James wrote a fascinating book called *The Man from the Train*, in which he investigated newspaper reports from the early twentieth century about families murdered in their beds by someone wielding an ax across the United States over a fifteen-year time period. The common factor in all of these wildly violent, middle-of-the-night mass murders was the proximity of each family's home to the newly built American railway system. Each house was a hop and a skip from the train. It was likely the first serial homicide spree west of England and Jack the Ripper. The sheer number of victims—over a hundred— put the Ripper to shame. (It was also an exceedingly rare, and possibly unprecedented, combination of mass murder and serial murder.) But there was no national newspaper syndicate in 1910, and no national police force. Each shocking attack was interpreted completely locally, and according to old-fashioned motives of jealousy, greed and revenge. More often than not, African-Americans were hanged for the crimes. Yet, at the same time, investigators repeatedly almost got it. "We will see this syndrome many times in this book," James wrote, "that the sheriff fairly quickly understood what had happened here, but then went into denial about it. Several days into [one] investigation, the sheriff told a reporter that the only thing he could figure was that the crime was committed by a 'fiend who may have developed a homicidal mania and satisfied his lust for blood' and who had disappeared via the train track after the crime. That was, in fact, exactly what had happened." But "as time passed the sheriff began to feel pressure to solve the crime, and began to rummage about for a prosecutable candidate."

It appears, in a very similar fashion, that Hamel almost got it, but then backed away after the drug theory appeared in the *Journal de Montréal* the very next day, as if to counter his deductions. Certainly an overdose seemed to hold some weight with PI Robert Beullac, Hamel's unofficial co-investigator, and it was most certainly the preferred option for Roch Gaudreault, who was otherwise busy at this time with the ongoing Charles Marion and Fernand Laplante cases. It is curious, if nothing else, that the *Journal de Montréal*, a tabloid usually focused on urban dramas—not the relatively minor concern of someone missing in the Townships—ran this one story about Theresa, this hypothesis about her involvement with drugs, and no other. Not an earlier piece on her disappearance, nor a later one on her discovery. The story was out of district and out of context. What purpose did it serve?

For Hamel and the other local investigators, the three young women's deaths could not have remained unconnected solely on account of jurisdictional blindness. Even if the different police teams tended to ignore one another, Sherbrooke is a small place. Louise Camirand lies buried within metres of Manon Dubé in the same Catholic cemetery. Clothes potentially belonging to Theresa were found in the same patch of forest as was Camirand's body. Local media were making the connections. You couldn't miss the potential links unless you were in denial, or didn't want the headache, or some combination of both.

After we learned about Louise Camirand, I phoned Kim Rossmo. Experience had taught him to be prudent and highly skeptical. "First," he told me, "you have to confirm that it's a cluster of homicides. You need to know how many female stranger murders there are, on average, in the Sherbrooke area. You need to confirm this as an unusual cluster."

We looked into that. Murder in the Sherbrooke region is— not surprisingly—quite uncommon. This small city and its rural environs have an average of two homicides per year, with occasional spikes up to four or five, largely due to the presence of the bike gangs. In Canada, over the period from 1974 to 1986, sexual homicides accounted for 4 percent of all murders. Fifty-seven of them occurred in Quebec. Montreal and its south and north shores accounted for the lion's share, as one would expect. I'm talking about a lion's share of roughly four per year. Three dead females dumped in fields and forests in the Sherbrooke region within eighteen months of one another seemed very much a cluster. Rossmo was sufficiently suspicious to have us draw a map marking the sites of the abductions and the bodies. He wanted to see what the geographic connections were.

I had read about the Robert Pickton case in British Columbia, which Rossmo had been involved in, although it wouldn't be until an inquiry in 2012 that the full picture emerged of how police officers kept almost-getting what was right before their eyes. It was the most astonishing crime story in Canadian history. Robert Pickton was a scraggly, balding brute who lived with his brother and niece on their farm, although he had his own trailer, which also served as his abattoir. There was a booze can on the property as well, known as Piggy's Palace, which was popular with the Hells Angels. If the police and politicians hadn't been so blind to what was unfolding, Pickton would have been caught much earlier than 2002—because, for one thing, one of his victims escaped.

On March 23, 1997, a woman identified publicly only as "Ms. Anderson" was hitchhiking in Vancouver around midnight en route to meet a friend in the Downtown Eastside when

Pickton stopped for her in his muddy red pickup. He offered her twice the usual sex worker's rate for oral sex if she'd come home with him. Anderson preferred safety to profit. She countered with the normal rate—forty bucks—in a nearby location that she knew. But the farmer pressed and ultimately promised to drive her all the way back to the Downtown Eastside if she'd agree. Then they were off, in silence, for a drive that took almost an hour. At one point, Anderson asked him to stop at a gas station so that she could use the bathroom. He refused. "I know now why he wouldn't pull in," she later told the police. "I wasn't expected to get out of there. I'm sure I wasn't." He didn't want any witnesses.

In his trailer at the far end of the property, Pickton and Anderson had sex on a quilt on the carpet. There was no bed. When they were done, she used the bathroom and then consulted his phone book to look up the number of the hotel she was headed to, planning to spend the night with her girlfriend. At that point, he grabbed her wrist and clicked on a handcuff. Alarms went off like air raid sirens and Anderson "went ballistic," as she told the police, realizing that she was in mortal danger. "I started fighting him, and we fought and we fought and we fought and I started hitting him with any object I could get hold of." She noticed a knife on the kitchen table while he slammed at her with a two-foot board. Dodging and swinging back, she inched Pickton closer to the table. "I got ahold of this knife and I jugged him right across the neck."

They continued to struggle while he pressed his hand to his bleeding jugular. She demanded to be let out of the trailer, waving the ten-inch blade. Eventually, growing dizzier, he opened the door and she fled toward his truck, but he gave chase and somehow wrenched the knife away. He stabbed her in the stomach and lifted the weapon up through her abdomen, inflicting serious damage, before sagging to the ground, his energy seeping away with his blood. Clutching her body and breathing raggedly, Anderson ran to the road, climbed over a fence and banged frantically on a neighbour's door. A couple passing by in a car saw her and drove her to the hospital, where she died twice on the operating table before being revived.

"I know it," she vowed to the police. "I just know there's broads on that property." In the truck, before he turned demonic, he had told her that he picked up a prostitute once a week, and she was fully aware that her acquaintances had been going missing. She told the officer interviewing her from her hospital bed that she would go to the needle exchange on the Downtown Eastside to find more names of missing women, presumably because she would recognize them more by picture than official birth name. But the investigating officers never followed up on that. Instead, they drove out to the farm for a look around while Anderson slowly recovered in hospital. Although they found condoms in his trailer and a bra in his truck they took the word of Pickton's brother that Robert never saw "hookers." He had neither wife nor girlfriend, his brother said. He didn't drink, he didn't smoke, he did no drugs; he was the miraculously vice-free proprietor of the Piggy Palace.

Anderson's credibility, on the other hand, was dismissed by the Crown prosecutor on the grounds that she was addicted to drugs. She wouldn't make a good he-said-she-said witness, given that both of them had ended up hospitalized with life-threatening injuries. (Interviewed by police from his own hospital bed, Pickton described Anderson as a crazy hooker who'd gone nuts and attacked him.) Even though Pickton had been investigated for a rape and stabbing seven years earlier by the Surrey detachment of the RCMP (the charges against him were dropped), his word with a jury might prevail. The prejudice against Ms. Anderson proved deadly.

Women who were still alive at that point—still calling their kids and visiting their doctors and methadone clinics and attending family birthday parties—would later be found as remains on his farm, some ground up and mixed with pork sold to the public.

As early as 1998, Detective Inspector Kim Rossmo had proposed that his colleagues at the Vancouver Police Department consider looking for a serial killer. He had recently been involved in Project Eclipse, an investigation into twenty-five murders in Victoria and Vancouver between 1985 and 1991 where the victims were mainly survival sex workers. The murder rate for sex workers, he knew, was estimated to be 60 to 120 times higher than for all other women. What was needed here, he thought, was to establish a kind of base rate for how often women on the Downtown Eastside typically went missing, because that would tell you whether what was happening now was statistically unusual. (It was the same advice he would give to John and me a few years later). Reviewing twenty years' worth of reports on missing persons from the same neighbourhood, Rossmo found that in the years between 1978 and 1994, most of the people were ultimately located. That changed in

1995, and the annual tally of unfound women grew, with eleven women unaccounted for in 1998 alone. (Note that 93 percent of people reported missing are located within three weeks, and typically within two days. That's another base rate.)

"If these numbers represented incidents of tuberculosis," Rossmo later wrote, "officials would suspect an epidemic and begin searching for the vector [cause] of the disease outbreak." There was a cluster of missing women that required an over-arching explanation. Was it not likely that some of them had been murdered? As the Commission of Inquiry later wrote, "Police awareness of the risks to women engaged in the sex trade based on these investigations in the early 1990s supported an assessment that the missing women were likely murdered. . . . The fact that police did not form this conclusion amounted to a type of short-term memory loss."

The cops just wouldn't link the cases. Each one, individually, got chalked up to a different potential scenario, just like the Township deaths in Quebec. Maybe the Vancouver women had died of a drug overdose. Maybe they went on vacation, or took off with a boyfriend. But Rossmo insisted that investigators had to ask themselves why all these women were missing *now*, not ten years ago, and why in Vancouver and not in Toronto, say, or Seattle, and why no bodies were being found if overdoses were to blame, and why no *men* were going missing. Men, after all, also worked in the sex trade; they also took drugs on the Downtown Eastside. (Likewise, in our case, Rossmo urged us to consider whether low-risk women were being found sexually murdered in nearby areas, such as upstate New York and Vermont, at the time. They were not.)

When it comes to victims, says Melina Buckley, a lawyer who oversaw the writing of *Forsaken*, the Pickton inquiry report, "there is systemic and individual emphasis on social value." Who matters and why? "These biases are very hard to break because they're so unconscious. If there is any history of partying or drugs, that will shift complicity to the woman. Even after evidence is shown to the contrary, [we found that] the officers couldn't shake their belief that the woman was doing drugs, or had an erratic schedule that meant she wasn't 'missing'"—just transient. "Their lives could be very regular, organized around children, and it was still considered plausible that they just wandered off or went to the States. You have to break open some deeply ingrained stereotypes."

On November 5, 1998, a community liaison officer with close ties to the Downtown Eastside sent a memo to his bosses at the Vancouver Police Department. "I feel very strongly that a large percentage of the women have met with foul play," he wrote, in agreement with Rossmo. "I feel this way for the following reasons: 1. The majority of women are on social assistance and have stopped picking up their cheques; 2. There has been no family contact; 3. Street friends or associates have not seen them; 4. They are among the most vulnerable group that exists."

Detective Constable Lori Shenher, with the Missing Persons Unit, also agreed. On August 27, 1998, Shenher wrote to superiors: "A large percentage of these women have children either living under the care of the Ministry or with extended family and they have not lost contact with these children or with family for more than very brief periods of time until they went missing. None have contacted family."

By Shenher's tally, eleven women had disappeared from the neighbourhood in 1998, eight in 1997, two in 1996 and three in 1995. When Rossmo analyzed these statistics in the spring of 1999, he grew even more certain that a serial killer was involved. Yet the brass continued to resist this possibility, and women continued to vanish.

"It is difficult to understand the continued currency of nonsensical theories, such as extended vacations or a sudden rise in deaths due to overdoses without leaving a trace," Commissioner Wally Oppal observed. "The serial killer theory was repeatedly dismissed and discounted in the face of a mounting assessment that it was a viable theory.... Senior police officers appeared to consider Detective Inspector Rossmo's analysis to be 'speculative' despite the fact that it was grounded in solid empirical evidence and factual analysis."

But there were no bodies. "Police officers start from the premise that a homicide always begins with a 'body,' and 'no bodies, no crime' was an oft-repeated mantra in the evidence before the Commission," according to *Forsaken*. This echoes what happened in Theresa's case, where the Sûreté du Québec refused to get involved without a body, leaving a novice investigator and a young PI as the only investigators for six months. No body, no crime. No semen, no rape. No nudity, no sex crime. No wounds, no murder.

Ultimately, in the Pickton case, there were several issues that caused an upsetting divide between people who cared about the victims—including constables who knew the community, medical providers and social workers, families and friends, and escaped victims like Ms. Anderson—and the distanced thinkers in the upper echelons of law enforcement. "A review of 1,400 killers over the last century," the Commissioner found, "identified seven major pitfalls in police investigations of these crimes." These weaknesses included an "inability to find linkages between the crimes" and "investigators [who] are often unwilling to admit they have a serial killer in their jurisdiction."

Kim Rossmo left Vancouver and, as part of his doctoral thesis at Simon Fraser University, went on to pioneer a method of homicide investigation called geoprofiling, a criminological technique that can narrow down the area in which a serial rapist or killer lives by analyzing the geography of the attacks and, where relevant, the body dump sites. There are several premises behind geoprofiling. One is that predators will operate along routine pathways in their work and home lives. They seldom stray into unfamiliar areas to attack, so there's no point in feeling terrified at the summer cabin or an isolated farmhouse. On the contrary, like all of us, criminals have their comfort zones. They also have routines. As such, they will often pass the same victim—or type of victim—dozens of times at a bus stop or parking garage near their work, say, before they summon the nerve to act.

Where victims disappear and where their bodies are found are significant clues in geoprofiling in light of routine activity theory. Geoprofiling then draws on mathematical equations to locate serial offenders. Early on, Rossmo offered law enforcement a proposition: if detectives could provide at least five or six incidents traceable back to the perpetrator, his algorithm could reduce the search area for the criminal's residence by more than 90 percent. The algorithm produces a "jeopardy surface," a geocoded map with a topographical surface showing peaks and valleys, ramped and coloured to highlight areas where it is most likely that the suspected criminal resides.

In putting together a Townships map for Rossmo, John and I found that we had one further point of reference to use. Theresa's red wallet had been found on the outskirts of Sherbrooke on chemin Macdonald. That road is an extension of rue Belvédère, and if you follow rue Belvédère from the downtown armoury that Camirand frequented, then travel out of town heading south, after a kilometre and a half you will pass the caisse populaire where Manon Dubé went sledding in the parking lot. After a few more kilometres, the road starts to bend to the left and travels down a steep incline as it switches names to chemin Macdonald. Pass an apple orchard, and you are where Theresa's wallet was found. Follow chemin Macdonald to its conclusion, eight hundred metres farther down the hill, and you run into Route 143. Turn left, and within three kilometres you will be at the corner of College Street and Queen / 143, home to the Golden Lion Pub, where Theresa often stood and hitch-hiked. All of these points are within five kilometres, all located on or near the main artery route of rue Belvédère.

It was important to know precisely where the wallet was found. Was it in the ditch on the right or left side of Macdonald? This could indicate whether the vehicle was travelling into or out of town. John's guess was that Theresa's killer had used the rue Belvédère artery to drive back into town after dumping her body, tossing the wallet out the driver's side window on the way. If this theory was correct, the wallet should have been found on the left, or south, side of the road. The police had given John access to the statement by the farmer who found the Buxton wallet. John searched for his number in the phone directory and was surprised to find him still living there. "I called and got his wife on the phone," he told me. "She remembered the incident well. She apologized for not letting her husband speak for himself, but he was deaf." Indeed, it was this fact that had led to the discovery of the wallet in the first place. The farmer had been deaf all his life, and to compensate, his other senses were more attuned. Only his exceptional eyesight allowed him to spot the wallet where it lay amidst spring melt and gravel. His wife confirmed that the wallet had been found on the south side of Macdonald—the driver's side if a car was heading up into Sherbrooke.

She remembered one other thing that, she offered, might be significant. In the autumn of 1978, their teenaged daughter—whom we will call Ms. X to protect her anonymity—had had a deeply frightening encounter on that road. This would have been the weekend of the Quebec National Assembly, the farmer's wife remembered. She was away at the political convention and her husband and daughter were home. Thinking back, she placed it as the first week of October. At about seven thirty one night, Ms. X was out walking their German shepherd. She was on the edge of chemin Macdonald, near the spot where the family kept an apple stand. A car came speeding around the corner from the top of Macdonald and stopped just in front of her. The driver jumped out of the car and began to chase her. The young woman ordered her dog to attack, then ran to hide in the orchard adjacent to the road.

Almost immediately, a police cruiser appeared from the top of Macdonald and stopped in front of the attacker's car, where the man was now confronting an enraged dog. Ms. X remained hidden in the orchard. The police issued the man a ticket for being parked illegally, and then both cars went on their way.

The following morning, Ms. X's mother returned from her trip to Quebec City. She heard what had happened and understood that there was nothing ordinary about it. There had been many occasions when her daughter had been walking the dog and drivers had slowed to call out, "Hey, baby, do you wanna . . .?" But this wasn't any "Hey, baby." Ms. X had instantly been afraid for her life.

By 2002, all she could remember about her attacker was that he was small—a small, dark-haired man with, to judge by his speeding ambush, a feverish appetite for predation. At her mother's urging, Ms. X had gone to the local police department and filed a report. Subsequently, the family heard that the police had traced him through the traffic ticket issued that night. They also heard rumours that the police had advised him to get out of town.

All we had for certain was the attempted attack itself. It had happened. It was witnessed by Ms. X's father and corroborated by the ticket. So now there was another reference point for Rossmo's map: an attempted assault on chemin Macdonald in early October 1978, one month before Theresa's disappearance. Six separate reference points, all within a short drive: the assault at College and Queen in January 1978, also where Theresa may have been hitchhiking, the wallet, the apple orchard assault, the Caisse Populaire where Dubé had been playing, and the armoury where Camirand worked.

Where the bodies were discovered was equally important. In all three cases, the dump sites were fifteen to twenty-seven kilometres south of the environment in Sherbrooke the victims frequented. Theresa was found on chemin de la Station, roughly a kilometre from the village of Compton and fifteen kilometres from Lennoxville. Manon Dubé was found off chemin Brook, approximately thirty kilometres south of Sherbrooke. So, Theresa dumped off 147; Dubé, off 143. The two sites were separated east to west by a distance of just eight kilometres.

As for Louise Camirand, there is a direct path from where she disappeared to where her body was found. Whether she went missing from the Sherbrooke armoury or from the bus stop near her house, both places are located on or near King Street. Travel west on King — away from King and Belvedere and then the bus stop—and the street turns into Route 112 and eventually bends southwest. A series of obscure turns along dirt roads finally brings you to the one where local men Robert Curtis and Florent Henri found Camirand's body.

We sent the map to Washington. Once he ran our data through his algorithm, Rossmo sent me his formal report:

> *Each of these incidents involve multiple locations that, when combined, form a persuasive pattern. Camirand disappeared in Sherbrooke, close to where Dubé went missing. She was later found in Magog, near what may have been Allore's clothes. Dubé, in turn, was found a few miles from Allore's body outside Compton, just off a route linking Compton to Magog. Allore's wallet was found just south of the area where both Camirand and Dubé disappeared, very near an attack on a fourth woman.*

The locations associated with these three deaths are inter-twined, woven together in the landscape south of Sherbrooke. Three murders of low-risk young women in a 19-month period, in such a tight geographic cluster, is highly suspicious, and not likely to be a chance occurrence. These cases should be fed into ViCLAS [Violent Crime Linkage Analysis System], and re-examined as a group of potentially linked sex murders. Serial murderers typically live closer to the victim encounter sites than body disposal locations.

This offender was most likely based in Lennoxville or south Sherbrooke during the period from 1977 to 1978.

Rossmo's report exhilarated, sobered and terrified us. What now?

ELEVEN

RIDDLES AND DARK WORDS

"The town was freaky-deaky, man—the entire police force was schizophrenic."
—former member of Quebec law enforcement

SOMETIMES HELP ARRIVES FROM THE MOST SURPRISING quarter. More rarely the surprise source is a colourful and animated character who breaks through the stone wall you've been hitting and beckons you through the gap. Less than three months into our investigation, John heard from a former member of Quebec law enforcement who was sympathetic to his efforts. Gilles, as John refers to him, offered to supply information, provided his identity remained anonymous. Being an insider, Gilles had first-hand experience with problems in Quebec law enforcement. The police officers were too bureaucratic, he thought. They weren't creative thinkers, and they had a terrible reputation for not communicating with the public. Gilles was aware that we had started working on a story for a national newspaper. He wanted to assist us, hoping the story might force Quebec police brass to change.

"So, what is it you need?" he asked John.

"I need the file."

"You not gonna get it."

"Can you get it?"

Gilles paused, considering. "Are you coming to Sherbrooke anytime soon?"

"I could come back."

"Let me see what I can do."

John had been planning to drive to Saint John to visit his parents with his eldest daughter, who was five at the time. He could build in a detour, he figured, take her on a road trip to the scene of a crime. "Any suggestion that I was living a Jim Thompson novel must be squashed right here," he told me, laughing. "My daughter and I were not Ryan and Tatum O'Neal in *Paper Moon*. I was not driving a GTO; it was a Honda Odyssey. We did not stop at roadside diners for coffee, cigarettes and a bag of gumdrops; it was hot chocolate at Denny's. I am an ordinary man with a normal family; it was the circumstances that surrounded us that seemed like fiction."

They arrived back in Sherbrooke at the same hotel across from SQ headquarters on rue Don-Bosco, and had the buffet breakfast in the dining room. John equipped Amelia with plenty of crayons and colouring books, and waited for Gilles.

"Now, when the man comes, I need for you to sit quietly and let us talk," he told his daughter.

"What man?"

"The man we're meeting."

"What's his name?"

"Gilles. Eat your pancakes."

John didn't know what Gilles looked like, so he watched the dining room entrance door apprehensively, but when the man arrived, it was obvious: studded earring, cowboy boots, braided ponytail running down the back of his jacket. Only a Quebec cop could look like a biker.

"John?"

"Yes, and this is my daughter."

"Hi there."

"Do you want breakfast?"

"Just coffee."

Gilles sat, his gun peeking out from his holster. He looked rough to John. "Like an ex-everything—ex-boozer, ex-pill-popper, ex-wife-beater. Maybe this was a bad idea." The cop smiled a vacant smile and, in one motion, reached beneath the table and from nowhere produced a thick legal-sized folder. It was Theresa's file. John wasn't sure whether he could just pore over the whole thing right away or should make small talk. "I just wanted Gilles to go away." Amelia coloured. (She could keep this up for hours and, in fact, got a job, years later, as an animator in Los Angeles.) Gilles sipped coffee while John glanced through the file. Most of it was in French. He'd have to somehow find time to concentrate. For the moment, that seemed rude. Gesturing at the file, he asked what, if anything, was missing.

"Statements, some mug shots, some things of your sister's."

"What things?"

"Personal papers belonging to her—ID cards, a driver's licence." It struck John as bizarre and wrong and almost maddening that the cops felt entitled to hang on to these family mementos when they'd tossed any actual evidence. He brought that up, the evidence that could have contained trace DNA.

"Do you know about the scarf?" Gilles asked.

John knew about Theresa's scarf. Apparently it had been recovered, but no one was ever sure where it was found. Andre had heard it was with the wallet.

"It was found near your sister's body—in the cornfield. It was torn into two pieces."

This was a huge revelation. The scarf, unlike all her other clothes, had still been with Theresa's body and *ripped apart*? John considered the implications, which must have been clear to Gilles or he wouldn't have raised the subject. That long Isadora Duncan scarf hadn't been some old, paper-thin garment; it was a recent gift to Theresa from their mother. "Take one of your scarves," John told me later, "silk or wool or linen, and try to rip it in half. It's not easy. Nor is it easy to strangle someone. It requires persistent, straining force for upward of five minutes. *That* kind of force would maybe tear your scarf." When he'd recovered his wits, John asked where the scarf was now. Gilles assumed it had been chucked out with the other items of clothing.

They talked about theories—an isolated murder or a serial event connected to Dubé and Camirand? Because he was French, Gilles was familiar with both the Dubé and Camirand cases. He had seen their files, but he hadn't known about Theresa's case until he heard of our investigation. This was part of the linguistic and cultural divide that would have impeded any public awareness of possible links. They discussed suspects—teachers, students, local crazies that Gilles knew about. John wondered if he should share what we were learning with the SQ.

"Don't do it. They will only resent you for the work you've done. They'll suppress it—your investigation will go nowhere."

Gilles kept scanning the room, looking for people he knew. The buffet was knee-deep with sales reps, techno-geeks in town for some local trade conference. He was fidgety, and John couldn't figure him out. Had he come here to help, or was he *sent* here to find out what John was up to? "I was so nervous that I kept playing with my packet of Kraft peanut butter," John wrote to me later. Struggling to be nonchalant, he accidentally punctured the packet, and the viscous condiment spurted across the table. To distract Gilles, he waved cheerfully for a coffee refill and asked some more questions.

"If the three cases were connected, how could investigators have missed it?"

"Lots of reasons. They may have been too stupid to see it. They may have been too lazy to put in the effort. Or maybe they didn't miss it. Maybe it was covered up."

"I find that hard to believe," John said.

"Why? This isn't Mayberry. In the seventies, Sherbrooke was a tough town. A lot of bad things happened here. The line between cops and robbers was pretty thin."

John suddenly remembered that in December 1999, the Hells Angels and Sergeant Guy Ouellette of the Sûreté du Québec had coincidentally ended up at this same hotel. The bikers brazenly stole Ouellette's briefcase from his room while he was downstairs having breakfast.

As they spoke further about the three cases, John revealed that he'd never been to the locations where Louise Camirand and Manon Dubé were found.

"Well, I'll show you those spots if you show me yours," Gilles joked. "C'mon. We'll go for a drive."

In the hotel parking lot, Gilles decided to take them in his car. "He seemed very sure of himself as he whisked Amelia into his Crown Vic," John wrote. There was nothing in the car—nothing that would tell John who this guy was. Doubting the sanity of the venture, John reached back and latched the seatbelt around his daughter's waist.

"Daddy, where are we going?"

"We're just going for a drive with Gilles."

"I don't want to go. I'm tired."

"Lay back and have a nap."

"Leather seats," recalled John. "The interior was about as comfortable as a hospital gurney." Gilles got in the driver's side and there was that gun again—a little shy, peeking around his coattail. He said they'd go to the Dubé site first. While he drove, John flipped through the police file, which he was going to have to return. He had no pen. From what he could tell, he was reading the preliminary report. There were references to the crime scene, a list of students interviewed, with their dates of birth and social insurance numbers, a list of the recovered evidence, including the wallet and pieces of scarf. Aha. This was new: bus drivers had been interviewed. They hadn't seen Theresa on any of the shuttles the night she disappeared—not at 6:15 and not at 11:30. So she *must* have been hitchhiking that night. There was no information on suspects. There was no conclusion from investigator Gaudreault.

John looked up from the file and realized that he didn't know where he was. They were headed through an industrial part of town. Everything looked out of place—warehouses and over-grown weeds. Gilles kept driving. He said nothing, his focus straight ahead. John began to silently panic. *This guy said he was a cop, right? Well, did he ever show you any proof he was a cop? He could be anyone. Shit, this guy is a hitman! Maybe I know something I'm not supposed to know. Maybe he's been sent by the police to do a job. Oh shit, he's going to take us to some field and shoot us! Two bullets in the head at point-blank range. And you brought your five-year-old daughter along. You stupid, stupid shit!*

Then they were back in familiar territory, heading south on Route 143 in the direction that, John knew from the map on his office wall, led to Manon Dubé's dump site. They slowed and turned left toward chemin Brook, following it until Gilles brought them to a stop in front of a cottage beside a brook. The property was remote and secluded, with forest encroaching along both sides of the narrow road. It seemed such an odd place to arbitrarily dump the body of Manon Dubé if you were a family member who wanted to distance yourself from an accidental hit and run. Why drive all this way from Sherbrooke and leave her in the open on family property when you had miles and miles of forest to choose from?

Gilles pointed out that the brook flowed from upstream near a beaver dam, passed under a small wooden bridge, then bent west and trickled past the cottage, eventually emptying into the Massawippi River. Dubé's body had been found right at the bend in the brook. It was believed she had been dropped in the water at this point—either off the bridge or from across the property.

John looked at the small cottage. "Was that always there?"

"No, that house is new. But the one that was there originally was similar."

"Did the first one have a small attic window like that?"

"Yes. Why?"

"I don't know."

He did know. He had once had a dream in which his sister was held captive in a cottage like this. She was locked in an attic and tied to the bed. Marilyn had had a similar dream. It was frightening. They hadn't known what it meant.

John and Gilles got back in the car, where Amelia was fast asleep. Driving to Compton, Gilles told stories of the Eastern Townships—*L'Estrie*, as it is known in French—in the bad old days, when things were "wide open." Sherbrooke was a frontier town. The police divided the land into separate fiefdoms. Gilles knew all the players. He described a braggart without a brain, who couldn't solve a word scramble, let alone a crime. Another was paranoid, bordering on psychotic. Gilles described hand grenades being kept in car trunks, and offices being bugged in the cop shop to see who was saying what.

"The town was freaky-deaky, man—the entire police force was schizophrenic."

When they reached chemin de la Station, John pointed out the details of the site he was coming to know so well.

"She was found all the way over there?" Gilles asked.

"That's right."

"Someone must have driven into the cornfield."

"Or dragged her. There were bruise marks under her armpits."

"And the scarf in two pieces. It's pretty clear that your sister was murdered. And probably strangled."

. . .

Next, they headed to where Louise Camirand had been found. Along the way, more tales of the Townships. In the seventies, the area was rife with drugs. The trade was controlled by Les Motards—bikers who preyed on the local college and high school kids. LSD was a big seller. In the fall of 1978, police raided a trailer in the woods near Austin; it was a mobile drug lab capable of producing enough acid to supply the whole of North America.

"Gaudreault's theory was that my sister overdosed on acid and died," John told Gilles.

"That's ridiculous."

"Why?"

"You take too much acid, you trip out. You don't die."

"Still, it can't be good to take that much acid."

"Look, the average person would need to consume between 50 and 250 hits of LSD in order to die from the stuff. It just doesn't happen."

They drove through Magog, a tourist town that would feel familiar to any American who's spent time in Bar Harbor, Maine. It was June, so there were lots of people on the streets and crowding the shore of Lake Memphremagog. Gilles looked hot and sweaty. John thought he needed a drink—maybe a shot of tequila—or a bowl of chili. They inched through three blocks of traffic until they hit the other side of town, then continued toward the north shoreline of the lake.

John asked Gilles why he had mentioned the idea of a

cover-up, back at the hotel. The man looked like he regretted tossing that out there.

"It was common at that time for some cops to fraternize with college students," he said. "And some cops were known to deal drugs. They would seize evidence, then sell it back to the community. I knew these two guys—these cops—who used to cruise at night in unmarked cars. They wouldn't wear uniforms. They'd hang out with girls—college girls. They were bad numbers. It wouldn't surprise me if they were involved in a cover-up."

"Are you saying that you know something?"

"No, I'm not saying that. I'm trying to help. You've got to keep an open mind. You've got to look at everything."

John couldn't glean Gilles's motive, but he was growing to like him. "He was like my tour guide for all things dark and dangerous. He copied the file for me. What did I care how he got it?"

They reached chemin des Pères and turned left. Lake Memphremagog sprawled outside the left window. The water sparkled blue. The forests that bordered the lake were deep and green. It was beautiful. "It also," John told me, "made the bottom fall out of my stomach. It looked like such a nice place. But it was not a nice place."

They turned right on chemin Giguère (now chemin Duval), then drove about a quarter of a mile and pulled over to the side of the road. Gilles got out of the car and John followed. In the back, Amelia was still sleeping. At first John didn't know why they had stopped, but then he saw the back road, overgrown and misshapen, with large divots and underbrush. Only a tractor could get in here—like the one Florent Henri and Robert Curtis were riding the morning that they found Louise

Camirand's body. They walked in about fifteen metres, and Gilles pointed to where the body had lain. John found it strange, as he recounted later. "Where my sister was found was different: right in the middle of an exposed valley, off a road that was heavily travelled. This was different. It was completely hidden in a thick, dense forest. Why would anyone think to come here unless they had been here before? And unless they didn't want the body found. What if getting away with murder made you less cautious? The thought of it made me fear the world."

John and Gilles got back in the car and sat talking for a moment while Amelia continued her nap.

"I'll take you back to Sherbrooke now."

"So what do I do?"

"Keep doing what you're doing. You've found out more than anyone else has."

"Can you get copies of the rest of the file?"

"I'll try."

Gilles drove them back to the hotel. They promised to keep in touch. He never sent the photocopies from the police file. John had the information in his hands for a couple of hours, and then it was gone.

Before leaving for his parents' home, John had one more appointment to keep. In the previous weeks, he had managed to track down many of the witnesses to the events of 1977–79. Aside from the farmer who had found the wallet, he also spoke with Bernard Camirand; Robert Ride, the muskrat trapper who'd found Theresa's body; and Robert Curtis, one of the young men who'd discovered Louise Camirand lying in the snow. And then there were her friends, people John had never known, who could bring his sister closer to him in some ways. "Solving the crime is one objective," he said, "but there are other things that matter. Sharon Buzzee could tell me about that encounter on the staircase, but it was when she said that she remembered and respected Theresa that my heart beat a little faster. Suzanne DeRome sent me a photograph of Theresa taken in residence just days before she died. This meant more than piecing together a timeline for the events that took place on November 3, which was why I'd called her. I was sifting through facts, but every so often I'd feel a little tremor. I'd stop and listen, then go back to work, foolishly believing that just because I couldn't see her, she wasn't there; thinking she was some twenty-three years and 613 miles behind me. One day, I took my hand and placed it up against my chest. She was that close."

Now, before taking Amelia east, he wanted to connect with a man who hadn't known Theresa at all but was still a part of the puzzle. Samuel Burnham was one of the hunters who had found the clothing in the woods shortly after she vanished. He agreed to meet with John and take him to the place. John drove to Burnham's house and knocked on the door. Burnham greeted him in hunting fatigues, stepping out onto the front porch to light up a cigarette.

"So you're the brother, eh?"

"Yup."

"How come you're gettin' involved in this?"

"Oh, I don't know . . ."

"Follow me in the four-by-four and I'll take you there."

"Okay."

"It's not far. Just down the road."

They backed out of the driveway and headed toward chemin Duval. Burnham slowed his four-by-four and pulled to the side of the road. *Wait a minute,* John thought. *What are we doing here again? I was just here.*

They got out of their cars. Burnham lit another cigarette and pointed into the forest. "There."

"You found the clothing there?"

"A pair of blue pants and some sort of shirt. Right back there."

"But the other girl, Louise Camirand, was found right *there*." John gestured to the rutted turnoff where he and Gilles had been, not a hundred metres down the road from where they were standing now.

"That's right, that other girl was found in there."

John found himself wanting to scream. Camirand's body and the clothing thought to have belonged to Theresa were not only found off the same forest road, they were found off the same side of that road, within a distance of ninety metres.

"Hey, you okay? You look a little freaked out."

John asked, "When you came back with the police to look again for the clothes, could you not find them because you couldn't find the spot, or because they had been taken from the spot?"

"We couldn't find the spot," Burnham said. "They were there. They're probably still there. Whatever's left of them."

John stared hard into the forest. He wanted to go in—take a shovel and pick and find out what was in there.

"We always heard it was teenagers that killed that Louise girl, but they never could prosecute them 'cause they was too young."

"It wasn't teenagers . . ."

"Oh, so you know?"

"No."

"Oh."

From somewhere John heard a steady, dead thud. *Dunk-dunk-dunk-dunk-dunk*. He looked over at the car. His daughter was crying, pounding on the glass.

Map made of the Theresa Allore crime scene by Sûreté du Québec agent Normand Grégoire.

SQ investigators Roch Gaudreault (light jacket) and Jacques Lessard search through the found garbage bag of clothing (Archives Madame Karine, inc.).

Theresa's wallet discovered by a farmer at the side of the road outside of Sherbrooke (Archives Madame Karine, inc.).

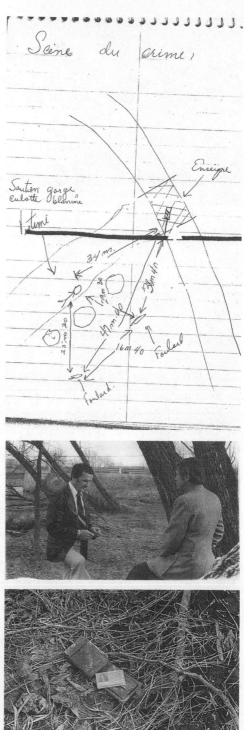

In the boat at Stoney Lake, 1968. Andre and John in front, our cousin Kathy Allore in the back with Theresa.

Theresa with her mom.

Left to right: Robert, Marilyn, John, Andre and Theresa Allore, dining out in Montreal, 1978.

John and Theresa,
Pierrefonds, Quebec.

Theresa Allore, Edmonton,
Alberta, summer 1977.

Looking down the path to
the Champlain college
residence at King's Hall,
Compton (Archives
Madame Karine, inc.).

Passport photo of Vlad Kulich taken August 31, 1978. The photo was discovered in Theresa's wallet, water damaged from having being discarded in the snow.

Theresa arriving in Saint John, New Brunswick, with Vlad Kulich, summer 1978.

Party at Haidi Muller's, July 1977. Deborah Ferdinand is in the bottom row, second from the left. Theresa is in the bottom row, to the far right.

Staircase in the King's Hall residence where Sharon Buzzee said she saw Theresa the night she disappeared.

The curious "Histoire De Drogue?" article from the *Journal de Montreal* was the only story published in that era about Theresa in the tabloid.

DISPARITION MYSTÉRIEUSE: UNE HISTOIRE DE DROGUE?

(G.R.) — Le chef de police de Lennoxville, M. Léo Hamel, se demande si la disparition de Thérésa Allore, 19 ans, n'est pas reliée à la drogue.

FORTIFIANT PAGE 12

La jeune fille est disparue du Collège Champlain de l'université Bishop depuis le 3 novembre dernier.

Sa disparition demeure complètement inexplicable du fait que la jeune fille avait ses études, avait beaucoup d'amis et avait même donné rendez-vous à l'un d'eux quelques minutes avant de disparaître et de ne laisser aucune trace.

De plus, la jeune fille n'a apporté aucun effet personnel et a même laissé tout son argent à la banque.

M. Hamel a multiplié les démarches depuis ce temps

et son enquête l'a amené à fouiller plus particulièrement le milieu de la drogue, ces jours-ci, qui est fort actif dans la région de Sherbrooke.

Fugue ou assassinat?

«La fugue ou l'assassinat sont deux hypothèses plausibles. Je suis plutôt porté vers la deuxième hypothèse alors que certains de mes confrères croient davantage à la première. Mais nous apprécierions grandement avoir un nouvel indice dans cette enquête difficile», a mentionné M. Hamel.

Le père de Thérésa, Robert Allore, est retourné passer les fêtes dans sa famille, au Nouveau-Brunswick, après avoir séjourné quelques semaines à Sherbrooke, dans l'espoir que sa fille soit retrouvée.

Mais cet espoir s'amenuise, au fur et à mesure que les jours et même les semaines passent. M. Allore croit quand même que sa fille est toujours vivante, mais ce n'est pas le cas de sa femme qui croit que sa fille est enterrée dans un lieu inconnu.

Photo Le JOURNAL

Thérésa Allore s'est-elle enfuie ou a-t-elle été assassinée?

Police sketch of unknown assailant as reported by assault victim "Marie," from the Sherbrooke *Record*, November 25, 1981. Her description resembles Luc Grégoire.

Police seek would-be rapist

SHERBROOKE (TB) — The Eastern Townships division of the QPF published yesterday an artist's sketch of a would-be rapist who assaulted a 27-year-old North Hatley resident November 13.

The attack, which took place in the late afternoon, was foiled when two passing motorists came to the intended victim's aid. The assailant received scratches to the face before the two passing women were able to rescue the object of his attack.

The suspect, who is believed to be between 20 and 30 years of age, attacked the young woman while she was jogging along route 143. After attempting to

tear off her clothes and meeting resistance, the assailant then punched the woman repeatedly in the face. It was at this point the two rescuers arrived and after freeing the woman successfully escaped in their own automobile.

Anyone able to supply information concerning the identity of the individual in question is requested to contact the Sherbrooke division of the QPF.

Léo Hamel

Leo Hamel, Lennoxville
chief of police.

Private detective Robert
Beullac.

The authors dressed up for
a university formal.

Denise Bazinet (Archives Madame Karine, inc.).

Reporting on the murder of Manon Dubé, from *Allô Police*, October 2, 1977.

Other unsolved murder victims, including Louise Camirand and Hélène Monast, from *Allô Police*, 1977.

Profile
of a
Predator

A surviving victim of
Luc Gregoire says his hands
were deadly weapons

22·08-12

Luc Grégoire

Hi John, I received your letter yesterday
Trought your letter I can feel your pain.
I'm realy sory that they aren't found the
person responsible for the death of your
sister.
Has you know, the Cop question me on this
matter, I haso Voluntarily consented to take
a Polygraph examination and they Touke
me of the list of suspect.

Johh I realy have nothing to do with
the death of your sister.

You also asked me if I heard of anything,
I havin't I'm sory

Hope they find the person responsable.

Luc Grégoire

Luc Grégoire revealed in the *Calgary Herald* by reporters Christina Mungan and Bob Beaty, June 29, 1994.

Luc Grégoire's letter to John, dated August 22, 2012.

A gathering of victims' families at Montreal's Hotel Bonaventure in April 2016. John, left. Stephan Parent, centre. Ugo Fredette, right (photo courtesy Stéphane Luce).

Theresa Allore, 1978.

PART TWO

TWELVE

RAVING AND DROOLING

"Anything one man can imagine, other men can make real."
—Jules Verne, *Around the World in Eighty Days*

WHEN OUR NEWSPAPER SERIES "WHO KILLED THERESA?" CAME out in the *National Post* over the 2002 August long weekend, we reached women whose response—as one of them told us—was to feel electrified. They recognized our witness Ms. X's description of her assailant near the apple orchard on chemin Macdonald, where Theresa's wallet was found. Either the physical description rang long-dormant bells, or readers related to the unsurpassed malice directed toward her by the predator's gaze.

"I can remember the intent look in his eyes," one woman said, about a man who tried to force her into his car in downtown Sherbrooke in 1987. "It was not a look of love or interest, but a look that is hard to describe because you are not used to seeing [it]. In a sense, it is almost a look saying, 'You're going to pay for this.' Your sixth sense kicks in, and you can't describe the fear."

Wrote another, who had been hitchhiking in 1981, "I remember feeling very afraid pretty much from the get-go. . . . I tried to open the door while the car was moving and it wouldn't open. . . . He told me he could drive down any side road and no one would ever see me again . . . I started to cry and he pulled over and let me out . . . he terrified me. . . . What happened to your sister is often on my mind."

A waitress was raped repeatedly in her apartment after being followed home from a restaurant shift in Magog. Multiple witnesses saw the man. His prints were all over her flat. "It took me almost eight months to go out of my apartment," she wrote to John, "and never again alone, even in broad daylight. Do you know what, Mr. Allore? I never ever heard from the police again. They never called, or followed up with this case."

There were, indeed, several accounts featuring total police indifference, some of which we described earlier in this book, such as the woman attacked in Lennoxville a day before Manon Dubé's abduction. But with Kim Rossmo's hypothesized south Sherbrooke offender in mind, two stories in particular caught our attention. One incident (described to us in an e-mail) took place in the summer of 1977, a few months after the murder of Louise Camirand. A woman we will call Margaret, who was at the time a twenty-one-year-old dental assistant, stood one day at the corner of Portland and Jacques Cartier Boulevard, hoping to hitch a ride to the Carrefour de l'Estrie, a mall where she needed to do some shopping on her lunch hour. She was, specifically, at 1855 Portland Boulevard, a one-minute drive from the street where Camirand lived. A short young man pulled over and bade Margaret hop in his car. It was a ten-minute drive to the mall, but the man said he needed to take a slightly different route so that he could check on a house under construction, presumably a job site. According to Margaret's brother, writing to John, "the guy took her to a building that is located on Beckett Road," about a five-minute detour. "He had to drive along a dirt road north to get to Beckett, and then would have gone east. This was an electrical building or some such. It looks like a house but I don't believe there are any windows. It has been there forever. Back then it was just a field with that one place."

The driver got out of the car to fetch something from his trunk. Margaret, feeling nervous, shook a cigarette loose from her pack, and when the man came around to the passenger side and lunged at her with a screwdriver, she responded by jabbing her lit cigarette into his skin and kicking him before scrabbling out of the car and bolting away.

Margaret's mother called the police to report the incident. No officer followed up.

The attack on Margaret was another violent assault by a man driving the same stretch of Jacques Cartier Boulevard from which Camirand disappeared. It raised a new question. Might the abandoned building he took Margaret to also have been where Camirand was raped and murdered before her body was transported southwest into the forest? Kim Rossmo has written that "the most powerful behavioral predictor of crime linkage is spatial-temporal proximity. Crimes that occur near to each other and close in time are more likely to be connected than those separated by distance and a significant time interval." Could Margaret's assailant have been Camirand's killer?

The second case that heightened our interest took place on another routine pathway for these crimes: Highway 143, south of Lennoxville. In November 1982, a student at Bishop's was out for an early-afternoon run near her home in the village of North Hatley. A man lunged from behind and attacked her. He had actually driven past her once and U-turned, parking his early-seventies gold car at the side of the highway. He grabbed her by the neck (she remembered he had "thick heavy hands") and began punching her repeatedly in the head in order to subdue her. Cars passed by them as if nothing was happening. Marie, as we'll call her, had taken self-defence classes, and yet she was completely overpowered; although she raked at his face with her nails, she eventually passed out from the hammering blows. When she regained consciousness, he had stripped off her clothes. Seeing that she was awake, he began pummelling her again, so ruthlessly that she feared she might die. "God save me!" Marie cried, and for some reason that worked a certain magic. It's one thing to destroy sinners, but a woman who calls out to God? He put her clothes back on her battered body, including her underwear, dragged her out of the gold car and told her to go.

He then drove away north. Marie hauled herself dizzily back to Highway 143, where passersby collected her, delivering her to a Sherbrooke hospital. The doctors said she was so badly beaten, it was astonishing that she'd survived the trauma to her brain. Detective Fillion from the Coaticook detachment of the SQ was assigned to the case, and because she was an artist, Marie managed to produce two sketches of the suspect. The car, she said, was a "boxy North American two-door model, with beige interior. . . possibly a Buick." An ice pick was found in the bushes. No one was collared for the crime.

Twenty years later, when Marie read our *National Post* series, and in particular Ms. X's description of the man barrelling toward her on chemin Macdonald, she thought, *That's it; that's how it happened to me.* The devouring rage on his face was like nothing she had ever seen before, she wrote. It terrified her most of all.

A man this aggressive must, sooner or later, have been caught, or so we could only imagine. John and I combined Rossmo's analysis of an offender living in south Sherbrooke with the accounts we were gathering of women being accosted by a markedly short, dark-haired French-Canadian man. Marie's police sketches suggested that her attacker had heavy eyebrows, a moustache and bangs, almost a bowl cut. We provided this information to someone familiar with the files on all sex murderers incarcerated in Quebec in 2002. (He asked to remain anonymous.) His response was immediate.

THIRTEEN

DOWNWARD SPIRAL (THE SUSPECT)

"Reality seems valueless by comparison with the dreams of fevered imaginations"
—Émile Durkheim

IN THE EARLY 1990S, A VIVACIOUS YOUNG BUSINESSWOMAN named Deb Alouis moved to Calgary from Montreal to be closer to her mother. She and her husband, Tony, rented a modest house in Castleridge, a new neighbourhood of brick bungalows on the expanding eastern edge of this young city near the foothills of the Rockies. Their local pub—a five-minute walk away—was Tops Bar, set back in a tiny strip mall that also featured a liquor store and a 7-Eleven convenience store. From time to time, the young couple would run into a fellow Quebecer at Tops. He was a bit of a pipsqueak, height-wise, with coke-bottle glasses, heavy chestnut hair with bangs, bushy brows and a Burt Reynolds moustache. He chain-smoked and knocked back Labatt Blue beer while shooting pool, a game they began to join him in. Luc Grégoire, thirty-three, dressed indifferently, in baggy clothes, mostly sweatshirts and tar-stained jeans.

Skilled as a roofer, he had come to Calgary because of the construction boom. He was friendly but seemed a little lost, or out of his element. When he told Deb in the winter of 1992 that he was about to lose his basement apartment, she offered him a room in her house. It would help to offset her own rent. The basement had a separate entrance, its own washer and dryer. Why not?

So began a fifteen-month stint as a landlady that would end with Deb hospitalized on a psych ward for trauma.

"Luc was a good tenant," she told me, thinking back to what began as an ordinary year. He always paid his rent on time; he babysat their neighbours' school-age twins and took care of her black lab, Trooper, who often rode with Grégoire in his car. "Anything I ever asked him to do, he'd do it. Right away." He usually joined her and her husband for dinner rather than eat by himself.

Deb is an attractive person in her late fifties now, with a light-brown, chin-length bob, a stylish Montreal fashion sense and a warm, straight-shooting manner. She plied me with coffee and homemade chocolate eclairs when I dropped by her custom-built house north of Calgary, which she shares with her third husband—her last name now Horton—and two doting King Charles spaniels. You can easily see how she'd make a drifting young man feel at home. Later, she wondered why he hadn't killed her, but figured that maybe, in her down-to-earth, bossy way, she'd become a mother figure to him. "I was constantly at him: 'Luc! Clean this room!' or 'Luc, you can't go out without having a shower!'"

He never called his family, that she can remember, and barely spoke of them. She knew he'd dropped out of high school in

Sherbrooke, and that he'd been thrown out of the house at the age of fifteen or sixteen. (Another source tells us this was because he sexually assaulted a relative, but we cannot confirm it. We do know that early sexual violence against family members ought to be taken far more seriously as a red flag by the justice system.) "He had severe nightmares," Deb remembered. "He would scream and yell in the night, and I'd go check to see if he was okay." Although he was always calm with her, he was "a hot-headed Frenchman, and I can say that, because I'm from Quebec. He'd slam doors hard, and roar off in the car." The muffler on his beat-up hatchback was corroded—smoky and loud.

"One day," Deb said, nudging the plate of eclairs toward me, "I came home early from work and found Luc with a parole officer in the living room. I lost it. He said no, it was fine, it was just for a DUI. He drank and drove all the time, so that made sense." She often warned him about it; her aunt had been killed by an intoxicated driver. "I had no idea he had been convicted in Edmonton for armed robbery." Grégoire had been in the Alberta prison system for the previous six years and was now paroled under mandatory supervision. Deb and her husband were completely unaware of this; they likely confused the role of a probation officer, who might handle a drunk-driving sentence, with that of a parole officer, who oversees a prisoner's release.

For the most part, Luc would come home from roofing gigs, play fetch with Trooper, drink beer and snort coke. He never went on dates, or mentioned girlfriends. "Lay 'em and leave 'em," he'd say, as if he were a confident charmer. Deb's friend Gail found him slightly repellent. "His appearance was generally unkempt," she told me. "His hair was longer and straight, with bangs, and generally not brushed, or brushed well. I will say that he was a rough dresser. His accent struck me as uneducated. And I can't remember if this is an accurate memory or if I am confusing him with someone else, but I have a sensory memory of a stale smell . . . he smoked a lot."

Once, Deb remembers, he brought a woman home at two or three in the morning, and the woman started screaming. "It wasn't pleasure screaming," Deb said. "I got up and yelled, '*Luc*, what's going on?!' There was silence, and then I saw her leave." The screaming wasn't something Deb was able to compute. Were they fighting? Did the woman have a phobia of spiders? No matter—whoever she was, she was gone, and so Deb never found out what had upset her. She went blearily back to bed.

When Tony and Deb bought a house on Pinetree Place Luc moved with them, but he was deeply discomfited by the change. Deb remembers working in her garden in the spring, on her knees pulling up hollyhocks, when she turned around to find Luc standing behind her with a shovel held over his head "as if he was going to hit me." He lowered it, just foolin' around.

On Tuesday, May 4, 1993, Grégoire came home in the middle of the night and blocked Deb and Tony's Mustang in the driveway with his car. The next morning, before heading to her job at a radio station, Deb wanted to drive over to Walmart, to buy some things for the new house. Short on time, she asked to borrow Grégoire's car. He protested, but she pushed. "What's the big deal?" Unbeknownst to her, Grégoire's back seat was sprinkled with shards of glass and blood.

Close to midnight, she was changing for bed, was actually naked, when a SWAT team burst into the house. They shouted,

"Don't move!" and a cop threw his jacket over her. Luc was arrested in the alley behind the house. She remembers him shouting "I'm sorry!" Deb was hauled in for questioning and held until dawn, as was Tony. Her mind reeled. She couldn't process what she was learning. It was mad—a crazy revelation that her tenant was a sexual murderer, and she was being treated as his accomplice. The car in which she'd zipped over to Walmart that morning had transported twenty-two-year-old Lailanie Silva, a Filipina immigrant just recently arrived in Calgary. Silva had been working the May 3rd night shift at their local 7-Eleven, washing the windows outside. While her arms were outstretched to hold a cloth or squeegee, Grégoire must have grabbed her from behind and shoved her into his car. He then drove about ten minutes north along Calgary's eastern fringes. After destroying her with fists and weapons, strangling her and breaking her legs, he dumped her partially clad body in a field.

Earlier that night, Grégoire had attempted and failed to abduct another woman in the neighbourhood. Aida Yeou—whose car window he'd pounded on, wearing gloves so as not to leave prints—had then called the Calgary Police Service and provided a description. As it happened, the police had a matching description in Grégoire, who was in their system due to two charges in the previous months. On January 31, he had been hit with a DUI charge after being found passed out drunk in his car in front of the local 7-Eleven, and on April 6, a sex worker named Patricia Mongey had gotten into Grégoire's car on the city's main downtown stroll and then frantically escaped when he attacked her with a roofing hammer. The cops, moreover, were already vigilant, due to a spate of prostitute murders that had gone unsolved in the previous eighteen months.

By the time the police located their suspect, Silva was dead. Her body had been disposed of, and her killer was asleep. They put him under surveillance and watched Deb jump into his car, then followed her to Walmart and into the store. At first, they suspected Deb of being "in cahoots" with Grégoire, she told me, an impression that Luc cemented later that morning by digging Silva's clothes out of a Dumpster where he had ditched them and re-dumping them directly outside Deb's office at the radio station. She remembered that he had come by her office earlier in the day, offering her his rent money. She'd thought it strange that he couldn't just wait to give it to her at home. Now she understood why. He was connecting her to the clothes, trying to frame her, or maybe threaten her. "Police had seen him do it."

Deb became a trial witness after investigators realized she'd played no part in the crimes, and she staggered under the weight of her new reality. Who suspects a murderer in their midst? Did Bundy's mother? Did Dahmer's? (By coincidence, the year that Deb had Grégoire living in her basement, I talked to Jeffrey Dahmer's mother, Joyce. She was an articulate, thoughtful social worker who had begun living in a nightmare when she saw her son arrested on TV. She'd been visiting him in prison, trying to pull from him the why of it, but then he was murdered by a fellow inmate. Now she was in the midst of a surreal custody battle with her ex-husband over the disposition of their son's brain, which she wanted to donate to science in hopes there might be some explanation that could mitigate her grief and shame. Her husband prevailed, and Joyce died of cancer five or six years later.)

In Calgary, Deb's sense of reality was shattered. "Luc put me in a really bad spot. You're just stunned. It ruins your ability to trust." Her marriage to Tony fell apart, and it would be years before she could feel any confidence in her judgment. She lost her job at the radio station; they gave her a full year's pay, but "there was too much news" to separate her from Calgary's most shocking sex murder. She was part of the story. Journalists were constantly at her house or office. "I couldn't move." She never spoke to any of them.

Luc-Yoland Grégoire pled not guilty to first-degree murder, arguing that he might have been caught with Silva's *clothes*, but that didn't mean he'd killed her—where was the proof of that? His conviction was a slam dunk. The trial mesmerized the western city, which generally had a very low murder rate. Sentenced to life in prison, Grégoire was sent back east, behind the clanging metal gates of Archambault Institution, a prison north of Montreal, where he disappeared from view until our source identified him in 2002. There was never a mention of his crime in the Quebec press. However, one of the journalists covering the trial, the *Calgary Herald's* Christina Mungan, did reach back through time and across the country to a 1981 rape victim in Sherbrooke named Nicole Couture.

Grégoire grew up in the 1970s in a small detached home at 3253 rue Delorme, in a working-class neighbourhood on the southern flank of the narrow Magog River threading through Sherbrooke. The closest convenience store for anyone living on Delorme—should one run out of smokes or Labatt Blue—was the Provi-soir at the corner of Jacques Cartier Boulevard and

King Street. This was where Louise Camirand was last seen buying cigarettes and milk. The main artery leading into and out of the neighbourhood, Jacques Cartier Boulevard, was also one block from Portland Boulevard, where Margaret (whose brother wrote to John) had stood and hitchhiked in the summer of 1977 during her lunch hour.

On a cold night in February 1981, Nicole Couture, a mother in her early thirties, was returning to her car in a municipal parking lot in the area after a girlfriends' night at a discotheque. Grégoire, extremely drunk, pushed her into the back seat and pummelled her with his fists. "He didn't need a weapon," Nicole told Mungan of the *Herald*. "His hands were his weapons." He punched her repeatedly in the head, "as if in a panic," and then began choking her until she stopped struggling. After that, he raped her and did things so unspeakable that she couldn't voice them. "She was quite willing to talk, once it was clear I was female and francophone," Mungan told us. "The only thing she could not bring herself to tell me was something Grégoire tried to make her do. '*Et je ne pouvais pas, je ne pouvais pas*'; she couldn't even describe it. Since she did describe anal and vaginal rape, I didn't choose to speculate."

Couture began pleading for her life, saying her four young children needed her. Grégoire agreed that children needed their mother alive. His own mother, he said, didn't love him. He spoke of his rage, of being kicked out of the Canadian Armed Forces, of other women he had raped since his military discharge. He said the only way for him to have sex was through violence, because he wasn't sufficiently attractive. "Though he promised not to rape again," Mungan wrote in the *Herald*,

"Couture says she knew that he would, 'because of his incredible rage, his frustration.'"

After demanding money for a cab home, he locked the doors of her car as she lay inside bleeding, telling her it would keep her safe. Two weeks later, Sherbrooke Municipal Police arrested him lurking in the same parkade.

Mungan's *Herald* article contained a full-length photo of Luc Grégoire. It is one of the only photos of Grégoire, and in it the tattoos on his forearms are prominently displayed. It is worth noting that around this time, Grégoire left (was again turfed out of?) his parents' home on Delorme and moved into an apartment at 135 rue Brooks, walking distance from the parkade and just southwest of the King-Wellington corridor—the same neighbourhood where the taxi driver had dropped off Jean Charland and the "tattooed man" after the murders of Raymond Grimard and Manon Bergeron in the summer of 1978. The man convicted of those murders, Fernand Laplante, did not have tattoos on his forearms. Grégoire's rue Brooks apartment was also one block away from the apartment where Carole Fecteau lived in June 1978 before she was left naked and murdered beside a stream in East Hereford. Make of that geography what you will.

In May 1981, Luc Grégoire, then twenty-one years old, agreed to plead guilty to the lesser charge of indecent assault against Nicole Couture. (He was also charged with robbing a female gas station clerk at gunpoint while out on bail for the Couture assault, and pled to that as well. This second crime involved another robber, suggesting that—in Sherbrooke, at least—Grégoire sometimes ran with other thieves. On May 27, according to the *Sherbrooke Record*, "By fighting and screaming, a young woman foiled an attacker who attempted to rape her last night . . . [while] walking down Ontario Street by Howard's Park." This was the same area of south Sherbrooke. Had Grégoire violated bail conditions and attacked again?) Under English common law, the difference at the time between indecent assault and rape mattered greatly to sentencing. Canadian law started changing in 1982, but in England as late as 1994, one British parliamentarian clarified for the House of Commons the failings of that distinction, and why it made little sense that any attack that didn't involve penile penetration should carry far less weight in sentencing guidelines: "Also excluded [from the legal definition of rape] is the use of objects such as bottles, broom handles, knives and men's hands," MP Mildred Gordon told her colleagues as they considered new legislation. "There was a famous case involving a Queen's guardsman, Thomas Holdsworth, who was freed by the court on the grounds that a [jail] sentence would ruin his Army career. In legal terms he had not raped the woman involved, although he had used his fist, full of rings, which tore her internally. The distinction made by the law, and by many men, between penile penetration and other sexual assault has nothing to do with the trauma that women suffer, or with women's perceptions."

Somehow, thanks to the plea deal, not only was Luc Grégoire's punishment lighter, but the *story* of his intense violence against Nicole Couture got lost in the legal translation. On July 29, 1981, after his sentencing, Sherbrooke's *Tribune* characterized the crime this way: "Grégoire had sequestered a girl on February 6 for the initial purpose of having sex with her, but she resisted and he stole her money instead. He hit her and squeezed her neck when she tried to escape." In another version filed by the parole board, he made her masturbate him in the parking lot and hand over taxi fare. The narrative was controlled by the predator and by the press, not the victim. (That this bothered Couture is suggested by the fact that she agreed to an interview with the *Calgary Herald* only because Christina Mungan was a female reporter.) Couture told Mungan that she was so traumatized her marriage fell apart. She left the city.

Grégoire served a little over a year in prison and was paroled to a group home in Montreal. Within months, as Nicole Couture had predicted, he was rearrested for assaulting a sex worker.

What John learned about Luc-Yoland Grégoire's time in prison, as he patiently and persistently traced the killer over several years from his North Carolina home office, came from two sources, Quebec parole review hearings (known as decision registries) and a Correctional Service of Canada internal review from 1993. The task assigned in that review was, in effect, to answer a spectacularly awkward question: How did Grégoire manage to commit a DUI, an assault with a weapon, an attempted abduction and a murder while under mandatory supervision on parole? Or, in the words of the document, the review's mandate was "to analyze pre-indicators to the [murder], the quality of case preparation and supervision, and the quality of communications and the sharing of information, as well as to provide its findings relating to the circumstances surrounding the incident, the adequacy and effectiveness of the operational framework, and the effectiveness of staff."

The first thing John gleaned from these reports was that Couture was not Grégoire's first victim on record. He had beaten and raped a woman in Germany while serving with the Canadian Armed Forces. "As regards your two previous acts of sexual aggression," observed the Quebec parole board, "the one was committed in 1981 where you took the victim by the throat in a car and demanded money for a taxi. At the same time, you demanded that she give you a blow job. You were in a state of advanced inebriation." This was, at least, one iteration of what had happened. "The second aggression characterized as sexual would be committed in 1979, when you lived in Germany. You beat a woman because she was sticking too close to you. You explained that you were intoxicated. You sexually assaulted the victim after having beaten her, and then left her on the sidewalk."

Grégoire, as he'd told Nicole Couture, had been in the Canadian Armed Forces for a time, perhaps sent by someone attempting to straighten him out. There is nothing in his history to suggest that he cared about serving his country or was interested in structure, hierarchy and discipline. Yet in 1979, he seems to have been stationed at a Canadian base in Germany, either at CFB Baden–Soellingen or CFB Lahr. Grégoire admitted the assault to a prison psychologist, but there is no evidence of a court martial archived at the Department of National Defence. Maybe his superiors never knew. One report stated that he was discharged for drug use. But in the 1960s and '70s, and particularly during the Vietnam War, rape in the military was often an *authorized transgression*, as feminists called it. "So long as knowledge about sexual violence remained confined to the victims and the military community," historian Joanna Bourke wrote about this period, "very little was done." In other words, the Armed Forces might well have known what Grégoire did, but that didn't lead to his discharge. The Canadian Armed Forces has been plagued by scandals involving sexual assault and harassment. In 1998, *Maclean's* magazine ran an investigative feature about a gang rape in the mid-eighties at CFB Gagetown for which no one was rebuked. Retired Brigadier General Al Geddry, who wasn't familiar with the specific case, told *Maclean's* that in the seventies and eighties the Canadian Armed Forces took a "wash-your-dirty-laundry-in-the-family" approach to transgressions. "Therefore," he said, "we ended up with a lot of coverups right up until the recent past."

One effect of this "family" approach, of course, is that sex offenders in the military don't build a track record that can alert judges to the danger posed by one who later commits a civilian crime. Grégoire was sentenced for the first time on July 28, 1981, seemingly for a first offence, and was given a release eligibility date of January 28, 1982 (at least for temporary absences and day parole). We believe he was housed at Cowansville Institution in the Eastern Townships. His prison intake report identified his problems as "influence of peers, work skills, and alcohol abuse." Who were these peers who could have influenced Luc Grégoire to rape and beat women? The low-level thugs who hung out on rue Wellington, stole cars and took out hits on each other for petty drug disputes? Those peers? Or Grégoire's military buddies? Or both?

As rape rates rose across North America in the 1970s, alcohol abuse emerged as the explanatory driver that it remains to this day. It wasn't the behaviour so much as the booze that had to be brought under control. In one 1986 study, college students who were given a placebo drink (something like "near beer") became more violent and sexually reckless based on their assumption that they had been drinking and that alcohol elicited aggression. The underlying belief was that sexual violence was normal—*not that difficult to trigger*. The 1978 book *Understanding Sexual Attacks*, according to Joanna Bourke, explained rape this way: "Men who attacked women were experiencing 'a chronic feeling of dissatisfaction, real or imagined, with their own masculine performance, social or sexual.' They also harboured 'strong and ambivalent emotions towards women, who tended to be perceived as agents of frustration and guilt.' Typically, these men developed violent sexual fantasies as a response to anxieties that rape was (as one rapist put it) 'the only way I would ever be able to have intercourse.'" Grégoire said something along these lines to Couture.

What this pervasive belief led to, in prison therapy, was an emphasis on teaching men how to have better social and dating skills, as if one were house-training puppies who didn't *mean* to hurt you when they jumped about and nipped. "These schemes were designed to give men who had sexually offended some basic tips about conducting relationships in a healthy manner," wrote Bourke. "If, as one forensic psychiatrist diagnosed it, rape was a 'courtship disorder,' that is, a flawed performance of 'normal' courtship behaviour, then men could be trained out of it." In the 1950s, Nathan Roth, senior psychiatrist for the New York State Research Project on Sexual Offenders, went even further by suggesting that rapists felt distressed and ashamed of their inability to not rape. Masculine institutional sympathy for rapists ran deep.

A host of theories, many of them directly contradicting one another, came into play about the rapist personality as more and more women reported the crime. By the time Grégoire was imprisoned, there were literally hundreds of therapeutic techniques being applied to sex offenders in North American prisons. Yet, according to one major survey, over half of the offenders resisted treatment entirely. Why wouldn't they? Their offences were tacitly sanctioned by the military, implicitly supported by the culture and largely ignored by the cops. Lay 'em and leave 'em. The criminologist Dr. Candice Skrapec remembers interviewing another serial killer housed in Cowansville in the late 1980s who had committed his first murder at the age of sixteen and was receiving the same "work skills" and behavioural counselling that Grégoire might have been offered.

A year after his brutal attack on Couture, Grégoire was denied his first bid for day parole due to "poor introspection regarding violence and his varying story concerning the offence circumstances." In July, a psychiatric report "notes no serious sexual pathology, but states that inmate Grégoire has difficulty understanding and relating to women. Aggressive tendencies are rated as moderate while under stress." By October 1982, day parole had been formally granted. The report makes no mention of whether he already had permission for unescorted temporary absences, such as to visit a doctor or family members. There are two redacted lines immediately above the "day parole granted" line. Each of these lines begins with a date, and the redacted one covers a word longer than October, which would be September. Something was requested or recommended that month that needed privacy shielding. One possibility: Grégoire's father had a birthday in November (only a few years earlier, serial killer William Fyfe committed his first murder while similarly out on a day pass, from the Bordeaux prison in Montreal).

In early November 1981, we have Marie's account of being ambushed and beaten, in a manner very similar to Nicole Couture's experience, while she was jogging on Highway 143. Marie drew two sketches of her attacker that were evocative of Grégoire. The location of the attack was by no means out of the way for someone returning from Sherbrooke on a day pass from Cowansville Institution, and the assault occurred mid-afternoon. Whoever it was that left Marie near death on the road that day, they committed no further rapes reported in news accounts during the time that Grégoire remained behind bars.

In late January 1983, Grégoire was fully paroled to a community residential centre in Montreal. Within weeks, a case manager noted that he needed to "improve his reaction to frustrations," as he was ignoring house rules and continuing to use drugs and alcohol. In March, he was arrested for assaulting a sex worker. "Apparently, offender Grégoire wished to have sex with her, and her injuries resulted when she refused." (There is no record of how badly she was hurt; given what we know from Couture, anything is possible.)

On March 28, a case management worker reported to parole authorities that Grégoire "tries by all means possible to camouflage his sexual offences. I consider him as a potentially dangerous offender and in his case, the protection of society (violence against women) should outweigh his liberty . . . recidivism is more than likely." Although he didn't know it at the time, this case worker would have had solid research to back up his warning. According to criminologist Eric Beauregard and his colleagues, "A criminal record of violence (severity of prior crimes against persons) is a significant predictor of sexual murder."

Grégoire's parole was revoked, and he went back into the correctional system until February 13, 1984, after which he was released on mandatory supervision until late July. He was arrested at some point that fall for theft over $200—and then there's no trace of him in Corrections Canada records until August 1985, when he was charged with DUI in Saanich, British Columbia, on Vancouver Island, nearly five thousand kilometres west of where he'd lived most of his life. What propelled Grégoire to the westernmost point of Canada in those intervening months is a mystery. After he'd been kicked out by his family (according to Deb Horton and another source), and then the military, it seemed that someone or some group had now thrown him straight out of Sherbrooke. Had he committed another crime? Why not move to the more familiar ground of Montreal or the Gaspe? We know that the Hells Angels established their first western foothold on Vancouver Island in 1983, although their members may have been more connected to California than Quebec. Grégoire would have been acquainted with some of the lower-level gangsters—his "peers"—given his lifestyle and penchant for robbery and drug use. Did he follow gossip about the gangs out West? And did they, then, also tell him to scram? By November, he had boomeranged a thousand kilometres eastward, as evidenced by a DUI charge in Slave Lake, Alberta. By May 1986, he'd been convicted in Edmonton of the armed robbery of a fur coat store using a sawed-off shotgun. As the

Parole Board of Canada would say to him years later, "Your criminality is polymorphic and persistent since adolescence. Your violence seems often impulsive, encouraged by intoxication. Your crimes are associated with the presence of grave damage for your victims." He was hell on wheels, this guy.

Grégoire was sentenced to serve seven years for the Edmonton robbery. He bounced around Alberta prisons for four of them. He was first transferred after being caught trying to escape from one institution, and then transferred again after getting stomped by other prisoners at another, for reasons unknown to us. He would ultimately commit ten prison infractions, "four of which were classified as violent," before his parole date was set.

In August 1988, Grégoire underwent another psychiatric assessment. It reported that he had "little ability to postpone gratification or control his impulses, but [was] without entrenched hostility or alienation." Did this psychologist perceive him as Deb Alouis later would, as friendly, a little lost and unkempt, a bit hot-headed? Was Grégoire trying to play nice with parole fast approaching? In the few pictures we have seen of him, Grégoire is always smiling. His mother, Claire, described him to the *Calgary Herald* as having been a "cute little boy." A dog lover, a babysitter, someone eager to help. He wasn't a sophisticated charmer, but he could project the right quality—a certain earnestness—when it suited him. Now, he had apparently decided to "recognize" that he drank too much. According to the Board of Inquiry, "this report contains the first indication that inmate Grégoire recognizes an alcohol abuse problem, although the assessment does not address the issue at all."

Later that month, transferred to yet another institution, Grégoire was, for the first time, diagnosed with antisocial personality disorder (the approved term—not *psychopath* or *sociopath*—included in the American Psychiatric Association's *Diagnostic and Statistical Manual of Mental Disorders*). Why no one had caught this earlier has to do with when the concept itself spread. In 1985, clinical psychologist Robert Hare at the University of British Columbia refined an assessment tool known as the Psychopathy Checklist (PCL). The PCL-R (with the R standing for *Revised*) is a twenty-item checklist of behaviours and personality traits that guide clinicians through whether the criminal before them is wearing what psychiatrist Hervey Cleckley once called the "Mask of Sanity." Hare's list soon went into very wide circulation amongst forensic and prison psychologists. In fact, the Parole Board of Canada approached Hare to have the entire incarcerated population tested, because one of his UBC studies had found that 80 percent of PCL-R-rated psychopaths reoffended within three years, compared with only 20 percent of non-psychopaths. Although the system-wide tests didn't happen, Hare published the checklist in 1991, allowing officials to make use of it as they saw fit.

The checklist's twenty items include glibness/superficial charm; need for stimulation/proneness to boredom; lack of remorse; lack of empathy; promiscuous sexual behaviour; early behaviour problems; lack of realistic, long-term goals; impulsivity; juvenile delinquency; criminal versatility; and failure to accept responsibility. It appears that the prison psychologist applied this checklist to Luc Grégoire, who rated highly enough to earn his psychopath pedigree. But shortly thereafter, he again switched prisons, and the treatment focus resettled on his alcoholism. Fix that, his new minders decided, and maybe he'd be fine. In September 1989, he was assessed by someone else as "a suspicious individual with significant assaultive tendencies who may be at a high risk of abusing some form of intoxicants." In the ensuing months—the date in the report was redacted—a detention review determined that Grégoire was, indeed, an alcoholic, but "serious harm has never resulted."

It was a deeply consequential game of broken telephone, from Couture's experience in that parking lot to some highly alert and concerned Quebec psychologists warning of violence against women, dwindling through shuffled files of paper and prisons to an Alberta team worried that the offender, upon release, might get drunk and disorderly. The greatest communication gap of them all, according to the 1993 Board of Inquiry, was language: "There was no translation of file documents produced during an earlier term in Quebec, which may have had some effect on case management decision making and assessment, and parole supervision." The Alberta penal system couldn't read French. Two solitudes, as Canada's French and English nations have sometimes been called, have rarely led to such a deadly outcome.

Grégoire was released on January 21, 1991, to Edmonton's bleak midwinter. We don't know what he did for money. At a parole meeting in February, he reported "attending bars to test himself," by which he presumably, and insincerely, meant refraining from drink. He was cautioned. A condition attached to his freedom was that he "participate in counselling as deemed necessary by a clinician." He finally got around to meeting this condition in July and "became agitated at the length of time required for assessment." The psychologist decided there would be no point in counselling such an unwilling client, or even referring him elsewhere, so they closed the file. Apparently, that didn't affect his parole because Grégoire agreed to meet with the pastor of a local church instead. What else he did with his time is unknown. Criminal psychologist Candice Skrapec told me it was highly unlikely that he didn't engage in rape. "I don't think he was clean," she said, referring to his criminal proclivities during this parole period in Edmonton. But he would have been careful, at least initially, not to do something too headline-grabbing. The RCMP later reviewed several of their cold cases in and around Edmonton but could find no evidentiary links.

At his August supervision appointment, his parole officer noted that "offender Grégoire is observed to have a black eye and scratches. He explains that he was at a night club drinking and intervened on behalf of a woman who was being beaten. Case notes report this is the first indication that he is drinking again." The missing-the-pointedness of this case note is almost exquisite.

At around the same time, coincidentally, a Calgary teenager named Jennifer Joyes, who'd lost her mother in a car accident and was living as a ward of the province, was reported to the police as unaccounted for, having last been seen at her group home on August 10. At some point before she disappeared, she'd been seen by police on the city's main sex-work stroll, although it was never clear why she was there. Her body would be found in a wooded area near Springbank, west of the city limits, on October 7, 1991. Another teen, Jennifer Janz, was found murdered at a construction site on August 13, after disappearing in July. The cause of death wasn't released by the Calgary Police Service. These two slayings would mark the beginning of what became known as the Calgary Prostitute Murders.

Grégoire was due to be assessed again by his case managers in November, but couldn't attend "due to employment in Calgary." By December, his alcohol use was no longer deemed problematic, and he was considered low risk for reoffence. His supervision was transferred to Calgary, where he'd been cobbling together odd jobs as a roofer.

On January 18, 1992, a young woman named Anita Gilavish was found murdered in a bird sanctuary about a six-minute drive south of the National Hotel, which was known at the time as the "main stroll" for prostitutes. Her family didn't know if she had become a sex worker, only that she'd started running with "a rough crowd," according to the *Calgary Herald*.

There are no parole notes on Grégoire in Calgary from March 1992, when it was affirmed that there was "no benefit in forcing him to attend" counselling, to July, when it was decided again that "alcohol is seen as a major focus of supervision," although the supervision frequency was reduced to one meeting per month. By now, he was working as a freelance roofer, living paycheque to paycheque and sleeping in the basement of the home rented by Deb Alouis in Calgary's Castleridge neighbourhood. (It must have been around this time that Deb came home and encountered the parole officer in her living room, to her unnerved surprise.)

The main north-south through road for the Castleridge area is 68th Street. New home developments began rising off this road to the west, while fields and parks still flanked its eastern side.

The first body found dumped off of 68th Street, in Elliston Park, was that of a transsexual named Jean McMaster, found August 8, 1992. Her cause of death wasn't released. The newspapers made no report. She was a victim considered to be without consequence, the most vulnerable of all.

In October, Grégoire headed to Edmonton for a week to pursue a lawsuit against the Correctional Service of Canada for having been beaten while in custody in 1988. (We assume by other inmates, but we have no details. We know from his parole records that he was prone to feeling aggrieved.)

On October 28, a single mother named Tracey Maunder disappeared from "the stroll" in downtown Calgary at 3rd Avenue Southeast. She was reported missing immediately when she didn't come home to relieve the babysitter, and was found stabbed to death in a field south of the Castleridge neighbourhood, off of 68th Street, near the highway that heads north to Edmonton. She lay—rather eerily—across from the Garden of Peace Cemetery. Her mother couldn't conceive of Tracey being unable to defend herself. "She was a fighter. She would have fought to the death, that's the type of person she was," she told the Herald. But what if you don't see the weapon coming? How easily do you fend off a murderous rage? Missing from the crime scene were Tracey's black Chicago Bulls jacket, her spandex pants, her black boots and her purse.

A December parole report stated that Grégoire's alcohol consumption was "reduced to the point that offender Grégoire is now saving money through a Registered Retirement Savings Plan." (It is highly unlikely this was true.) At around the same time, Deb

Horton told me, he was actually beginning to career out of control with his drinking and drug use. Between January and May, he really fell apart. He would drive absolutely shit-faced, she said, and was doing a lot of cocaine. (To support the habit, he would rob Calgary women at ATMs, something he admitted years later to a prison psychologist.) Horton attributed Grégoire's spiralling behaviour to the fact that she and Tony had bought a house and were leaving the rental home in Castleridge. "The move was a stressor," she mused. "He had been comfortable, and he may have worried about what people would find." Did he perceive this as being thrown out of another family home? Another stressor, likely related, was receiving a letter in January from his mother, Claire, exhorting him not to "bring me any more misery to my heart." Claire Grégoire told the *Calgary Herald* he had visited her in Sherbrooke that winter. (The trip would have been news to his parole supervisors, but Grégoire had taken an unauthorized trip to the town of Banff, and would drive to Edmonton with his roofing boss, Glen Guttinger, so a Quebec trip is possible.)

In the study of serial murder, there has long been a theory that stress can act as a trigger for predation. Jeffrey Dahmer, for example, killed his first victim in 1978, with, according to criminologist Mike Arntfield, "the breakup of his family [as] a key factor—a psychological trigger known as decompensation." This idea was first proposed by FBI agent Robert Ressler in 1988 and has since been refined by other researchers. One pattern observed by the criminologist Candice Skrapec, after interviewing serial murderers in prison, is that these killers (ironically) have a highly overdeveloped sense of themselves as victims. They see the world, and their conduct in reaction to it, through the lens of their aggrievement. Skrapec's perception was later the subject of a doctoral thesis at the University of Toronto by Sasha Reid, who explored how serial killers develop vivid fantasy lives in which they enact the power they feel keenly deprived of in their real lives, where they exist as victims. Stress, for them, is felt as a *re*-victimization that compels them to try to regain control. If at first that control involves fantasized violence, it can evolve to incorporate living targets. After being rejected by the Canadian Armed Forces, as he perceived it, Grégoire may have been regaining control in this way when he raped several women (by his own account). In a sense, according to Reid, the violence engaged in by Grégoire and his murderous peers amounts to a coping mechanism.

On the last night of January 1993, Grégoire was found passed out and slumped in his car in the parking lot of the Rundlehorn Hill 7-Eleven, a few minutes' drive from Deb's new house. He may have been prowling but run out of steam, as this would be where he would ultimately abduct Lailanie Silva. The police rapped on his window to rouse him and issued an appearance notice for driving under the influence. Unaware that the dozing man in the car was on parole, they made no notification to the Alberta Justice duty officer who was tracking Grégoire's mandatory supervision.

Two weeks later, a twenty-year-old Cape Bretoner named Rebecca Boutilier, known to those who loved her as Becca, disappeared from the 3rd Avenue stroll. She was found dead some days later in a field off 68th Street, beside a pile of roofing shingles. The location was a straight six-minute drive from the 7-Eleven. She had been killed by a weapon undisclosed by police.

Her black suede jacket, black purse and black leather boots were never found. A full set of women's clothing, however, had been placed near her body. The police traced these clothes to another sex worker, who warily told them about a "bad date." The man had made her remove her clothes, but then pushed her out of the car. Now, of course, learning that her clothes had been deliberately placed with a murdered colleague in a snowy field, she could only be terrified. (When the police originally sought her, according to the *Calgary Herald*, other sex workers eyed her mug shot and clammed up. The detectives complained to the press that this was how street workers could be frustratingly unhelpful. Did these women not get it? Actually, the women got it quite clearly: *The killer was still at large*. Given the deliberate and incredibly menacing positioning of her clothes beside another woman's corpse, not one of them would have wanted their friend and co-worker to feel more vulnerable than she already was.)

On April 6, sex worker Patricia Mongey was picked up by Grégoire on the stroll on 3rd Avenue. She agreed to oral sex for $75. He parked his car in a nearby alley and started to fondle her. When she asked for money up front, he pulled out a sharp-edged roofing hammer and pressed it to her neck, telling her to do what he wanted or be killed. "I was scared," she later testified in court, since her request had been totally pro forma, not something most johns objected to. She knew this was trouble, and when she saw a police cruiser passing by, she fled from the car, leaving her patent-leather heels behind. Grégoire, for his part, testified at the assault trial in 1994 that he paid her $60 and got frustrated when she quit fellatio before he was finished. "I squeeze her neck a little bit to get her attention because I was not going to pay for something

I wasn't going to get." This hearkens back to what one of his Quebec parole officers said: that Grégoire "tries by all means possible to camouflage his sexual offences." *He's* the victim, after all.

Although the police arrested and charged him, Grégoire was released and the assault was not brought to the attention of the Alberta parole team. His parole officer last saw him on April 15, less than three weeks before Silva's murder. "Starting to celebrate," the officer noted about Grégoire's reaction to the imminent end of his sentence. "Take it easy." Cool it with the booze!

That April, Deb and Tony took a vacation to Hawaii, leaving Grégoire to care for their Labrador, Trooper, whom the basement tenant had grown very attached to. He brought the dog everywhere in his car. When the couple returned, tired from the flight, Deb noticed blood spatter on her foyer wall. "What is *this*?" she asked Grégoire, alarmed. "Luc went red in the face," she recalled, and stammered something about Trooper cutting his paw. That made enough sense for her to let it go in the moment, but later she would think, *No, the blood was too high up.* Everything, mercilessly, in retrospect. She wondered if she'd triggered his violence, getting on his case about this and that. Did he take out his rage on other women? For years, this prospect haunted her.

What actually happened in the foyer, nobody knows. Did the blood belong to a woman, knifed but able to escape? Was a corresponding body ever found? There were seventy-two reported incidents of assault and sexual assault against Calgary's sex workers in 1993. Many more, it is likely, were handled by the victims themselves. By coincidence or not, it became less likely for them to need protection from murder after Luc Grégoire was arrested in May. No sex worker was murdered in Calgary for another six years.

FOURTEEN

ECHOES

"It's a poor sort of memory that only works backward."
—Lewis Carroll, *Through the Looking Glass*

AFTER WE MANAGED, IN 2002, TO IDENTIFY AT LEAST ONE suspect in the violent mayhem of the quiet Townships of the seventies, I drifted away from this story. My mother-in-law was dying in Cape Breton, Nova Scotia, and my husband was her only child. Throughout that fall, we took turns flying out to Halifax from Toronto and then driving five hours north to Cape Breton Island. In January, after the funeral, we gathered our small children and went to live in Mexico for six months, working via slightly dodgy Internet connections in a valley west of Mexico City.

John was left at the centre of a stirred-up wasp's nest in Quebec. As he later wrote me: "The tragedy of Theresa's death finally got everybody's attention"—in ways both good and bad. The fallout from our newspaper series had been immediate, with Champlain College the first to sound off. In the *Sherbrooke Record*, Champlain Lennoxville director Bertrand Daigneault expressed his outrage at such a "gratuitous, unfounded and untruthful attack" on the college's "sterling reputation," one that had been "carefully developed during the past 30 years." The director's stunningly defensive response seemed at odds with the facts, including the most obvious one: Theresa's disappearance and death had occurred twenty-four years before our articles were published. Much had changed since then, including the directorship of the school. Daigneault went on to argue that, despite the meagre bus service during Theresa's time, if a student chose to hitchhike, it was a "personal decision." A Champlain alumnus, Tom Cavanagh—who was an associate dean at Champlain in the seventies—told the press that everyone had assumed Theresa was a runaway. "Violence just wasn't on the radar screen," he said. But Cavanagh's perspective would seem to be contradicted by the existence of two editorials in student newspapers in February and November of 1978 about violence against women on campus. There were assaults being reported to cops, a local woman had been found naked and strangled, and another had been found naked and shot. Violence wasn't merely on the radar, it was screaming "Red alert!"

The upwelling of indignant denials left the Allore family with a disheartening case of déjà vu. "My father's prediction that this would be 1978 all over again, where the school was concerned more about its reputation than harm to young women, proved correct," John wrote me. The ensuing shouting match, which played out through the press, was debilitating. "I found myself asking, what would my sister have made of all this? Was I championing her cause or making a fool of myself? Our series had taken the police and the school totally off guard, and I was enjoying every minute of it. But was Theresa laughing along-side me, or scorning me for being petty? The problem was that she couldn't speak for herself. It would have been better if she did. My sister was ten times as eloquent as me, twice as funny, a hundred times more impassioned and incisive. I was a pale substitute. Who was I to speak for the dead? If she'd have told me to shut up, I would have obliged; but I heard nothing."

On August 20, 2002, ten days after the series ran, the police decided to weigh in on the matter. The SQ said they would look into the information brought forward in the *National Post* articles and consider whether a reinvestigation had merit. "Many of the elements are still there in the file and we have a team and the technology to support them that wasn't available 20 years ago," said the SQ communications officer, Corporal Jean Finet. The media immediately took this information and misinterpreted it, according to John. "Girl's death in '79 gets second look" announced *The Gazette*. "Montreal SQ to revisit Theresa Allore case" touted the *Sherbrooke Record*. Neither statement, strictly speaking, was true. Still, John felt encour-aged. Maybe some smart detective(s) would see now that these cases had never been properly handled.

Theresa's case files were to be transferred to the SQ's central headquarters in Montreal. That was home base for Marc Lépine—a young investigator who had been handling the case of a killer named Guy Croteau, arrested that February for the 1987 stabbing (fully 173 times) of a sixteen-year-old in the city, after which Croteau had committed several sexual assaults before being caught. (Croteau's criminal arc defied the FBI rule of thumb that killers escalate their violence.) John knew of

Lépine, who struck him as highly astute. Perhaps Lépine could be that dedicated "super-cop" he was struggling so hard to find, the Quebec Serpico.

Though the story had generated interest in Canada's English press, so far the reaction in the French media was tepid. In the 2002 aftermath, *La Tribune* managed to publish just one piece, basically a canned version of the *National Post* series. "This was a problem," John wrote. "It wasn't just an English story; we were talking about a cluster of young women—two of whom were French." The same media divide had occurred in 2001, when Chantal Dubé's reinvestigation of her sister Manon's murder had created a buzz in the francophone press but failed to elicit any English media response. John continued, "With Champlain College issuing a gag order, and the police sitting on the sidelines deciding whether to decide, the anglophone press began to focus exclusively on just how far I'd grind the ax. Shock jocks from local radio stations offered me five minutes to unveil my plans for a major lawsuit. Everyone fixated on the conflict between Quebec authorities and myself. Recently, another young woman from Sherbrooke had been murdered, Julie Boisvenu, and a second one, Julie Bureau, was missing. No one wanted to talk about them." The idea of a David and Goliath drama appealed to the media more, it would seem, than the ongoing matter of missing and murdered women. "Frustrated, I began to write letters to the editor—but editors would cut my submissions and edit out all the parts that included any mention of the victims. I was tired of hearing my own voice. I was beginning to sound like the Tokyo Rose for lost causes."

John found an ally, of sorts, in a young journalist from Radio-Canada named Jacques Taschereau, who also worked for a Quebec television newsmagazine called *Justice*, which typically produced segments about underdogs fighting the system. Taschereau wanted a story focused on the women who'd died, so John agreed to meet him in Sherbrooke in early September. "To my wife and family, I pretended that returning to Quebec for a third time in six months was a burden," he wrote. "And it had been, before. But I began to crave it. I would think about these places—the Sherbrooke streets, the bridges, the fields and farmland. In my head I'd pass through the landscape—across the college campus, down hallways and student corridors, over highways and little back roads. I couldn't wait to get back there. As someone living in the United States, all of this work—dating back to Andre's quest in '96—had been a virtual exercise. I would be sitting in the Carolinas and piecing things together through the Internet, with computer maps, essentially in my head. It was a work of imagination; so, at a certain point, it became important to connect it to three-dimensional reality, to see these places and give myself some physical assurance that these events actually happened."

Families contending with violent death in a peaceful society have a badly shaken sense of reality, I have come to learn from the Allores. They are constantly dancing in a realm of surreality, even if they don't mention it to others. This is what makes them so sensitive to the pain of being gaslit by authorities who want the crimes to just go away. When violence crashes through the gates of a loving family, every truth, suddenly, is terrifyingly suspect. Mitchell Maunder, Tracey Maunder's son, devoted much of his adolescence to wandering the downtown Calgary strolls, trying to find someone who knew what had happened to her, to find some unambiguous truth to hold on to as a route back to sanity. "There's a part of me that's still really upset," he told the journalist Sherri Zickefoose in 2011. "It hurts me how torn up my grandmother is. . . . Thank god I'm a good person; I could have gone one way or another. I took it upon myself to become a gentleman and a good person. I didn't want to be a part of what took my mother out of this world."

In Montreal, the Sûreté picked two detectives to review the files, including Marc Lépine, which excited John. He drafted a letter summarizing what we knew, and made contact with Lépine by phone. John was disconcerted to find the detective's attitude careful and guarded. He didn't have the files yet; he would need some weeks to analyze them. John asked Lépine if he would share the files. "No, he would not let me see them. I had the ring, watch, earrings and wallet, the evidence from the case; did he want to see these things? Yes, he wanted to see them. Okay, then could I see the file? No, I could not see the file. Fine, then he could not see the evidence."

Lépine and John went back and forth like this through a series of phone calls. The chess match was turning into a headache. John fumed, *"Why couldn't these people just act like human beings?"* Of course, the answer, in part, was that he had become a major thorn in the SQ's side, so they probably felt the need to keep him at something of a distance. But in this case, that was only part of the answer. Lépine agreed that when he had completely reviewed everything, he would let John know what he knew. In the meantime, John could send him what information he thought was important.

"I drafted a letter and—to ensure there would be no misunderstandings—had my sister-in-law translate it into French." The points laid out for Lépine were as follows:

1. Contact the farmer's daughter who was almost attacked on chemin Macdonald in October of 1978. She said she had given a statement to the police, and that her attacker had been arrested and told to leave town. The police should have records of this and be able to determine the attacker's identity.
2. Check out Luc Grégoire, who had attacked Nicole Couture in the parking lot in Sherbrooke in 1981.
3. Re-interview Jeanne Eddisford. She was the former assistant residence director at Champlain, currently living in Montreal.
4. Verify whether there were teacher/student suspects from Champlain College in 1978–79.

As he waited for Lépine, John travelled to the Eastern Townships to assist Jacques Taschereau with his story for *Justice*. "I met him and his group at King's Hall over Labour Day weekend. They looked so young and fit; more like a bike team than a television crew. Taschereau was very assured. He had already filmed spots with Chantal Dubé in front of the school where Manon disappeared, and with Louise Camirand's brother at her former apartment building. Mine was the last spot. We would go to the place where Theresa's body was found. We got in the crew van. Along the way I started explaining all the details of the geographic locations. Jacques stopped me: 'John, it's okay. You don't have to justify it. I've driven the map. I believe your theory.'"

This segment for *Justice* was one of six interviews John wound up doing over the course of five days in Quebec. He couldn't shut up. He said anything he was thinking to anyone who was willing to listen. He raged against the authorities—especially the police and the school. Eventually, he would learn to tone it down, but not yet. "I was triggered, I suspect, by Champlain's instant circling of the wagons and impugning of the family, just as they had done when I was fourteen. This time, I had more agency." He petitioned provincial and federal ministries of education and justice, demanding that they launch a full inquiry. He jammed up Champlain College's e-mail system, sending long-winded diatribes asking for information and assistance. He was flailing, like someone who has been running so long that they can't stop when the path hits a cliff's edge.

The investigation we'd undertaken was supposed to bring him some clarity. But instead it had tapped deep wells of anger, anxiety and grief. Latency, as the psychologists call it, had kicked in. "Having obliterated the memory of my sister for two decades, I now began to obsess about her. I created a shrine in my house with photographs and mementos. At work, my office looked like a command HQ—I pinned a map of Quebec on the wall; I had medical reports, crime photos and grisly accounts of murder all over the place. In spite of the mess, I stood defiant, challenging any of my co-workers to dare ask questions. On my drives home from work, I relished the soundtrack of the seventies. I mellowed out with the Walking Man, James Taylor, grooved to the tunes of Fleetwood Mac and cried along with Cat Stevens. Through it all, my sister was right there beside me in the passenger seat. We hit the I-85 and rocked on into the fading sunset, laughing and raging and flying. We were coming together."

In reality, however, John was coming unglued. "I began drinking too much. I had an affair. Within two years, my marriage would unravel." He and Elisabeth got a divorce.

On September 18, 2002, the Sûreté du Québec announced there would not be a new investigation into Theresa Allore's disappearance and death. Police spokesman Jimmy Potvin issued this statement: "A complete analysis was made after the allegations made by the brother of the victim in the *National Post*. The file is still open and active but there isn't any new development or evidence to further our investigation."

"Open and active." By the police's definition, information in a crime dossier could be disclosed only once that case had been solved. But cases could get solved only if they were investigated. Keeping a case open, but never investigating it, virtually assured that it would never be solved. It was a cynical Catch-22. John wrote a response in *The Gazette*: "If the Sûreté du Québec doesn't want to help us, that's fine. We've got private investigators and law enforcement in the U.S. who are willing to . . . and that's a hell of a thing to say for victims in Québec, that I have to go to American law enforcement to help me solve this crime."

In truth, the "we" John was referring to—his team—consisted of a sympathetic retired insurance investigator and his hometown police chief, Carolyn Hutchison, who had read the story and offered moral support. "I was fighting the powers of Quebec law enforcement with Banachek and one half of Cagney and Lacy."

John called up Detective Lépine and demanded to know what had gone wrong. "Why did you say you were going to investigate, and then turn around and not do it?"

"Why did you embarrass the Sûreté du Québec?" Lépine reportedly countered. "Why didn't you first come to us with the information?"

John now worried that he'd made a tactical mistake, but he'd done what Gilles had advised him to do that day in Sherbrooke when they drove around with his daughter. Had he gone to the police quietly with the information, they would have ignored it, the way Corporal Robert Théorêt had. The stories of these victims would have remained hidden, kicked over with gravel and mud. He couldn't win, really.

John tried to at least get Lépine to cite specifics contained in Theresa's file. Lépine refused. "When I asked him if he knew how my sister had died, all he would offer was, 'I can't tell you.' This just felt mean to me, a senseless punishment." But it turned out Marc Lépine wasn't exactly on the case. If he examined the information John had faxed him, it was likely because Lépine had been tasked with ensuring no connection to the case of the murderer Guy Croteau, arrested in early 2002. Was Croteau, then, a suspect in Theresa's death? Lépine wouldn't say. In his youth, Croteau had visited a family cottage in the Eastern Townships on Lake Memphremagog. After that, however, he lived and raped in Montreal. There was no connection to the Township deaths. "I felt like a fool all over again for imagining the SQ might care," John told me.

...

When the police made the decision not to reinvestigate, now-retired PI Robert Beullac told Bob Allore that Theresa had been killed three times: once on November 3, 1978, once with the poor quality of the original investigation, and now again. No one articulated this sentiment publicly, though, until late September, when a letter from a retired Champlain teacher appeared in the *Sherbrooke Record*. It was a bombshell. Former English teacher Michael Benazon wrote:

> The news that the Sûreté du Québec has decided not to re-open the investigation into the tragic death of Theresa Allore will disappoint the many Canadians who have been following this case, and it will alarm hundreds of Townships residents who were hoping for some resolution to this sorry affair. Are we to be given no official explanation? Are we to understand that the investigation stands where it did 23 years ago with the absurd hypothesis that on the night of November 3, 1978, Ms. Allore overdosed on drugs and died, and that her friends and classmates, instead of calling for an ambulance or for the police, stripped off her outer clothing, transported her body to a small creek about two kilometres away, and then several months later tossed her wallet into a farmer's field thirteen kilometres to the north? Given the failure of the police to come up with some substantiating evidence, this dubious story will only serve to nourish suspicions that the provincial police are shielding their colleagues at the local level who mishandled this case, and others.

Benazon went on to point out that the people of the Townships were rightfully worried that a killer was still at large; Julie Boisvenu, after all, had just been found dead.

> They should give their reasons in an official report at a public press conference where their findings can be challenged by family members and other interested parties. If it turns out that the earlier investigations were mishandled by the local police, the public needs to be informed what measures have been taken to improve police efficiency and professional competence in the Sherbrooke region. Without these reassurances, young women will be afraid to go out alone at night, to walk to school, to hike, jog, cycle, or ski unless accompanied by others. An atmosphere of apprehension and fear is not conducive to leisure industries, tourism, and to the creation of proper study conditions on the various campuses in Sherbrooke and Lennoxville. And needless to say, people will lose their trust in the ability of local police forces to protect them.

Benazon then took blistering aim at his former employer for refusing to address the security issues our articles raised about how unsafe the female students were, and noted that not much had changed. (The pathway through the woods remained unlit, for example, as it would for the next 20 years. Only very recently were lights finally installed.) Finally, he asked,

> What, precisely, was the source of the apparently slanderous remarks made about Ms Allore following her disappearance? These remarks, as reported by Ms Pearson, added grievous insult to the terrible injury inflicted on the Allore family. They also

appear to have served as an excuse for the police and the College to dismiss the suggestion, apparently made by more than one person at the time, to undertake a comprehensive search of the fields between Compton and Lennoxville.

We had no idea, before hearing from Michael Benazon, that staff at Champlain in 1978 had pushed for a search for Theresa and been refused. Apparently this had deeply upset Benazon for years. "While a search could not have saved Ms Allore," he wrote, "it could have provided immediate conclusive proof that a murder had taken place."

This wonderful throwing down of the gauntlet made John feel much less isolated. His fingers flew on the keyboard from his office in Durham. "I launched new petitions with the ministère de la Sécurité publique, the Commissaire à la déontologie policière, the minister of justice, the leader of the opposition, Jean Charest, and Canada's Governor General, Adrienne Clarkson. (Clarkson was my mom's suggestion; I didn't see the point, but she's my mom.) In each request, I demanded that the complete contents of my sister's file be finally turned over to me and my family. This was the final effort. Attention was centred squarely on the police. If I ever had an opportunity to gain access to the secrets of my sister's death, it would be now."

The SQ relented.

On Monday morning, November 4, 2002, John and Andre arrived at the Parthenais Street headquarters of the Sûreté du Québec in the east end of Montreal. This was where Kathy Reich's fictional forensic anthropologist, Temperance Brennan, honed her craft in the Bones novels, and where Louise Penny's Chief Inspector Armand Gamache assumed command. But those are works of fiction. This wasn't. Entering the building, the brothers felt tense. The last time they had been here together was when their dad came to the morgue to identify Theresa's body. He had emerged a different man, a distanced father, and the family had broken. John remembered the colours, the green metallic glow of the lab hallway.

Now, "Andre and I dressed for this occasion. We wore suits, all business. I carried my *Kiss Me Deadly* briefcase with all the documents. It looked like a briefcase, but it was actually a black diaper bag. You are never very far from home." Inside, the guard with the metal detector asked them to check their guns. He thought they were cops. This struck them as hilariously absurd, and they snickered like kids. Their new SQ liaison, Michel Tanguay, greeted them and led them to a modest conference room. Waiting at the table was a young detective who had been assigned to the case, a close-shaved blond with an open and engaged face. Within a year, this detective, Éric Latour, and Marc Lépine would be selected to become Quebec's first profilers, travelling to New York, Los Angeles, Miami and Washington to undergo training. Latour "was a smart, thoughtful guy on the rise," in other words. For now, he was being supervised by the older Detective Tanguay, who had served fifteen years in the homicide division.

Before the four men could talk openly, there were ground rules. The Allore brothers were allowed to take notes, but no jotting down names and phone numbers. "He did not want me running off, conducting my own investigation," as John put it. In disclosing the information they had, Tanguay warned, they were pushing the limits of Canada's Access to Information laws. The police could get into a lot of trouble if John started using classified information from government files to track down leads and suspects. On the other hand, they had no objection to John handing over what information he had gathered. This included a summary of the attacks on the women from the Eastern Townships between 1977 and 1981, from Louise Camirand through to Nicole Couture, with all the attempted assaults in between; information on witnesses and potential suspects that should be properly interviewed; information about Champlain College; and Kim Rossmo's correspondence and theories. John also gave them the evidence found at the crime scene that had been kept at home all these years in their father's file cabinet: Theresa's watch, a ceramic ring, her wallet and her earrings.

Tanguay and Latour assured John and Andre that they were serious about investigating their sister's case, as well as those of Dubé and Camirand. Latour wanted to take some time to review everything before drawing up a plan of action. This was what Lépine had said, so . . . "It was my brother who finally popped the $100,000 question. What was the Sûreté du Québec's position, now, on what happened to our sister? Tanguay said he believed that Theresa had likely been murdered. No drugs. No students. No cover-up. Like the pathologist, André Lauzon, with whom I'd corresponded when I first got the autopsy report, who had stressed the importance of good police work in cases where the body stays silent, Tanguay suggested that detectives had done a poor job of working the crime. It never should have happened this way."

Andre remembers the senior detective saying, at this point, that our *National Post* series "shook the foundations of the

Sûreté du Québec." Tanguay didn't seem particularly happy about it, John added. "It seemed more that he felt duty-bound to clean up Sherbrooke's mess."

Latour took the evidence John supplied to the forensic lab for testing. Normally these tests could take up to six months, but in this case analysis would be rushed. Before he left, he returned to the brothers an envelope marked "*Papiers personnels de Theresa Allore*." Here were her driver's permit, her library card, a weather-worn photograph of Vlad, a ticket stub to the Edmonton drag races, her McDonald's employee ID, a Life Savers wrapper, a luggage claim ticket, a bus transfer and her Baldwin-Cartier High School ID card. A partially assembled history of someone growing out of her teens and into adulthood.

Tanguay invited them to look, *finally*, at Theresa's entire case file. Police dossiers are not usually works of organizational brilliance; typically, as John would learn, they are a jumbled mess, and his sister's was no exception. Though Roch Gaudreault had been the investigator assigned to the case, the file was a collaborative effort, a collection of scribblings and typed documents contributed from various sources and detectives. Over the years, investigators sometimes drop new information into a file, but that doesn't mean anyone else ever looks at it. A good investigator should, periodically, do a thorough review of the contents, but as of 2002 not even the FBI had established a cold-case unit, with resources allocated to reconsider long-dormant files. Marc Lépine, as it turned out, would head up the SQ's inaugural cold-case unit in 2004.

For the next five hours, hunched over the conference table in their business suits, pens in hand, the Allore brothers reviewed their sister's case file. Much of the information proved repetitive—handwritten notes that were later turned into reports, reports that were produced in triplicate. John had seen a lot of it already, and what he hadn't seen didn't seem important enough to keep under lock and key from the family. There was a statement from Marilyn, for instance. More student statements, a list of items recovered. "Every time my brother and I opened a new folder or envelope, it seemed to produce another disappointment," John said. The truth was out there, but it wasn't in here.

John had been anticipating a chance to review the list of suspects since his first meeting with the Sherbrooke police back in March, when Théorêt said he wasn't permitted to see it. "That was right before the director general of Champlain College, Gerry Cutting, told me he'd heard from Gaudreault about two suspects at the time of the original investigation—a student and a teacher." It had been for this reason that John had urged Marc Lépine to re-interview certain people when he thought Lépine would actually work the case. Now, he and Andre saw that only four male students had been looked at as potential suspects, and the depth of scrutiny consisted only of background checks. All four of the "suspects" were Champlain kids who had done nothing particularly suspicious on the night of November 3, 1978. What the quartet had in common was some association with the drug culture on campus. When the background checks had come up clean, it seems the inquiries were dropped.

The file also contained a series of fading mug shots, "fifty photographs of 'Sherbrooke's Most Wanted,' each one photographed in film noir black-and-white, *Les Diaboliques de l'Estrie*," John wrote. "They looked like a living history of every Hollywood villain ever to grace the screen: sloppy, truck-driving pedophiles; snaggle-toothed drug addicts; cab-driving wackos—the Quebec version of Travis Bickle. One guy looked like actor Richard Widmark and singer Elvis Costello all rolled into one happy bag of psychotic fun. Jeanne Eddisford, the Champlain counsellor, had mentioned these photos to me. They were shown to Eddisford by Gaudreault in hopes that she might spot a familiar face. 'All these men are loose in the streets of the Townships?' she'd asked Gaudreault. To which he replied, 'Lady, these are just the ones we've caught!' That had stuck in her mind." None, however, seem to have been interviewed. There were no statements from any of them in the file.

At length, John and Andre came across a piece of paper that made their day worthwhile, albeit in the worst possible way. It was a map of the crime scene, drawn on the day Theresa's body was discovered, April 13, 1979, and sketched in pencil by a detective named Normand Grégoire. The map detailed the location of her body, the distance to Compton, the location of the Gagnon farm, the cornfield and other geographical landmarks. Most revealing was the location of the two pieces of Theresa's scarf. Both were found in the cornfield to the west of where the body lay on the Gagnon farm property, about sixteen metres apart. It pretty much killed the idea, long entertained, that Theresa had been dropped off the bridge by panicking friends. Looking at the map, you could see how someone might have driven to the side of the road and dragged her through the cornfield, the Isadora Duncan scarf slipping away from her shoulders as she was hauled, the two pieces lying unnoticed by her killer in the shadowy field before he laid her by the pond's edge. The rest of her clothes were gathered up and taken away, or had been stripped from her in the car. The map depicted a green garbage bag of clothes found at the second bridge crossing the Coaticook River, about 325 metres from the crime scene, near the tractor access path to the Gagnon farm field. The bag contained clothes belonging to either a man or a woman, but no other details were given. A pink sweater was found at this entrance to the field as well. It wasn't Theresa's.

On a single sheet of green legal paper, someone had handwritten the names of Louise Camirand, Manon Dubé and Theresa Allore, and inserted it into the file. Next to the names were some brief, jotted notes—"found with clothes," "found without clothes," "strangled" and so on. The sheet wasn't dated. There was no way of knowing how old it was, nor any explanation for why it was there. It was the only reference in the file connecting the three cases.

Toward the end of the file, John and Andre came across a series of statements from women who had been raped or sexually assaulted in the Townships in 1971. It was hard to understand why these were included. Was it an effort to show that the police had considered the prospect of sexual assault, while at the same time neatly avoiding the many reports that came in and were talked about in the local press in the actual lead-up to Theresa's disappearance? The 1971 assaults had happened in various places and made reference to known local felons. There was nothing to indicate that any follow-up was done related to these statements. Whatever their presence meant—whether they constituted a lead, or an early theory—it appeared that the line of reasoning was dropped. Was this the actual file, John found himself wondering, or a self-conscious imitation of what the police hoped a civilian would buy as a police file?

One of the last assault reports belonged to Ms. X, the farmer's daughter who was chased on chemin Macdonald one month before Theresa's disappearance. The statement in the file, however, described a completely different incident. "Michel Tanguay held her statement in his hands and looked patronizing, as if to say, *Okay, when you see this, you'll know just how far off base you and your reporter friend are,*" John wrote me. "I remembered then that a police PR rep had said on the TV programme *Justice* that Ms. X's allegation wasn't credible. This seemed to be why." According to the statement in the file, on the afternoon of April 30, 1979, Ms. X was out jogging on Route 143. It was approximately three thirty in the afternoon, just ten days after her father had found Theresa's red wallet. As she approached the junction of Route 143 and chemin Macdonald, she noticed a parked car. Leaning against it was a man in what appeared to be a uniform, maybe a security guard—his coat had epaulettes on the shoulders. He looked to be in his early fifties, possibly five foot seven and weighing 150 pounds. As she got closer, she noticed that he had his pants down and was exposing himself. Disgusted, she started yelling at him, calling him a pervert, telling him to fuck off. The man got in his car and drove off.

John was mystified. The two accounts were polar opposites. In one version, the incident took place during the day; in the other, it happened at night. By one account, she was walking her dog on chemin Macdonald; in the other, she was jogging on

Route 143. One took place in the fall; the other happened in the spring. The incident the SQ had on file was attested to by a signed statement from the victim; the attack in the fall, however, had been witnessed by her father from the family's living room window, and the Coaticook police had ticketed the man. "I asked Sergeant Tanguay what he thought might account for the dramatic discrepancy. He suggested fallible memory. Over time, the details of such things get lost and forgotten, or changed. Or, the girl had made the story up to gain some attention. In his experience, this was very common. I dismissed that out of hand because Ms. X only talked to me after I called her father about the wallet. Also, she asked to remain anonymous."

If experience has taught the police that in the vast majority of cases victims forget, distort or lie about the truth, John figured that common sense should dictate that you at least check with the source of the information first, before jumping to those conclusions. So, after the meeting with Tanguay and Latour, he contacted the family again. As it turned out, there had been two incidents, one in the fall and one in the spring. They hadn't mentioned the second one because it didn't seem as significant as the nighttime attack in October. Her mother remembered the timing of the autumn incident because she had been away at a political convention that weekend. It was easy to check the dates. Her daughter remembered it because she'd *feared for her life*. That was not how she'd felt about the spring incident with the flasher.

This difference is important, and often gets lost when male investigators make assumptions about confused or forgetful female witnesses. Dr. Jim Hopper is an American clinical psychologist and trauma expert who prepared remarks for the Senate Judiciary Committee hearing into the sexual assault allegations of Dr. Christine Blasey Ford. As he wrote in 2018, "When it comes to what will remain stored in our brains, [it] is this: How emotionally activated, stressed, or terrified we were during the experience. Decades of research have shown that stress and trauma increase the differential storage of central over peripheral details. . . . Seeing the enemy's face as our bullets enter his chest. Seeing the face of a boy we know as he holds us down and tugs at our clothes. Such details can be *burned into our brains* for the rest of our lives."

Ms. X did not provide two different accounts of one incident; she experienced two distinct events. We wondered why her statement on the second incident, in the spring, was the one placed in Theresa's file. Was it because it happened soon after the wallet was found? The same wallet that Roch Gaudreault had told Andre was probably carried that far by wild animals? If there was a link made between Theresa and Ms. X, why didn't anyone pursue it, or tell the family? "That the first incident should be missing, but the other one included specifically in Theresa's file was ironic, given that one referenced a man so unthreatening she freely shouted 'Fuck off,' while the other assailant terrified her," John told me. "But it was also just weird to have that statement in Theresa's file. It corresponded with nothing else, no police work, no follow-up. All it appeared to do was discredit the *Post* series."

The final item of interest in Theresa's file was Roch Gaudreault's case summary, at the end of the forty-page report he had prepared in June 1979. We quoted from it in an earlier chapter, but this was the first time John and Andre had ever seen it.

> *Before we can make a conclusion of this information, we need to look deeper. In our investigation, we discovered a surrounding problem of drugs in the environment [that the victim] frequented. Unfortunately, the autopsy could not give an exact cause of death, and I expect that this will be the same with the lab results. Notwithstanding these difficulties, there are still other people to interview, with the family, among friends, and the community. We will therefore continue this investigation, and in a new report we will record anything worth mentioning.*

But the toxicology report had been submitted *in April*; its determination was final—"no evidence of usual drugs or abuse." There were no other drug tests. Nor were there ever any further interviews. The investigation didn't continue; it closed.

"Andre and I left, deflated and confused," John wrote me. "We went to a bar across the street and had a beer, even though it was too early for a beer. After so many years of being left in the dark about what, precisely, investigators had done to determine how our sister had died, we had gained access to a kind of Funhouse Mirror file, where everything felt faintly illusory. Officers Tanguay and Latour had done more for us than had ever been done before by Quebec police. We certainly felt that. Before we left the Parthenais Street headquarters, Tanguay apologized on behalf of the Sûreté du Québec for the poor treatment my family had received. That was something we had yearned for."

But it wasn't quite enough. If a death isn't carried forward into grieving with a shared consensus about its meaning, families are stranded in some inchoate way, just as they are by the feeling of broken reality. It is a habit of society to do everything we can to defend ourselves against the prospect that such a horror could be inflicted on us; we defend ourselves psychologically against a common vulnerability, and that rebounds against grieving families.

"I think society as a whole really cannot comprehend or understand what a family goes through or the grief they suffer," Karen Venables, the president of the Calgary Homicide Support Society told me. "I remember back to when [my son] Devin died, I felt I had to defend him—as he died at a pub. I really believe that some of our society believes anyone who is murdered is a bad person or criminal." This sense is what's so hard to alleviate.

"Over lunch at an Irish pub on Peel Street," John wrote, "we mulled over our sense of deflation. Now the overriding question was what kind of an investigation were they going to conduct? We didn't trust them; why would we? Tanguay had showed little interest in pursuing our information. Were they going to investigate, or were they saying they'd investigate to get us off their backs? We had to wait to find out. Meek and hopeful, emotions roiling."

On November 21, John finally tracked down Roch Gaudreault. The former investigator was in semi-retirement, working for a private investigation agency in Sherbrooke called Enquêtes spécialisées de l'Estrie. On the agency's website, Enquêtes spécialisées claimed their mission was "to give you the information and proof you need." John called Gaudreault and asked him what proof he'd had that Theresa had died of a drug overdose. "At first, he pretended that he could not understand English. But I had seen him on television; his English is excellent. I asked him how many homicide investigations he had handled in his career. 'Many. I served twenty years,' he snapped. Again I asked for an exact number, but he claimed he didn't know. Then he burst out: 'With your sister, I am convinced of a drug overdose!'"

John pressed him, but Gaudreault just insisted that if John had new information, he should give it to police.

"But you were the lead detective on the Camirand and Dubé cases," John pushed again. "Camirand was strangled—"

Before John could finish his sentence, Gaudreault hung up on him. When he called back, Gaudreault's secretary said he had gone to lunch. "*Est-ce-que vous voulez laisser un message?*" she asked. Did he want to leave a message?

"Yes. Tell Roch he is a coward."

"*Comment?*"

"A coward!"

"A cow-ard? *Un instant, je cherche mon dictionnaire. Okay, c'est juste ici. Alors, un lâche?*"

John nodded, eyes closed, enraged and exhausted. "*Dit à Roch qu'il est un lâche.*"

The meeting with Tanguay and Latour, and in particular the contents of the file, such as the alternate statement from Ms. X, would mark one of many times that John and I felt as if we were dealing with a cover-up, as his informant Gilles had casually suggested. It wasn't that the SQ was attempting deception *now*.

It was the older, long-forgotten bits and pieces. There were just so many points of illogic. For me it began with the wildly implausible explanation for Manon Dubé's death, given the coroner's suggestion that she was possibly the victim of a sexual murder, and then the dubious propositions about what happened to Theresa and the information kept back from the family—like the torn scarf at the crime scene. So much gaslighting and foot-dragging for no discernible reason.

When the SQ officers came driving along chemin Macdonald, right where Ms. X had moments before fled into the orchard, why were they so conveniently on the scene to detain and then release the assailant? Were they keeping an eye on someone known? When the Lennoxville police seemed aware of the rapist in the green parka and denim jeans, but refused to investigate, were they protecting a local? When Dubé was found on a family member's distant property but no arrest was made, was someone covering by planting evidence? What if it *was* Luc Grégoire, an out-of-control kid since forever, a loose cannon, finally dangerous enough to boot all the way to British Columbia? He was a heavy drug and alcohol user, but got hit with DUI charges only once he'd left Quebec, and then almost immediately: once on Vancouver Island and once a few months later in Alberta, before his armed robbery arrest. Out again on parole, then another DUI in Calgary. Why was this chronic drunk driver never flagged in the Townships? Was someone turning a blind eye?

More than once, we came across a remembered rumour from the 1970s that a black-sheep son was being protected in the Townships by his policeman father. We even heard it from a journalist working across the border in Vermont. At one point we noticed that Detective Gaudreault's SQ partner in the 1980s was a man named Luc Grégoire. That piqued our interest. The SQ's Gregoire's brother was Normand Gregoire, a police technician who drew the Allore crime scene map in the spring of 1979. Could this be a family connection to the murderer who'd killed Lailanie Silva? If a family connection existed, we didn't find it. Luc's father, Roland, was a drummer who performed big band tunes at pubs in Magog. He wasn't a cop. Later, a researcher tried to help us with the genealogy of Quebec Grégoires, but ran into too many loose ends to conclude anything. It's a common last name in the province. We googled extensively, but backed off when a link I'd bookmarked about the SQ officer Luc Grégoire suddenly turned into a 404. One day it was there; a few days later, the page had gone offline.

On a rainy August afternoon, John and I walked through the Catholic francophone cemetery in Sherbrooke, scanning the tombstones to find possible family connections. All of them, the dead and the murderous, lay buried within yards of one another: Louise Camirand, Manon Dubé, Luc-Yoland Grégoire, the other Luc Grégoire—the SQ officer now also dead—and even a tomb for Nicole Couture, with no end date yet. If these souls could only rise and sing. We lingered, and wandered, in the wet grass, daring the silence, helpless to unearth any truth.

John sent me an article from *The Atlantic* about the mystery of the Malaysian airplane that plunged into the sea in 2014, "A close observer of the MH370 process said, 'It became clear that the primary objective of the Malaysians was to make the subject just go away. From the start there was this instinctive bias against being open and transparent, not because they were hiding some deep, dark secret, but because they did not know where the truth really lay, and they were afraid that something might come out that would be embarrassing. Were they covering up? Yes. They were covering up for the unknown.'"

Maybe that's all that this was.

FIFTEEN

THE SEXUAL MURDERER

"La vérité d'un homme c'est d'abord ce qu'il cache."
—André Malraux, *Antimémoires*

ÉRIC LATOUR, THE YOUNG DETECTIVE ASSIGNED TO THE CASE IN
2002, turned out to be a dedicated investigator. He set his sights
on Luc Grégoire, doing what he could without much evidence
to work from, since so much had been tossed away. What
remained had been returned to the Allore family in 1979. Several
people had handled the watch, wallet and jewellery. John agreed
to a DNA test that would exclude his family—who had handled
the wallet—from any matching specimens. Nevertheless, a
DNA comparison with Grégoire, who was still serving time
at Archambault and would admit to nothing, proved frustratingly inconclusive.

Latour confirmed that Grégoire had indeed worked in the
Canadian Armed Forces, from some time in 1976 until his dis-
charge in 1980. For a time, he was stationed at Petawawa, east of
Quebec near Ontario's Algonquin Park. The CAF could offer

no record of his whereabouts for November 3, 1978. In order to have travelled back and forth from Petawawa to Sherbrooke, he would have to have been driving. Grégoire, Latour learned, had driven a number of cars including a Chevy Camaro, which in 1978 was at the height of popularity as a mid-range sports car, or "pony car." His father, Roland, favoured big American cars, perhaps Buicks; his mother did not drive. How Grégoire could afford any kind of car beyond the muffler-ravaged beater he was seen driving years later in Calgary is a mystery. Maybe he was hanging with the two-bit car thieves in south Sherbrooke.

Latour wanted to put together a composite of eight shots of different offenders from 1978, but the only photo he had on file of Grégoire from the time was of poor quality, while every other archived mug shot was sharper. The contrast, he thought, would draw attention to Grégoire, thereby threatening to bias anyone who looked at the composite to identify him. Latour mulled whether he should show just Grégoire's photo to the women we had heard from, but that strategy wouldn't stand up as well in court. In the end, he refrained from showing them any pictures at all.

At one point, Latour grew very interested in talking to a Bishop's student who had jumped from a moving car to escape her abductor in 1978. For whatever reason, he believed her experience sounded like it could have been an encounter with Grégoire. Latour doesn't recall now whether he left messages on her answering machine, but John did, and she didn't call back; he surmised that she was too scared, or wanted to handle the trauma by moving on, eyes forward. There is irony there: so many women pressed the police to investigate their attacks, and when one cop was finally willing to do so with full attention, he had a victim who wouldn't or couldn't revisit the crime.

Latour also found another case, one we hadn't been aware of: a woman who had escaped from a man who'd called himself Luc. But there was little to work with but old memories.

Later, the SQ arranged for a plant to cohabit with Grégoire in his cell at Archambault Institution; the effort yielded no shared secrets. The killer was aiming for day parole. For the same reason, presumably, Grégoire was all sunshine and rainbows in a handwritten letter to John, who had asked him directly if he'd killed Theresa.

"Writing him was quite obviously a point of desperation on my part," John says, "in that I had nothing left to lose. I was probably emboldened by being assured by Éric Latour that Grégoire wouldn't get parole, that he'd eventually be ruled a dangerous offender who would never be let out of prison. But up until this point, I had been pretty much anonymous where Grégoire was concerned. He would have been aware that I'd asked Corrections Canada for his parole requests, since that interest has to be disclosed to the inmate. But I was a blogger writing about Quebec crime; there could have been many reasons to justify my curiosity. Putting the question straight to Luc, 'Did you murder Theresa?' was taking things to a new level. I felt like I was attracting the Eye of Sauron." (Later, Latour's assurances proved misguided. By the mid-2010s, Grégoire was applying for parole, and close to receiving it, a fact that outraged the Silva family in Calgary. When he died of undisclosed causes in 2015, everyone felt relief.)

In child-like scrawl on one page of lined paper, Grégoire denied any involvement but wished John good luck. This was hardly a surprise. Nor was it convincing, because the letter was cheerful and shallow, as if John had lost track of his jacket and asked a flight attendant if he'd left it on the plane. Unsure what to make of the letter, John scanned it and sent it to a couple of criminal psychologists familiar with forensic linguistics, to solicit their analysis. One wrote back:

> Off the bat, the fact that he writes "I really had nothing to do with the death of your sister" vs. "I didn't kill Theresa" is noteworthy. It's what's known as a weak denial, where the victim isn't named and is neutralized; it's also a subconscious neutralization/deflection method where the offender puts as much time, space, and superfluous wording between themselves ("I") and the event they're denying. It occurs almost universally among offenders of all levels of sophistication.

The second analyst thought the phrasing strongly implicated Grégoire. They were mindful of his application for parole and his desire to appear earnest and helpful, as he had while seeking parole from the Alberta justice system.

> It's impossible to tell if he's being sincere but a few things stick out. 1. He never mentions Theresa by name. This is significant given that you mentioned her name four times in your letter to him. 2. Notice that he does not mention murder or apologize that your sister was killed, rather, he apologizes for the "death." There is an emotional withdrawal from the seriousness of the event. He also only mentions that he had nothing to do with the "death." He says nothing about his role in her disappearance.

Also, it is not uncommon for serial offenders to put the blame on the victim (i.e. it was their fault . . . if they only acted differently . . . if they only did this or that differently). In his mind (if he did kill her) he may perceive your sister's death as an act that was avoidable if only she was more compliant.

Some other things the criminal psychologist picked up:

He's attempting to present himself as prompt ("I received your letter yesterday.") Trying to make you feel important in his eyes. He's also trying to appeal to you on an emotional level ("I feel your pain.") Notice that he never actually expresses sympathy. Only that he feels your pain. His words are like an echo. He's parroting back the pain you described to him in your own letter without any additional affective component. . . . He avoids responsibility completely: "I'm really sorry THEY haven't found THE PERSON . . ." He's smart not to implicate either a man or a woman. . . . He is aware that he is a suspect. . . . When he says "I have voluntarily . . ." he's trying (again) to build an emotional connection with you. As though voluntary submission to a polygraph is a big deal. Polygraphs are inadmissible and there is no empirical evidence to show that they detect deception.

For offenders like Grégoire, polygraphs are particularly useless because these individuals are unlikely to manifest fear. People with antisocial personality disorder (more colloquially, socio-paths or psychopaths) suffer no anxieties of conscience, or even of consequence. Grégoire had failed to show up for court appearances for the Nicole Couture crime. He committed armed robbery while on bail. In Alberta he violated his parole six ways to Sunday. Years later, at a 2013 parole hearing, a board member said to him, "You have indicated [to us] that your priority was always immediate satisfaction of your needs, and the only person of importance is you. You have been very exact that you haven't any empathy for others." This was at a hearing at which Grégoire was appealing a denial of day passes by taking issue with their assessment of whether he had raped Lailanie Silva before or after he strangled her. He was trying to nail them on a technicality: they had erroneously, he felt, denied his parole by misunderstanding when he had raped her (as opposed to when he'd abducted and killed her, and broken both of her legs, and lacerated her groin). The board responded with what must have been extremely well-contained horror at these quibbles: "It seems much more plausible in view of your modus operandi that the victim was sequestrated, sexually assaulted and then strangled."

The second criminal psychologist offered one final, intriguing observation: "Lastly, where he says 'hope they find the person responsible . . .' notice that he doesn't write "I hope . . ." This is like the inverse of a Freudian slip. He's omitting (albeit subconsciously) that he actually does not want you to discover who killed your sister."

Years later, we set up a sort of control experiment, with John sending the same wording in a letter asking about Theresa's murder to a killer we knew had not been in the Townships when she died. This man took many weeks to reply, referred to Theresa by name in his response and expressed his condolences, explaining that he hadn't been in the Sherbrooke area since he was young. The difference in responses may be coincidental. It was always so frustratingly speculative with Grégoire—but still, it was hard to avoid the smell of smoke.

Before being reassigned, Detective Latour flew to Calgary and conferred with investigators about the Silva case and the unsolved sex worker murders. Years later, a Calgary Police Service cold-case detective told John that Grégoire was a main suspect for some of the crimes in their city, but they hadn't been able to establish an evidentiary link. His colleagues had doubtless told Latour this in 2004. "DNA was handled much differently than it is nowadays," detective Ken Carriere explained to John. "Back then, you had to have a significant amount of sample, such as a full blood droplet, in order to get something. They would have got results back [from the lab] saying 'insufficient.' But as that technology got better, a cold-case investigator could come along and resubmit those exhibits, and determine if, now, the level is acceptable for them to create a profile. On the other hand," he added, "you now have to fight the natural degradation of the exhibit itself." DNA deteriorates, which is one reason that Latour couldn't get a conclusive answer either way on whether Grégoire had handled Theresa's wallet.

Carriere is planning to resubmit samples from the murder file of Rebecca Boutilier, the Cape Bretoner who was found at the corner of 68th Street and McKnight Boulevard in the winter of 1993, around the time that Deb Horton remembers Grégoire "spiralling downward" after she and her husband bought their new house. "I believe that Rebecca Boutilier is potentially the victim of Luc Grégoire for a number of reasons," Carriere told John.

Part of his calculus had to do with the geography of the abductions and disposals. "Boutilier goes missing on February 11, 1993. She's picked up on the stroll at the corner of 3rd Ave and Fourth Street." It was a stretch of pavement adjacent to the run-down National Hotel, known as "the Nash," a marketplace for drugs and sex. Boutilier, who had wide, dark eyes and a mane of soft blond hair, disappeared that night and was reported missing by her ex-boyfriend and her best friend. She was twenty, had a fourteen-month-old son and was close to her attentive mother, Sandy, who determinedly raised the alarm, speaking to reporters and distributing leaflets. (Sandy Boutilier had no idea that her daughter had been doing sex work in the last months of her life. What she did know was that she loved Rebecca, feared for her and wanted her home.)

"Because of previous murders," Detective Carriere said, "the homicide unit took a big interest in this file. She's not found until March 11, in a field, nude, except for a pair of panties that are kind of rolled down, and she's face down." There were roofing shingles piled by her body. Carriere continued, "On April 6th, one street away from where Boutilier was last seen, a woman is picked up at 3rd Ave and Third Street SW, and is threatened with a particular weapon I will keep under wraps for now." (It was a roofing hammer, a tool designed to rip and tear with one end and to pound or beat with the other, according to the prosecutor at Grégoire's trial for assaulting Patricia Mongey in 1993.) Carriere went on, "This weapon was held to her throat as he drove forward and told her to remove her shoes. I believe that was for the purpose of lessening her ability to run away. He then asked for oral sex, and as it happened a police car was driving by.

The woman spilled out of the vehicle and hailed the attention of the officers. He was charged with kidnapping and assault with a weapon. He gets released on a condition—that he's not allowed to go anywhere downtown near the strolls."

Once again, the justice system wildly underestimated the danger a man posed to women. Mongey was traumatized. She—or another of Gregoire's Calgary victims with a virtually identical experience—later wrote under a pseudonym in a crime victim's forum, "I repressed so much of that incident that I couldn't understand why the mere thought of visiting Calgary made me sick to my stomach." No more women went missing from the strolls that year. Instead, women in the city's northeast started to report being followed "by a vehicle that matched his," Carriere said. Then, on May 3, in Castlebridge: Aida Yeou, escaping, and Lailanie Silva, destroyed.

Carriere never did disclose—or the file didn't identify—the weapon used to kill Rebecca Boutilier. Might it have been a roofing hammer? Tracey Maunder, picked up from the same stroll the previous October and discarded near 68th Street in a field across from Garden of Peace Cemetery, was reported by police to have been stabbed and beaten. Might that have been with a roofing hammer? Boutilier was found a four-minute drive north of the 7-Eleven that Silva worked at; Maunder was found four minutes south. Like Boutilier, Maunder—shipped to the morgue on her twenty-sixth birthday—was missing her clothes, boots and purse. She had briefly resorted to sex work in order to raise enough money to send her son, Mitchell, to his grandmother while she was hospitalized for cancer treatment. That son, as I noted earlier, searched for her killer for years.

After flying to Calgary and familiarizing myself with the geography, I told Detective Carriere I was comfortable stating that it was well within the realm of possibility that Luc Grégoire had killed Rebecca Boutilier and Tracey Maunder using a roofing hammer. The detective, who had corrected me on a number of small details about his unsolved files, made no objection.

Driving past the intersection where Boutilier was abandoned by her killer, I found myself struck by the pattern of cross-referencing personal belongings: another victim's clothes left alongside her, the bloody garments of Silva's stuffed into Deb Horton's work dumpster, the wallet found so coincidentally on the farm where Ms. X had escaped ambush, the clean clothes in the woods near Camirand. If this wasn't the same man it was an awfully similar psyche.

In the fall of 2002, at SQ headquarters in Montreal, John and Andre saw one other statement in Theresa's file, attached to Ms. X's chemin Macdonald account of the flasher whom she told to "fuck off." The report, of a rape in the spring of 1979, identified a suspect that was not Luc Grégoire. It included the names of the victim and rapist, but for the purpose of confidentiality we cannot mention them. Here's a brief summary: In April 1979, a young woman visited a friend in Waterville, Quebec, about halfway between Lennoxville and Compton. She was offered a ride back home by a local man with whom she was acquainted. Along the way, he made the vague statement that he needed to "go somewhere" to "check on something." Detouring off-route, he eventually pulled to the side of the road and went to fetch something out of the back of his car.

A moment later, he returned brandishing a large, red-handled screwdriver. He told her to do what she was told and she wouldn't get hurt. He instructed her to take off all her clothes, except her underwear. He then raped her in the car. When he finished, he told her to put her clothes back on, and then drove her home, warning her not to tell anyone what had happened. She said he flashed a badge and told her it was pointless to go to the police because he was an officer himself.

This account raises the clear and unsurprising prospect that there were multiple sex offenders roaming the unlit roads of the Townships, taking advantage of police indifference. One of them had a rigged passenger door that couldn't be opened from the inside; another exposed himself; a third used a screwdriver as a weapon. One might well have been Robert Leblanc, a foster home kid from the Sherbrooke area who was arrested in the nineties for rapes and a later murder in Montreal. Given the fifty mug shots of Travis Bickles and snaggle-tooth drug addicts, and the Hells Angels zooming around on their Harleys, the bucolic countryside, with its pretty college buildings and dairy farms, was a mirage; it could turn into the Upside Down (from the Netflix series *Stranger Things*), all uncanny shadows and menace.

The key question is, what type of sex predator goes so far as to *murder*? Most homicide investigators never encounter a sexual murderer. Extremely few men—indeed, less than 5 percent of all male killers convicted—engage in the sexual homicide of strangers. According to criminologist Eric Beauregard, a professor at Simon Fraser University in British Columbia, the vast majority of incarcerated sex offenders commit either a single rape or serial rape. A handful may commit a one-off sexual murder. A fractional subset are serial killers. In 1998, Beauregard and his research colleagues approached every inmate in Quebec who was serving time for the sexual murder of a woman. There were fifty-seven, of whom forty agreed to be interviewed. One of them had been convicted of serial murder. That was in keeping with the national average, as only 3 percent of all incarcerated sexual murderers in Canada at the time of the study were serial murderers. The likelihood that more than one was operating in the Sherbrooke area in the late 1970s and early 1980s is vanishingly small.

In most cases, a sexual murder is essentially a sexual assault "gone wrong," which is to say that the victim resisted more powerfully and required more force to subdue than the rapist expected, triggering an escalation in violence. One example from Beauregard's research is the case of a man involved in youth athletics who attempted to molest a ten-year-old boy on the team he was coaching. After inviting this boy to his home on a pretext, the man started sexually touching him. "The little boy reacted violently and started to scream. [The man] had not expected this reaction. [He] panicked and started to strangle the victim into unconsciousness." Having unexpectedly killed the boy, he then wrapped him in a bed sheet and buried him quickly in some nearby woods. He confessed to the crime almost as swiftly. One-off sexual murders are generally unpremeditated and occur under circumstances that don't lend themselves to secrecy. The suspect is often quickly identified.

It is more likely with serial sexual murderers that they will drive their victims to the murder site, or transport their bodies to be dumped, with the likeliest sites being, according to

Beauregard, "outdoor public spaces." It's common for them to leave the body "as is," with no attempt at burial or concealment. In a field, by a ditch, in a creek. One-off sexual murderers more often leave the victim where they died, in a home or bar or parking lot, or attempt some panicked hiding job close to the scene of the crime. As most of us would be, they are terrified by the prospect of driving any distance with a body in their car. (In fact, this is one of the reasons that the case of Manon Dubé eludes any obvious conclusion about her uncle's guilt. She was clearly transported and dumped, with no further effort at concealment. If anything, one could argue that she was planted there, like Silva's clothes.)

That isn't to say that multiple murderers necessarily engage in murder every time they assault a victim. "Pre-crime anger," Beauregard found, can be a significant predictor of whether there will be a rape or a murder. The murderer may be catathymic, which refers to the "displacement of intense matricentric rage towards another woman." In January 1993, Grégoire received a letter from his mother—"Do not bring me any more misery to my heart"—and on the last day of that month he was caught asleep on the prowl outside the 7-Eleven from which he later abducted and killed Lailanie Silva. On February 11, Rebecca Boutilier disappeared from the Calgary stroll.

When compared to rapists, sexual murderers in the Quebec study were more likely to have been physically and sexually abused in childhood. It was more common for them to have dropped out of school at grade seven or eight, and to have had disciplinary problems in class. They were also more likely to exhibit "inappropriate behaviours" in childhood and adolescence, such as habitual lying, running away or reckless behaviour. More serious or disturbing behaviours were found in the childhoods of the most severely violent men. (Other literature on serial homicide cites violence against pets, aggressions toward fellow children and the setting of fires—in other words, random acts of cruelty.)

There is little difference between rapists and murderers, though, in terms of committing other adult crimes, such as robbery. "Sexual crimes against women appear to be more closely associated with polymorphic antisocial behaviour than with any specific sexual problem," noted Beauregard and co-author Melissa Martineau in *The Sexual Murderer*. This finding parallels research done in Switzerland, where a study of 21,347 army recruits found 30 who admitted to rape; among this cohort, 80 percent had committed other crimes such as theft or selling drugs. In other words, there isn't some Freudian dysfunction in their sexual psyche that drives them to rape, specifically; these men are indifferent to social norms in general. One exception: phallometric assessments, which measure sexual arousal when the subject is exposed to various images, indicate that sadistic aggressors have "a sexual preference for rape." This was conceivably true of Grégoire, who never had a girlfriend or a date, and was assessed as a sadist by prison psychologists at Archambault Institution in 2014.

It is painful to imagine what this meant for the women who encountered him, and even for those who eluded him but saw the blended rage and lust in his eyes. He would have been there but not there, gazing *through* them. An important difference between garden-variety rapists and far rarer serial sex killers is the architecture of an internal fantasy life. "Deviant sexual fantasies are extremely important determinants of serial sexual murder,"

Beauregard wrote, "and are much less important in the aetiology of non-serial sexual murder." In the Quebec sample, 36 percent of the men nurtured fantasies, versus 86 percent in a study of serial murderers. What's important about the role of fantasy is the compulsive element, which prods the killer to reoffend. There is a commitment to the world they inhabit, which is separate from the humdrum, and more reassuring or familiar to them.

Theresa, Manon and Louise are highly unlikely to have been victims of three separate one-off killers. The odds are simply against it. The fact that one was ten years old, or that one appears to have been strangled but not beaten while the third was both strangled and beaten, is not as significant as the shared facts of the crime's rarity and the transportation to a distant location to dispose of their bodies. "What plagues criminology," criminologist Keith Soothill has argued, "is the insistence that offenders either specialize or are versatile. We need to recognize that they can do both."

John asked Calgary Detective Ken Carriere for his thoughts on whether Luc Grégoire could have killed in both Quebec and Alberta over the years. Carriere was careful to emphasize that he was speculating, but said, "I think a predator such as Grégoire, if he stalked his prey in Quebec, like he did in Calgary—he stalked a number of people—if you take someone like that out in the country where they find people hitchhiking, people along abandoned roads that are easy targets," they are going to get away with it more easily. "If we're thinking about a sexual predator back in 1978, that was probably the bogeyman that you would see on TV that nobody actually believed in. Unless you're faced with solid evidence to the contrary, you would try to find excuses out of it, because that's not the norm that makes up our murderers. I can tell you that being in the Calgary homicide unit since 2011, very few of our cases are motivated by sex. Now, apply that to a smaller town in Quebec and rural areas, it's almost unfathomable. So, I would say that if somebody had committed all those murders because they were sexually motivated, and something caused that person to move to a big city, such as Calgary, now it's different. You have neighbours looking out the windows. You have to redevelop what you might do as a sexual predator. Who are the targets who will now get into your car?" Sex workers. "So, Grégoire is now picking up high-risk targets, and [after he] attacked one physically, he just so happened to get caught. I would think the big city is not such a great place. He can't take risks like he did before."

The challenge escalated when he got banned from the stroll. "You take Mr. Predator, who's been kicked out of the downtown, and now he goes back to a place he knows," which is to say Castleridge. Now it's hard *not* to get caught. As Deb Horton remembers the investigators telling her in 1993, Grégoire became sloppy. "This is speculation, of course," Carriere reminded John, "but I can see a sexual predator having to change his style of attack, moving from rural countryside to big-city Calgary. And we can't look away from the fact that he did murder Lailanie Silva, and left her in a similar state to two other victims that we're aware of [Rebecca Boutilier and Tracey Maunder], so it makes me go, hmm, and it makes me want to follow it. We can't ignore similarities and similar fact evidence. We have to keep our minds alive to it."

The question is how.

. . .

In 2005, with the Sûreté du Québec appearing to give up on investigating the Township deaths, John set up a website. It was around the time when everyone was figuring out WordPress and how to showcase their causes and careers on the Internet. Into that firmament went *Who Killed Theresa?* He posted our newspaper series and all the follow-up articles and letters, some pictures and a number of blog entries. Like a spider who'd spun a web, he waited uncertainly until into that web flew crazies and crime fetishists and sympathetic supporters and even long-lost family friends.

When I next saw him, for a visit to North Carolina after my own sister died, he caught me up a little bit on this endeavour. The website had attracted other victims, some of whom are quoted in this book. But John was like a rookie cop handling a tip line. "Initially, I was being led by the nose by a lot of these people," he said, lounging on the couch in a small white clapboard house he had rented after his marriage broke up. It was nearing Halloween, and his lawn was covered in handmade tinfoil aliens lurching toward the road in the Carolina dusk. "There was this one woman," he recalled, pouring a glass of red wine, "who was convinced her two brothers had done it. Her main piece of evidence was that they were at [Quebec's] Mont-Orford the week that Theresa went hiking there. She claimed to see them interacting. But then, later, she'd send me a photo, saying that her two brothers were at a mafioso's funeral, and I'd say, 'But this is from now—these men are in their twenties.' She'd write back, 'They're masters of disguise.'" He laughed. "She got me to look at this Hells Angels footage from New York in the seventies that purportedly showed her brothers. And I'd say, 'But they would have been fourteen!' And she'd say, 'You don't understand. They can fool anyone.' She started embellishing her premise. They weren't just hiking; now they were skiing, and Theresa was skiing. But I checked and there was no snow." Yet he checked. He ran down the clue.

Later, via Snapchat and Instagram, "it would be someone saying, 'I just love what you're doing for victims'—and then they'd send a late-night text flashing their boobs at the crime scenes."

"Seriously?" I asked.

He nodded. One woman took time off work, travelled to the Townships and visited the crime scenes related to Louise Camirand, Manon Dubé and Theresa. Then she sexualized them. It was like an iteration of women falling in love with Charles Manson or Ted Bundy, testing their own sexual power and immortality against those who had fallen.

More recently, "there was the French woman who phoned me in a panic one Friday evening, convinced that her former abusive boyfriend was the killer. In broken English, she explained her reasoning: 'He looks just like the suspect you posted on your site last night!' I checked my website. I had uploaded the famous composite sketch of the Unabomber—not because he was a suspect, but because at the time I had been working with James Fitzgerald, the FBI criminal profiler who cracked the case. This woman was from rural Quebec and had never heard of the Unabomber." John took a swig of Merlot and rubbed the stubble under his chin, gazing into the middle distance. "What I'm not getting across to you is the way that your heart ticks up in hope every time, *every time*, right before the sense of absurdity follows."

We talked for a long time that night about the alchemy of grief. How our very atoms get rearranged by the violence of loss, so that for a time we are nearly dissolute, as dysregulated as toddlers—rageful, hollow, terror-stricken, lustful, lawless, impelled by the highest yearnings and the basest wrath. We compared notes on drinking to black out, and on nightmares both sleeping and waking. Once, John drank so much that he had something like a psychotic break. The walls of his home dissolved and he glimpsed the alien beings that stared inside, implacably curious, and there all along. He wept inconsolably through that night. I pointed out that the Halloween aliens on his lawn must be some kind of art therapy.

The grieving stay sane by forging purpose and finding new meanings. The first is far easier than the second. John taught himself to be more fluent in French by watching movies, so that he could befriend other Quebec crime victims and draw supporters to their shared cause. One was Sue Tayachi, "a former criminology student from the University of Montreal who, in 2008, took an interest in the *Who Killed Theresa?* cases. She voluntarily organized a search party for evidence in the forest near Magog. We thought we might recover the clothing spotted by the deer hunters on November 4, 1978, or something belonging to Louise Camirand," John said. "Some tantalizing items did turn up: a woman's black purse and the sole of a black sandal or slipper that could have been a Chinese shoe."

Other siblings and parents of the victims of unsolved murders volunteered that day. Yvonne Prior, the mother of teenager Sharron Prior, murdered in the Montreal area in 1975, showed up with her two surviving daughters, Doreen and Moreen. This is the kind of thing that Quebec crime victims resort to after the police move on. John said, "They threw out or lost the evidence in so many of these cases. When I met Solange Blais after researching her sister's murder—Lison had been strangled in her Montreal backyard in the summer of 1978—she said the police had told her they would actively reinvestigate Lison's case. But she also received a letter from them saying, 'We're sorry but we destroyed all the evidence.' She's like, WTF?? Sharron Prior's evidence had all been destroyed as well. Her mother, Yvonne, showed me the letter when I had coffee in her apartment. Three years later, she got another note saying, 'We found a brown suede coat. It might be Sharron's; do you want to come see it?' And sure enough, it was Sharron's. I mean, you have to cry." Instead, he laughed. "Over the years, this had become a consistent theme for many of us, learning of the destruction of case evidence, but gradually understanding that we were not alone, that we were all being gaslit together."

What *was* it with the systemic destruction of evidence? Was it incompetence? Or was it a directive? Most police forces are mandated to hold on to evidence in perpetuity. Consider the case of human remains found off Mulholland Drive in Los Angeles, California. It took detectives forty-six years to make a positive identification of Reet Silvia Jurvetson, a woman from Montreal who had vanished shortly after arriving in Los Angeles in the late summer of 1969. But because they kept the evidence, and thanks to eventual improvements to DNA technology, they were finally able to make a match.

. . .

In 2013, John learned that the crime magazines *Allô Police* and *Photo Police* were still technically in operation in the Montreal suburb of Longueuil. Or at least, their archive was active, and was often tapped by investigators and journalists who wanted to look at back issues for details on biker-war stories. The Quebec tabloids changed their focus around 1982. Did sexual homicides stop around that time, or did the tabloids stop reporting them? Maybe a little of both. Certainly, in the Eastern Townships, the crime was less common after the seventies. Indeed, it became extremely rare. "There was the murder of Isabelle Bolduc in 1996," John said. "You had the killing of Senator Pierre-Hugues Boisvenu's daughter in 2002. A couple of others, but that's it. Not a lot was going on. Then again, readers may have had enough. They didn't want to see a dead body on the cover of a magazine anymore. By the early eighties, murder coverage fell out of favour and the magazines went more for sex and drugs. You'd have a woman sitting on a chopper bike with big breasts, and inside would be articles about the Hells Angels. The back page, for people sitting on the subway or something, was puzzles."

John's discovery of the tabloid archive opened some potentially valuable doors. "The way we made the original links was cross-referencing in newspapers," he reminded me, "so I thought, *What do we still not know?*" He reached out to the publisher and asked if he could look through the back issues. "I had to get special permission from their lawyer and owner—who was, in fact, Jean-Pierre Rancourt, the guy who had defended Fernand Laplante and the ruffians accused in the Charles Marion kidnapping back in 1978–79. They told me I was the only civilian who had been granted that kind of access." The exclusive invitation, he suspects, had something to do with his being related to a victim, as well as his advocacy for other victims. He drove up to Montreal and spent hours in the archive. "By the end of the day, I had eight hundred photographs on my iPad."

There were many cases in this dubious trove of tabloid stories that John would go on to research, bringing them to the attention of the SQ, for they had otherwise been long forgotten, unsolved, with evidence misplaced or tossed, yet acting as a source of lingering anguish for individual families. It would be for this dogged tracking of untended sexual homicides that John won a Senate of Canada medal for victim advocacy. "People's lives are worth saving and their deaths are worth vindicating," he told me. "If we ask nothing of our institutions, then it's like saying we expect nothing from ourselves. It does not take 'knowing' these people to get involved. You know them. They are of your communities. They are you. And they are lost."

There were two stories chronicled by *Allô Police* in particular, however, that John wanted me to think about when we next met in the Townships, after Labour Day in 2018. One occurred late at night on Saturday, September 10, 1977, in the pretty tourist village of Chambly, along the shore of the Richelieu River. We had lunch there in an old stone mill house, on a patio overlooking the water. John's energy was tamped down and guarded. Where he'd once felt excited to be in southern Quebec, pursuing his mission, now he was eating quietly, gazing across the river.

Almost exactly forty years earlier, in September 1977, a teenager from Chambly named Hélène Monast had celebrated her eighteenth birthday with some friends at a diner called Chez Marius. The milestone birthday was exciting. In the weeks leading up to it, according to *The Gazette*, "she had already started scribbling the number 18 beside her name on the back of the pocket-sized, 25-cent photos she would take at the mall." After dinner, she set off to walk a short distance down a poorly lit street to stay with her aunt. She never appeared. The next morning, she was found strangled in a very public place: a treed parkette in the town centre, half a block from the riverside restaurant where John and I were now having lunch. She was left semi-naked on her back on the grass. Evidence of rape was indeterminate. She had been beaten around the face. Her clothes were left nearby, but her purse was missing.

After lunch, John walked me to the parkette to give me a sense of how brazen this dump site was. Hélène Monast's assailant would have to have been relying on the entire town to be sound asleep for him to elude arrest. "A crazy person must have come through town," Hélène's then-elderly father told *The Gazette* a couple of years ago, still unable to fathom what had happened. He had spent half his life, from the age of forty-six, trying to unravel his daughter's murder. John has since become friends with his other daughter, Nicole, as they bond in the pain of not knowing.

Once we'd stood in the parkette and imagined this old crime, John told me what he'd relayed to Nicole: that in the *Allô Police* archives he had discovered something curious. Five weeks after Monast's murder, and about a fifteen-minute drive south of Chambly, another victim had been found. On Monday, October 24, 1977, Denise Bazinet was left naked and strangled in a ditch beside Highway 35 at the Chambly exit, as if rolled out of a car en route from Montreal, where she lived. The twenty-three-year-old, who shared a home with ten siblings and worked at a St-Hubert chicken franchise, had disappeared from Montreal less than twenty-four hours earlier, and was spotted by a driver in the culvert on Monday morning. Her wallet was missing. Police theorized that the motive was robbery, and scarcely investigated. John felt sure there was a link between these two autumn murders, and wondered how, if at all, Luc Grégoire might fit in. Over the nearly four decades since, no serial killer had been arrested in Quebec who covered this particular territory south of Montreal and east into the Townships during the late 1970s. (The so-called Vampire Rapist, Wayne Boden, had prowled Montreal a decade earlier. William Fyfe killed women in their fifties in Montreal in the 1990s. A third man, Serge Archambault, was convicted of three murders in the early nineties, but lived northwest of Montreal in Saint-Eustache.)

Riding on the gently rocking train back to Toronto from my weekend of touring murder sites with a haunted man, I got to thinking about where Grégoire would have been in 1977. SQ investigator Éric Latour had confirmed that Grégoire had joined the Canadian Armed Forces. (He turned eighteen in late September 1977, being almost the same age as Hélène Monast.) He would have had to do basic training, as all recruits do. For new military recruits who aren't attending university, the training takes place over three months. All French-speaking recruits do this boot camp at one facility: the Canadian Forces Leadership and Recruit School in Saint-Jean-sur-Richelieu, about eighteen minutes by car away from Chambly along Route 35.

. . .

John and I decided to send brief summaries of five murders—Camirand in March 1977, Monast in September 1977, Bazinet in October 1977, Dubé in January 1978 and Theresa in November 1978—to the criminologist Eric Beauregard, who was both an expert in sexual homicide and a Quebecer familiar with the geography. We didn't tell him that we had a suspect in mind.

"I've reviewed the material you gathered," he replied. "It is very interesting but at the same time, scary. To see so many events that are somewhat similar in a limited geographic region is suspicious. There are a few things that come to my mind when reading these cases." He then isolated certain factors. The first was distance. "To me this is very important. When you have so many incidents of the same nature in a small city or in the general same area, you need to pay attention. Sex offenders do not travel very far to commit their crimes. However, in my research we have seen that sexual murderers are willing to travel farther than most sex offenders. This is especially true for body disposal. Another aspect that is important to consider is whether the offender had a reason to be there. Sometimes we focus on the offender's residence. But it's not enough. Again, research is showing that it is also important to consider other anchor points that the offender could have in a specific region. For example, where family members live, friends"—or where someone was undergoing military training.

Then Beauregard highlighted the method of the killer's approach. "This is another important aspect that is somewhat tied to the distance component. In most of these cases the offender seems to encounter victims of opportunity. The offender can be driving around but it doesn't seem like he has a specific victim in mind. It looks like what Kim Rossmo termed 'premeditated opportunism'—meaning that he's ready to act out but he doesn't know where, when, and with who exactly. He's probably driving around in areas that he's familiar with, which are part of his routine activities."

The missing purses caught his attention. "Only a minority of sexual murderers commit theft on their victim. Some will steal some objects to remember the victim but, again, it's only in a minority of cases. What you have identified doesn't seem to correspond to that. The cases involving theft seem to be motivated by a desire to get money. This would make sense if the offender is not working or has a job that doesn't pay much. Moreover, if an offender has a problem with alcohol/drugs, he will need extra money to sustain his consumption." Luc Grégoire, for example, was often on the hunt for extra change for booze and cocaine, robbing women at ATMs in Calgary and holding up a cashier in Sherbrooke. For Dr. Candice Skrapec, to whom I also sent my notes, the missing-purses-for-cash component was a notable pattern as well. "His crimes are instrumental as much as they are brutal. They are both."

Both criminologists thought the five deaths we sent them were very plausibly linked. Skrapec highlighted the youthful age of the victims as well. None were middle-aged or elderly. "If it could be established," Beauregard told John, "that the same person was around when these crimes were committed, I think he would be a person of interest to investigate. This would be enough to force me to consider that one guy could have been responsible for many of these crimes. I think it would be worth examining."

· · ·

A final postscript on my own trip to Calgary in late May 2019, when I visited Luc Grégoire's former landlady, Deb Horton. She had more to say. In the aftermath of his arrest, her new home, which she had just started to decorate, was overrun by investigators. Lailanie Silva's murder had been so violent, the entire city was ablaze with chatter about it. Then came the news that Grégoire had been on parole, under mandatory supervision. His crimes shouldn't have happened. Media hounded Deb; her neighbours stopped speaking to her and Tony. But what she remembers from the execution of the search warrant in her house is this: the investigators found a handful of women's jewellery in Luc's basement apartment, tucked into a shoebox. "There were earrings, rings, necklaces," she told me. "Young girls' jewellery, inexpensive." She looked at it and noted a "private school cross," which put her in mind of a news story about a young woman murdered in Alberta who'd been at a private school, although she can no longer remember the details.

When her friend Gail found this out, she told me, "I remember thinking and feeling two things. Revulsion that he would collect jewellery from these women and store it. Like trophies. If he had taken it for money, he would have pawned it. This was obviously some kind of reward for him. My second thought was to wonder how many women had he actually attacked. (And now that he's dead, how would we ever know the full depths of his crimes?) It made me sad."

"Are you going to find the owners of all this?" Deb recalls asking the investigators.

"He's gone for life," one of them told her, "so don't worry about it."

She wasn't sure what that meant. They told her, she remembers, that Grégoire had gotten sloppy, that he'd wanted to get caught, which implied, at least to her, that they knew or suspected he had killed before.

After she testified at the trial—"Luc was so cocky; he just stared at me"—letters began appearing in Deb's mailbox from Grégoire in prison, threatening to kill her when he got out. She lived with that terror for decades, until the day I made contact with her and she learned for the first time that Luc Grégoire had died in prison, of unspecified causes, in 2015.

Detective Ken Carriere, reviewing the Lailanie Silva file at our request, found no box or bag of jewellery logged into evidence. Did someone in Calgary in 1993 decide to let sleeping dogs lie? Or did Deb Horton sew that vivid memory from whole cloth? When I put this question to the lawyer who authored the Robert Pickton inquiry in British Columbia—whether it was plausible that someone at some level of law enforcement would toss a piece of evidence, a box with contents they'd prefer not to unleash, lest it open a whole new can of worms—she said, "Yes, that is entirely plausible."

I checked with someone else, a person who had actually worked with Calgary Police Services: "Is it possible? Consider the heat brought down on cops who miss serial killers."

"The least likely scenario," she said, "is that the arresting officers in the field forgot to log the evidence. The most likely scenario is that a decision was made higher up. That is possible, absolutely."

We'll never know.

SIXTEEN

WHAT'S IN THE BOX?

"The newspaper readers forget fast. It goes in one eye and out the other."
—William Conrad, *The Racket*

ON THURSDAY, SEPTEMBER 14, 2017, I WAS DRIVING IN downtown Toronto when an Amber Alert sirened through the regular radio programming. A child in Quebec had been abducted. He was thought to be in a grey Honda heading eastward into Ontario. The alarming automated voice provided a licence plate number. I remember turning onto Queen Street West, nudging forward through a press of cyclists and pedestrians, feeling irrationally guilty that I couldn't help the abducted boy, that the alert would never intersect with my life. I was wrong. John, at his office a thousand miles south of me, didn't hear the Amber Alert; instead, he saw his social media blow up. *Where's Ugo? John, have you heard from Ugo? Has anyone seen him?*

In the ancient Greek myth of Pandora's box, first written by Hesiod and then reshaped by Aesop, a woman is given a mysterious jar by the god Zeus and forbidden to examine its contents. Compelled by her curiosity, Pandora lifts the lid, and—fairly literally—all hell breaks loose. Evil escapes from the vessel. The contemporary casual reference to this myth is akin to the phrase *Be careful what you wish for* or *Don't open door #3*, and these are certainly adages that spring to mind when I look back at that early autumn day. To set up the context, I must first take you to, of all places, a true-crime convention that I later attended in Nashville, Tennessee.

When you enter the glossy halls of the Gaylord Opryland Resort in Nashville, your sense of orientation is, rather instantly, blown away like a gnat in a hurricane, and all the more so on the particular May weekend I went there. The place is as sprawling and complex as a cruise ship, a realm of high-end restaurants, tony shops and artificial waterfalls, all sparkling beneath vast, arching domes. Getting from one end to the other calls for a good pair of sneakers. This glassed-in fantasy world—right across the road from a string of rough motels and biker bars— was filled with Nashville teens and newlyweds in their sequined finest, celebrating the milestones of life. They posed on flowered walkways for studious hired photographers, and raised toasts in restaurants like the Old Hickory Steakhouse, where fancy entrees were on offer for $45. Skirting these prom-night celebrants on the landscaped pathways was another set of Americans, mostly women, wearing T-shirts that said SPATTER MATTERS, referring to how blood patterns are investigated in homicides, and carrying tote bags sponsored by the Oxygen network with the tagline FOR THE LOVE OF CRIME. These amateur sleuths and self-described "Murderinos" were, quite literally, dining out on death.

I was entering the second annual CrimeCon gathering, a fan convention that capitalizes on the popularity of true-crime podcasting and armchair detective work. The entertainment objective of CrimeCon, it felt to me, was still being worked out. There was, for instance, an interrogation room, more like a booth, erected in the lobby of the hotel so that you could be photographed with your BFF under a swinging naked light bulb, pretending that one of you is the gimlet-eyed detective and the other the nervous suspect. Down the adjacent hallway, a long line waited to hear (and be filmed with) the TV personality Nancy Grace, CrimeCon's resident rabble-rouser, who hosted four packed tapings—"Crime Stories with Nancy Grace LIVE"—in one day.

Another line snaked down a plushly carpeted hallway for a session called "Sensory Experience," which my twenty-two-year-old daughter, Clara, and I joined, curious. Women nursing their morning Starbucks were handed blindfolds and hand-cuffs by a volunteer while they waited to enter the ballroom. Once inside, with the lights dimmed, a criminology professor named Kimberlie Massnick bade us slip on the blindfold, raise our bound wrists above our heads and listen to a dramatic re-enactment of the writings of convicted killer Gerard Schaefer, who described the gross defilements he inflicted on terrified young women in Florida in the early 1970s. The soundtrack included the songs of a tropical bird, as if we, too, were on the isolated shoreline where his victims were hanged, choked, raped and dismembered. Were we engaging in role play, like civil war re-enactors? What were we doing? This was never made entirely clear. Massnick just engaged in further ruminations on the life and crimes of this man, who apparently befriended Ted Bundy in prison.

There was a raffle at CrimeCon. There were sloganed sweatshirts for sale (BASICALLY A DETECTIVE) and ripped-from-the-headlines books, like a memoir by Asia McClain, the missing alibi witness from National Public Radio's true-crime podcast *Serial*, which some people credit for kick-starting the whole trend. A session on "How to Catch a Liar," which over eight hundred people attended, seemed to blur the lines between criminal investigation and women who suspected the men in their lives of being assholes of one kind or another. Later, I heard a middle-aged blonde on her cellphone, warning her husband, "Don't lie to me. You can't anymore. I've just taken a class."

On the main exhibit floor, a booth was manned by an Indiana family whose daughter had been killed along with a friend in what were dubbed the Delphi Murders. The family struck me as ordinary and uncertain, even a little exhausted, as they positioned their donation bowl, offering buttons and bracelets to anyone prepared to help with their unsolved calamity. At the edge of their booth stood a life-size drawing of the suspect, whose image had been captured by one of the girls on Snapchat as he'd approached them. Nonetheless, the man had never been identified, and the family seemed game to try anything, to bring any attention to their terrible case that might help. After offering them my condolences, I sat on a nearby staircase to see if any convention attendants would visit their table. It was hard for a family in mourning to compete with the podcast and TV celebrities, for whom people queued excitedly, seeking autographs and selfies. One such celebrity was a man named James Renner, who participated in several panels as the podcaster of *The Philosophy of Crime*, having cobbled together a career out of cold-case speculation. He was part of the presumably self-appointed "Maura Murray Team," which referred to a particularly beloved unsolved mystery from Massachusetts in 2004 in which a nursing student vanished in a blizzard. (John once spent an entire summer working with NBC's *Dateline*, trying to develop an hour-long programme on Theresa's case. "At the end, they came to me with an ultimatum: say that the Quebec cases were linked to Maura Murray and another popular East Coast case, Brianna Maitland, or no deal. We parted ways.") On Podcast Row there were also celebs from *hey, girl.*, *True Crime Obsessed*, *Crawlspace*, *Martinis & Murder*, *Wine & Crime*, *And That's Why We Drink*. (John's favorite is *Neverland Whispers*, a true-crime YouTube channel that once featured a half hour on Theresa's case, all of it *whispered* by the host.)

In the lobby, a portable wall was covered with handwritten yellow sticky notes responding to the bannered question WHAT'S YOUR MOTIVE? The notes provided some idea of why people had paid hundreds of dollars to be here:

> *To solve every cold case!*
> *To lean on a tree with Keith Morrison!*
> *My BFF needs to be regulated in her consumption of Snapped*
> *To solve the Colonel Mustard murders!*
> *To meet all my favorite podcasters in person*
> *Fascinated by the craziness of others*

Paul Haynes a hottie

Obsessed with finding justice for victims

To get my boyfriend to finally understand my true crime obsession

To stay sexy don't get murdered

Promote my podcast!

To get my CSI nerd on

To meet all the people who get to do this for a living. What a dream job!

Friends help you move . . . best friends help you move bodies!

All of this reminded me, rather ruefully, of my own ridiculous insouciance when, fresh out of journalism school, I worked on my first TV show, a New York–based series called *Confessions of Crime*. I was sewing together tales of murder and woe from the newly available videotaped statements of arrested murder suspects. The existence of these tapes had been, for some reason, cottoned on to by a couple of Manhattan luxury soap purveyors who wanted to become producers. They'd met me at a party. I had read crime biographies by the armful and had all sorts of theories to weave around those videos. But it wasn't until I went to a Long Island precinct and saw my first crime-scene photos that I realized I'd been engaging in parlour games. The end result of violence is annihilation. It is a mother on the linoleum floor of her kitchen with her skirt blown upward over her belly by the force of her son's shotgun blast. It is her tongue come to rest on the top of her microwave oven. It's chaotic, not artful, and deadening of all that it means to be human.

John had refused to come with me to Nashville. For most people, he had mused in 2002, when we were working on our newspaper series, crime "is high comedy and Grand Guignol: the things that go bump in the night. Things that terrify, then delight you. It's nothing like that at all. It's really the things that haunt you, depress you . . . that drive you insane, create grief, despair, longing. That's what it's about." Then, as he e-mailed after I returned from the Opryland Resort, "Cut forward nearly two decades and today the Grand Guignol is more like a PS4 all-nighter of *Heavy Rain* jacked up on Fireball and Red Bull." Or wine.

Nevertheless, the truth is that, like the desperate family at that CrimeCon who sat patiently and largely ignored as they sought help with the Delphi Murders (which would indeed become fodder for a podcast produced by CNN), John was just as vulnerable to this latest wave of interest in crime—because you *never knew* what stone a casual sleuth might overturn. Like a compulsive gambler, he couldn't relinquish investing in the slim possibility of long odds. Around the time I was in Nashville, he had a dream that he was lost in Montreal, trying to get home to his parents, and two guys approached who half-mockingly offered to drive him. He didn't have any money, and he didn't know where he was going. He got into their car and "slowly it dawns on me that I'm not my adult self. I'm my child self." He knew the route was wrong, he saw no familiar markers, and they asked him to follow them into the woods. And then it further dawned on him that he wasn't even his child self. He was one of the women he'd been podcasting about. He was losing the shape of his own reality, the bounded edges, if they had ever been there at all.

In the spring of 2015, John received an e-mail in French from a man who introduced himself as a director: *I would like to know if you could give me details about Theresa Allore for a documentary?* Stephan Parent was a DIY figure in the true-crime culture of Quebec. After making a documentary about a torpedoed ship called *Empress of Ireland*, he'd bootstrapped a film together called *Novembre 84*, a docudrama about a series of child abductions and murders in the Montreal area in the mid-1980s. Neither film got a distribution deal, but *Novembre 84* did attract attention, largely due to two of the project's supporters, Claude Poirier and Marc Bellemare. Poirier was the former *Allô Police* reporter who'd gotten involved as a ransom deliverer in the Charles Marion kidnapping affair. Marc Bellemare was the minister of justice in Premier Jean Charest's cabinet in the early 2000s.

Parent became aware of Theresa's story because of one of John's periodic efforts to shake things up with a blog post. After he gained access to the archives of the Quebec tabloids in late August 2013, he posted about some of the cases he'd found, in a post titled "Quebec 1977: Who Was the Bootlace Killer?" Trying to reignite police interest, he discussed several unsolved sexual homicides, including those of his sister and Louise Camirand. (Neither case had yet been posted to the SQ's cold-case website, which is in part what had provoked him.) "The Bootlace Killer was a moniker I simply made up," he told me, "because Camirand had been found with a bootlace around her neck and some of the victims had been strangled. But this caught the imagination of Stephan Parent, who would talk publicly about the Bootlace Killer as if this was some long-established name like the Zodiac Killer. He began to ask for information on all my files. After consulting the other families, I provided him with everything I had: crime-scene photos, autopsy and police reports. I would get the occasional update: *John, I'm working on the Bazinet file now.* I tried to help out where I could, but I was busy with life in North Carolina." John figured they were working on another true-crime docudrama. He paid little attention. "About a month after Parent's first contact, I received the following Facebook message (in French): *Hi John. I'm the producer with Stephan Parent on* Empress of Ireland *and* Novembre 84. *Have a nice day—Ugo Fredette.* This was my first introduction."

In early 2016, all of the victims' families involved in Parent and Fredette's new film project—now named *7 Femmes* (*7 Women*)— were invited to meet in Montreal. There were several items on the agenda, but chiefly, Parent wanted to hold a press conference at which he and Marc Bellemare would formally demand that the Quebec government launch a public inquiry into the unsolved cold cases that had inspired their new film. On a Sunday morning in April, the families converged in a crowded second-floor conference room of the sky-scraping Hotel Bonaventure in the city centre. John knew most of them—not just families, but also by now grassroots victim advocates and their supporters. They listened respectfully while Bellemare read his manifesto to the government. Some sat for interviews with Stephan Parent, whose "co-producer" Ugo Fredette helmed the camera.

Afterward, a group of them went to the hotel bar, "and it was here that I began to know Ugo and Steph," John would later write. "Ugo Fredette was big, in his late thirties, maybe six foot three, weighing about 220 pounds, with a brush cut and round, bright eyes behind wire-rim glasses. He had gone to film school, but his day job was at a company that exterminated insects. Stephan was older, smaller and smarter." Where Parent struck

John as reserved, Ugo was boisterous. John noticed his nervous habit of shoving his glasses back with his left index finger whenever he felt uncomfortable, which seemed to be quite often. "On the surface, he comported himself like a bon vivant—generous with the compliments, quick to order you another drink. But that day, the booze kept coming, and it was the middle of the afternoon, and a Sunday. Ugo and Steph were urging on a party atmosphere; things got rowdy, the jokes felt forced, and I eventually made an excuse and cut out early. It was unsettling. For a professional undertaking on such a sombre subject, it seemed slightly unhinged."

After the meeting in Montreal, John heard through the grapevine that families who had worked with the documentary duo on their film *Novembre 84* "were no longer on speaking terms with Steph, or Ugo, or both." Soon, some families on the new project began to describe feeling bizarrely threatened by the producers if they expressed any hesitation about participating in the film. "These families quickly withdrew," John told me. "I began experiencing similar tactics of intimidation, even though I had made it clear that I wasn't an exclusive source; there was no written agreement or contract, certainly no promise of any money. I was a hired gun—I wasn't even hired; I was just a gun. Late one evening that April, I received the following Facebook message from Fredette: *You are the king or what John You Never talk about us and 7 women . . . You just talk about you . . . Do you know what youve done with Radio Canada? . . . RESPECT John . . . I AM VERY DISAPPOINTED.*"

John had done an interview with CBC Radio (not the French-language Radio-Canada as Fredette had presumed) that failed to mention the film he was advising Fredette and Parent on. "So what? Was I the brother of a murdered sister or a disappointing PR flack? It was weird." Despite Fredette's moodiness and the party atmosphere after the press conference, John noted that the two filmmakers were determined to make their work as professional and accurate as they could. Parent would send stills or short clips from the project for feedback on details. The young actor they'd recruited to play Sharron Prior looked exactly like her. They used a brown suede coat that was a perfect match to the one found next to her body. One day, Parent e-mailed John a photo with the message *I just found the actress to play Denise Bazinet.* The resemblance to this Montreal victim who had been found in a highway ditch near Saint-Jean-sur-Richelieu in October 1977 was striking, right down to her dark hair and pixie cut. Parent sent another image of her in stark black and white, exactly mimicking the crime-scene shot of Bazinet stretched out on a stainless-steel gurney, the strangulation marks clearly visible on her neck. *Who is this actress?* John wondered.

In May 2016, John flew back to Quebec to film an interview for a local TV show. Since he was in the Townships, with an extra day that weekend, he, his local friend Sue Tayachi and a "fellow crime victim survivor named Stéphane Luce" decided to revisit the Camirand site with metal detectors. Stéphane's mother, Roxanne, had been bludgeoned to death in her bedroom when he was a child. Luce had recently started a non-profit to help cold-case victims, Meurtres et disparitions irrésolus du Québec. He was keen to help John. "Our recovery efforts that day found still more ambiguous items: a woman's blouse deteriorated after decades, a comb. Down a narrow logging road, we found a cache of burned military documents and purchase orders, clearly some local unit that did not want to be charged any waste disposal fees." For John, the obsessive quest, the refusal to leave a single forest stone unturned, almost literally, was well worn. But for Luce it was something new, and there was an opportunity to alert media to his non-profit. So, by noon, some local camera crews showed up, perhaps to do a minor item on the Sherbrooke news. It was not a big deal.

"At five o'clock my cellphone pinged," John told me. The text message read: *NARRCISIST! How could you betray us!*

"Ugo wasn't just texting me, he was on a rampage to all three of our cellphones. As we sat there on the outdoor deck of a Sherbrooke burger shack, trying to comprehend the level of vitriol, at first we laughed, then we began to feel unnerved. This was not normal behaviour. I don't think we ever expressed it, but I remember becoming concerned that he might actually drive to Sherbrooke. I didn't want to provoke him. I remember my final text to him that day was to say that he was not my father and had no right to dictate what I could and could not do." John returned to the United States, wary and grateful for distance.

John never met with Stephan and Ugo again. After that, he would occasionally hear from them, and he would respond to their questions about cold cases. The working title for their docudrama, *7 Femmes*, had to be changed, and John heard rumours that it was because the filmmakers kept disconcerting victim families, who would back off. At some point, he wrote me, the title became *Soixante-dix*. John began to feel uncomfortable with the narrative the two men were pursuing (one that might explain their curious new title). "Parent had a theory that most of these women had been drawn into seventies party culture. Louise Camirand, the shy girl who 'would blush at nothing,' as one guy who knew her had told me, was in fact, according to Parent, spotted at a disco the night she died. Suddenly, Sharron Prior was no longer on her way to visit her boyfriend at a local pizza parlor the Saturday night she disappeared; she was on a bus to downtown Montreal, headed for the dance clubs on Crescent Street, despite the documented fact that the sixteen-year-old had left her bus pass and money behind in her bedroom. This was particularly unsettling because I'd spent years fighting the narrative of young girls engaging in promiscuous and risky behaviour. The majority of the victims I had profiled were doing mundane things when they disappeared: on the way home from work or school, going to visit a loved one, returning to their dorm room to study, like Theresa." These were beloved women, whose families had befriended John, and it felt horribly wrong that their story was now being shaped by two amateur filmmakers who acted like bullies. "Slowly," John said, "Pandora's box was opening, and it was me who had lifted the lid."

He last heard from Ugo Fredette on Thanksgiving weekend, 2016:

> "John. Are you There? . . . Do not worry about the past John. Like I said before, I love working with my friend Stephan. I believe in what he do, since November 84 . . . I never met a man like John Allore. You did more than other victims we've met before. More than Police and other detectives . . ."

It sounded like goodbye.

. . .

We pieced the news together later that Thursday night in September 2017, after I had heard the Amber Alert and John had called me at home: Fredette had triggered the alert. He had raced away from the town of Saint-Eustache, north of Montreal, with his six-year-old stepson in the car, after stabbing his partner, Véronique, seventeen times in the chest and head. The murder, in the kitchen of their shared townhouse, was overheard by Véronique Barbe's son and his nine-year-old friend, who had been playing in the basement. An eyewitness described seeing Fredette leave the home with a child under his arm like a *sac de patates* (a sack of potatoes). Fredette fled in a white Ford F-250 pickup truck that belonged to his employer. The insect exterminator was on the run.

Just under an hour's drive later, he stopped at a rest area. The only person there, by great ill fortune, was a septuagenarian who frequently enjoyed having coffee at the wooded refuge along Rivière du Nord. Fredette beat Yvon Lacasse to death, most likely crushing his skull by stomping on his head. He then loaded the body into Lacasse's grey Honda CR-V and drove off, with his stepson in the back seat. Farther up the road, Fredette dumped Lacasse's body in the forest and sped off. When Yvon Lacasse's body was discovered by police six days later, wild animals had chewed off his legs.

Ugo Fredette's wild flight lasted less than a day. The Ontario Provincial Police caught him northeast of Toronto after a citizen heard the Amber Alert on the radio and spotted the stolen Honda CR-V. With helicopter guidance, the police lay a spike belt that blew out Fredette's tires. He pulled the juddering car into a grove of maple trees near a white clapboard home, whose owners stood frozen inside, given that a calm September day now featured multiple police cars and helicopters. When the cops spotted Fredette hiding near some garden fencing, he shoved his hostage in front of him, held by the shirt collar and using him like "a human shield," as one officer would later testify. In his right hand, Fredette held a hastily grabbed stick, with which he repeatedly mimed a stabbing motion toward the boy. "Fuck you. Shoot me, kill me," he yelled at the cops. It took seven taser blasts to finally subdue him, with another officer swiftly taking the child out of harm's way.

There's a famous quotation from the German philosopher Friedrich Nietzsche that has become somewhat of a true-crime trope: "Whoever fights monsters should see to it that in the process he does not become a monster himself. And if you gaze long enough into the abyss, the abyss gazes back into you." The FBI behavioural profiling pioneer Robert Ressler reintroduced Nietzsche's quotation in his 1992 book, *Whoever Fights Monsters: My Twenty Years Tracking Serial Killers for the FBI*, which was, in turn, the basis of the popular Netflix series *Mindhunter*. "Gazing into the abyss" is a concept at the heart of every good creation story, from Genesis ("God's face a glass in which man sees himself") to Mary Shelley's *Frankenstein* to HBO's *Westworld*. For John, it had long been a question, however unconsciously held, of when the darkness would become more than he could bear: "When would gazing too long into cold cases and crime-scene photos and autopsy reports become the abyss?"

He already knew that his latent grief had morphed into post-traumatic stress disorder. Since 2002 he had been getting triggered, as he jogged along forest pathways in North Carolina, by seeing abandoned clothing and shoes or, once, a stomped-on, naked Barbie doll. "Any of these things would plunge me into an anxious temper for the day, losing my shit at co-workers or family for no apparent reason." One of his triggers is getting lost, not knowing the route or the plan. When his daughters were teenagers, he had frequent panic attacks about their whereabouts. "I had been cautioned about it, many times. By my parents, by my brother, by friends. But I never contemplated, never thought it was even conceivable, that my obsession would lead to September 14, 2017."

John was devastated by Fredette's murders. What role had he played? He pondered all the cases he had shared with the documentary pair. Were any of the stabbing victims featured in *Soixante-dix*? One certainly was. A woman named Joanne Dorion had been stabbed several times in the chest and suffered massive hemorrhaging to the heart and lungs. "Parent got very close to the Dorion family," he told me. "She would have been one of the main cases in their film." He began to think about the other victims. Parent had written, *I just found the actress to play Denise Bazinet*. That woman with the pixie cut. He went back through his computer files and located the production still for the murder scene of Bazinet. He found himself gazing, as he'd known he would, at the now-deceased Véronique Barbe.

"It is a theme in my life that guilt can be devastating in its reach; it has a vast span of control. Years ago, I consulted a psychic who told me she had a vision of my sister in which Theresa told her, 'John is stirring the pot.' If so, what precisely have I con-cocted? In my mind it went like this. I did open Pandora's box. If I hadn't gone to the *Allô Police* archive, if I hadn't written that piece about a 'Bootlace Killer,' if I never shared my files with two amateur filmmakers—then they would never have made a movie, they would have never re-enacted the Joanne Dorion stabbing, Ugo's partner would never have dressed up as Denise Bazinet, Ugo Fredette would not have played the part of a killer, and Véronique Barbe and Yvon Lacasse would still be alive. The boy wouldn't be traumatized for life."

Horrified, he called his long-time therapist, with whom he hadn't spoken in some years. "I told him I wasn't quite sure what was wrong, but that it was probably going to manifest itself in bad ways, and fairly quickly. Peter said he was retiring in six weeks; we didn't have much time, but he would try to help. He had worked with me on my PTSD. Now, I felt something more like despair. I can remember, for a long time, I didn't look people in the eye. I refused to look at myself in mirrors and windowpanes."

I had actually noticed this change in John when we met in Saint John and visited his old house on Leinster Street, although he didn't say, or couldn't articulate, what was happening to him. He seemed brittle, and somewhat aloof. When I hugged him hello at the hotel, he stiffened, as if braced. He has been bracing this whole time, I've come to see.

Incredibly, Stephan Parent decided to release his film about the unsolved murders in the 1970s, *Soixante-dix*, regardless of the turn of events. The families of the victims were appalled when they realized that the "killer" in the film—somewhat obscured, running around in a hoodie—was Fredette. Daniel

Barbe, Véronique's brother, called it "flagrant disrespect." He was further unnerved by the new dedication at the end of the documentary, *In memory of Véronique Barbe*. He told the press, "I'm in shock, really stunned. I do not understand it. The guy who is accused of killing my sister is in the movie and in the end, Parent makes a tribute. I'm completely down."

Unable or unwilling to grasp the implications of what he was doing, Parent remained unapologetic: "I felt the need to express in my own way a tribute to Véronique, because many people who were there knew her, and they knew Ugo too, so I knew that inevitably I would have to talk about it."

It's like the true-crime sleuths and DIY journos have lost the plot—the real-life narrative—and cannot see or understand their own acts of predation for what they really are. In popular culture and politics, we dance with evil, sexualize it, experimentally venerate psychopaths in shows like *Dexter* and *House of Cards* and *Breaking Bad*, and even celebrate them in business through books like *The Psychopath Whisperer* or *Snakes in Suits*. Power and greed entice us more than love, more than the sacred. Grieving families know better than any of us why it is love, in fact, that matters, and they are the ones we kill twice.

"Parent pledged to the press to reshoot the scenes with another actor," John told me. "I understand he edited Ugo out of much of the film."

Over the weekend after the murders, Marc Bellemare, the former Quebec justice minister and production partner of Parent and Fredette, gave an interview with *La Presse* defending Ugo: "Very few people in Quebec have been as dedicated to the cause of crime victims as Ugo Fredette," he insisted. Bellemare went on to say that, in his work, Fredette appeared very courteous, sympathetic, and did not seem to have a problem with impulsiveness. And so . . . what? He was innocent? What made him do it?

According to Hesiod, after Pandora opened the jar (as it was originally called), one thing remained when all hell broke loose: hope. "We are never told this," John wrote to me, "but I like to think that hope (sometimes translated from the Greek as 'deceptive expectation') later escaped as well. At least, that's how I'm rewriting the story."

In September 2019, John drove me in his pale-blue Nissan with Carolina plates north along Montreal's too-fast and too-narrow highways, eternally under construction, to the pretty town of Saint-Jérôme, where Ugo Fredette, having pled not guilty, was standing trial for two counts of murder. The day was bright with sunlight, and we parked beside a grassy park that bordered a meandering river. The courthouse was unusual, in my experience: airy with white walls and tall glass windows, more atrium than fort. John had already been attending the trial for a week, and nodded hello as we passed Véronique Barbe's two brothers, who wore pink shirts inscribed with the words JE SUIS VÉRONIQUE. John pointed out other family members: her mother, aunts, nieces and nephews, plus family friends representing both "Véro," as she'd been called, and the man who had been beaten to death, Yvon Lacasse.

One day, Yvon Lacasse's sister and her husband approached John and asked what he was working on. He told her a little bit about this book, managing to be as fluent as he could in French, then said how sorry he was about her brother. She began to break down, so he held her hand. She promised to come visit him in the States. "One day, she greeted me with a hug. This I have learned about crime victims: they have the warmest smiles and the most haunted eyes."

The families filed in and sat to the right of the centre aisle, while the media and court buffs took their seats to the left. An unexpectedly tinny electronic doorbell chime announced the arrival of Judge Myriam Lachance and the jury. The judge was young and very stylish. She had raven-dark hair that she wore in a straight, glossy fringe above her red glasses. The attorneys fluttered like crows in their jurist gowns. Ugo Fredette entered the defendant's glass box. Apart from being a few pounds heavier, he looked the same as ever, John thought. He wore his usual uniform, though a slightly dressier version: a black jacket, black dress shirt, black slacks, his glasses periodically pushed back with that left index finger. For most of the trial, he kept his eyes fixed in front of him on the jury that sat opposite the defendant box. He rarely looked out into the public gallery, and if he saw John, he gave no sign of recognition. Until the day he did.

John had taken a place at the press table during that first week, and had written to me in Toronto about what transpired. "The Quebec media arena is tight, everyone knows everyone, so I quickly stood out. Who was this new guy? I had a letter from [our editor, Craig Pyette] in case I was challenged as press. When I produced my letter, the lead Crown attorney, who looked like a cross between Tom Hulce and the lead singer from the Buggles, explained he would have to take the matter up with Judge Lachance. We broke for lunch. I assumed he was going to address the matter in a closed session, but instead, after the break, he addressed the whole courtroom. 'Madame Judge, before we bring the jury in, I have a matter to discuss concerning a gentleman who has made a request. A Mr. Pee-ette has a letter I will read to you . . .' This was all in French, of course, so it took me a second to clue in to what was going on. *Oh, he thinks I'm Craig Pyette!* I frantically realized he was going to read the entire letter, which was a short synopsis of this book, so I shouted out, '*Ce n'est pas Pee-ette, je suis John Allore!*' And then Ugo Fredette turned his head and looked directly at me. The abyss gazed back."

Among the materials that journalists were handed was a full transcript of the interview conducted with the nine-year-old friend who had witnessed the murder of Véronique Barbe. Actually, there had been more witnesses: a neighbour saw Ugo and Véronique fighting on their deck, then watched Ugo drag Véronique into the house "like a rag doll." A broken, bloody knife was recovered from the deck, and a second stained knife was found in the kitchen sink, the words BON APPÉTIT inscribed on the blade. Fredette had apparently stabbed Barbe on the deck first, then dragged her into the kitchen and finished her off.

The testimony of the nine-year-old boy (who cannot be named) was videotaped in an interrogation room on the evening of the murder. Throughout the interview, he described to the detective what he'd seen. "She said ouch," then "Ugo gave her a hug." About thirty minutes into the boy's interview, the detective said she had to leave the room for a moment to consult with her colleagues. She invited him to do some drawing on the whiteboard while she was gone. The boy, left alone, started slowly drawing a circle, then colouring it in with a black marker. *Is he drawing a planet?* John wondered, leaning forward to look.

About two minutes in, the drawing started to take shape: A face? A clown? "Everyone sat in silence, watching the tape on the courtroom monitors. Most looked bored, not really understanding what the boy was drawing. I understood. It was the death's head skull from the Marvel comic *The Punisher*."

The media was transfixed by the hourly disclosure of all of the crime details, giving their news updates on breaks, but John had ultimately come for another purpose. He was looking for a sign. Something in the fantasy realm of Ugo Fredette's film world, in his work on the unsolved crimes in Quebec, had triggered him to commit two murders. Of course, Stephan Parent had flatly denied this was the case. Speaking with the wire service Canadian Press just two days after the murders, Parent said, "Yes, he could be impulsive and scream. He could hit the counter, but from there to commit murder? Never!" Parent denied Fredette might have had a morbid fascination with murder. "This has nothing to do with it. He was fascinated by the world of cinema. . . . When we did re-enactments, it was staged, but he had tears in his eyes. He said he could not believe people could do that and he was crying." Parent went on to say that he also saw Ugo weep with the families of the victims as they shared their stories. "I really feel betrayal in the depths of my being. For years I have rubbed shoulders with the families of the victims, that we track down murderers, that we denounce these things in public." Parent ended the interview by claiming to question his work, fearing he would no longer be able to handle cases involving murders or kidnappings. (Apparently, he got over this quickly. Within a year he announced that he was working on a documentary about the 1999 unsolved case of a teen named Julie Surprenant.)

Before I got to Montreal, John ran into Parent in the courthouse. "He said he'd been called as a witness, but not that day, or any other day for the Crown. Was he a defense witness? That could be interesting. Nevertheless, on this day, he was hanging around outside the courtroom. We spotted each other, and I was hoping he'd turn away, but he walked right up to me. 'He betrayed me! I'm a victim too, John!' A victim how? Like being stabbed seventeen times a victim? Like being stomped on the head a victim? Parent introduced me to Daniel Barbe. They now appeared to be friends, or was this also an act? Then, again with the self-pity: 'John, I'm still in shock with this, look at my hands!' He held his arms aloft and deliberately shook his fingers, like he was suffering from the DTs."

After his arrest, while under detention with the Ontario police, Ugo Fredette requested a phone call to his parents. He knew the conversation—which took place on September 21, 2017—was being recorded. Some of what was said is startling. The call began with his parents explaining to him that he needed to raise $50,000 to retain an attorney. Fredette told his parents to sell all the furniture in his apartment, which is interesting given that the apartment came fully furnished, so it wasn't his to sell. He went on to ask his parents to delete some derogatory posts he'd made about Véronique on Facebook. Fredette had texted her 179 times over the day leading up to her murder, alternately pleading with her not to leave him and haranguing her. Next, Fredette complained about how Stephan Parent had never treated him properly as a fellow producer, wasn't respectful enough. His parents asked if his stepson had witnessed the murder of Véronique Barbe. Ugo responded,

"He was there when it happened, he saw everything . . . but he thought it was a movie."

Fredette's crimes bring to mind a strange 2008 case involving Edmonton's Mark Twitchell, a would-be filmmaker enamoured of the TV series *Dexter*, who wrote a screenplay called "House of Cards," casting himself in the role of a killer. Following the plot he'd invented, he proceeded to pose as a woman on an online dating site. When someone took the bait and went to meet him at a rented garage, Twitchell filmed himself murdering and dismembering the man. His and other cases are discussed in the book *Murder in Plain English,* in which the scholars Michael Arntfield and Marcel Danesi muse about the historic interplay between art, fantasy and violence. In cyberspace, this entanglement has intensified, and it presents interesting policing quandaries. The NYPD "Cannibal Cop" Gilberto Valle never murdered anyone, but he was convicted of conspiracy to kidnap in 2013 after his wife discovered he was immersing himself in chat rooms dedicated to the torture, rape and cannibalization of women. In this cyber world, he described his desire to murder his wife, which became evidence of intent. "Valle admitted to FBI investigators that the intensity of his virtual experience ultimately obscured the line between the online and offline worlds whereby his 'secret cyber life was "bleeding" into reality.'" As Arntfield and Danesi noted, "writing and story-telling—including writing and story-telling *as* paraphilias [abnormally extreme sexual desires]—can all evolve in tandem and concomitantly escalate to real murders."

Was this what was going on with Fredette in his film life? Was it bleeding into reality? John went back and reviewed the filmmakers' online personas, on social media and in text messages.

"One of the first things I noticed was that these two guys liked to play dress-up. On Ugo's Facebook page [which is still active as of spring 2020], there is a photo of an event they hosted back in 2015, the shooting of a disco scene, presumably for 7 *Femmes*. They're all there: Ugo as the disco bouncer, Stephan embracing Véronique Barbe, who is wearing a headband. In the comments, Ugo thanks 'all the John Travoltas and the girls with their seventies costumes, really flashy!' Where was the self-awareness? It sickened me. They were turning my sister's death into a fashion riff. The same thing for their first film, *Empress of Ireland*. Ugo and Véronique in turn-of-the-century costume. Ugo and Steph flashing peace signs. Steph dressed as the captain, Ugo as . . . I don't know what, presumably someone from steerage. Ugo and Véronique even appeared on a Quebec dating show. There they are in complementary red sweaters, lying on their backs with rose petals, strawberries and tea candles, talking lovey-dovey, nine months before he stabbed her."

One photo John found on Facebook was particularly troubling. It depicts Fredette standing on a suburban street in front of a red Acura. A small girl in a bicycle helmet stands in front of him, apprehensive. Stephan Parent is to the side, and seems to be directing. In a second photo, Fredette appears to be pushing the girl on her bike, the red Acura in the background. This was a dramatization of the abduction of a girl named Cédrika Provencher. She had been missing for years, and her father, Martin, had agreed to collaborate with the men, until Cédrika's remains were finally found in 2015. At that point, he asked them to stop filming, as the act of advocacy was no longer necessary. They refused. He had to threaten legal action to get them to stop. Did Ugo Fredette also play the part of the abductor in the unreleased Cédrika Provencher movie? Because he most certainly abducted his own stepson.

Ugo Fredette's defense was equally an act of dark fantasy. In presenting his client's version of events, attorney Louis-Alexandre Martin tried to argue that, despite the eighteen blood samples recovered from Barbe's home, all of which belonged to Véronique Barbe, it was Ugo who was first attacked with a knife by his partner. She was a "crazy harridan" who made his life a misery with her temper and her put-downs. After all the abuse she'd rained down on him, he just "snapped." Then he blacked out and didn't remember killing her. With respect to the second victim, Yvon Lacasse, Martin argued that Fredette went into a blind paternal rage when he came out of the rest stop bathroom to witness the seventy-one-year-old man trying to lure the boy into his car. He was a pedophile! There was no other option than to beat him to death. This defamatory account left Lacasse's family in tears.

The jury requested a review of testimony from the couple's therapist, who had seen Ugo and Véronique on the day of the killing and noted that Véronique seemed truly scared. They didn't accept Fredette's improbable sequence of one act of self-defence after another, appropriating the role of victim. They convicted him on two counts of first-degree murder. Lacasse's daughter, Jennifer, put it aptly: "The movie that Mr. Fredette created in his head, the jury didn't believe."

The stories that predators tell themselves, that they borrow and begin to inhabit, that they spin and then fall for—that is, for us, as much a revelation of this quest as the truths that go unheard.

SEVENTEEN

I DREAM A HIGHWAY BACK TO YOU

"Perhaps I am stronger than I think."
—Thomas Merton, *Conjectures of a Guilty Bystander*

WHO, THEN, CAN FULLY RELAY THE STORY OF THERESA'S DEATH?
In more ways than the most obvious one, that isn't an answerable question. People weave stories around themselves like bindings, to salve wounds, to draw courage, to keep sane. She will have had her own account, of course, but in the silence imposed upon her by slaughter-stained hands in the autumn of 1978, that narrative has become, over time, several tales told by others.

In the spring of 2019, I met Theresa's old boyfriend Vlad when I was visiting Los Angeles. John had found a letter from him, mailed on November 3, 1978, from his resort in the Rocky Mountains, addressed to Theresa at King's Hall, Compton. It had arrived in the dormitory mailbox after its intended recipient had vanished into the night. She never read the letter. Vlad dropped by my Airbnb in Topanga Canyon on his motorcycle.

He's a very tall man with clear blue eyes and a lined, faintly melancholic face. Life has not been all that smooth for him, and Theresa has taken on a deep, almost iconic importance as his lost, best love. We sat for awhile in the kitchen and talked about climate change, the current nightmare of politics and the ways in which lives twist and turn. I handed him the letter, still in its envelope, and he nodded his thanks, tucking it into his motorcycle jacket before heading back down through the canyon.

I wondered if what he'd written all those years ago would flow into what he remembered, or tear the vision apart.

For Marilyn, her daughter's death had so long been a story of her own guilt—she hadn't mothered enough, she'd failed to deter Theresa from hitchhiking, hadn't warned her sufficiently about drugs, hadn't been there when she died—that it was hard for her to absorb the idea that someone else was responsible. John had told her about Luc Grégoire: his criminality in the Townships, his tight proximity to the victims, and other things we had learned.

"Is he the man who killed my daughter?" she asked.

"Maybe," John said. And if not him, an extremely similar suspect who has never been identified.

I told her about Grégoire too, when I visited Saint John that windy September weekend. Her eyes slid away from me and she gazed into the middle distance with a look of vague consternation. The focused anger she felt toward Champlain College and the Quebec police was absent in this response. I wondered if it was a story that Marilyn didn't recognize, in a way. It certainly wasn't closure.

At the end of our conversation that afternoon, she accompanied me to the doorway of her and Bob's apartment, gesturing down the straight, well-lit hallway to where I could turn right and find the elevator and head back down to Leinster Street. That's where I'd last seen Marilyn, it occurred to me. Around 1981, on this street. As I walked along the carpet, zipping up my windbreaker, I could hear her bracelets jingle. I pushed the button and she called out, "Patricia? Wait, I'll come with you." I held the elevator door and she joined me, riding down four quick storeys and walking me out into the foyer. She pushed the front door open and reminded me, "Just turn right. Right there on the street." *Don't get lost,* she seemed to be urging. *Don't get lost.*

Sometimes, John thinks of this story in terms of his dreams. For years, they involved him being lost. "I often have dreams where I am in a terminus, a transportation nexus that is a point of transition; the metro leads to a bus line, an airport into a train station. Sometimes the space morphs into a shopping mall. I'm in the Montreal airport, but then it becomes the abandoned ruins of Man and His World and the fairgrounds from Expo 67, even though all those buildings were razed decades ago."

But as John and I neared the end of writing this book, his dreams began shifting. In one of them, he wrote to me from North Carolina after speaking to Calgary detective Ken Carriere, "There is an icefield on a frozen lake. The ice is covering ruins. You can see what appear to be church relics, ancient paraphernalia. Theresa is standing on this island. You want to reach her, but you will sink trying to cross the ice as it melts. You try taking a skiff to her, but the more you approach solid ground, the farther away you are. She says, 'It's all there below

319

me.' Meaning the answers to all of your questions are below that ice, hidden in those holy relics and mysteries."

Lost necklaces, overwintered Buxton wallets, women's clothing, tossed evidence, old photos, tickets to a long-ago play.

Then, finally, a dream about a woman he had fallen in love with after his marriage ended, who broke the relationship off. I met her once, at his rented house, whip-smart and vivacious and heading into a future she didn't want him to share, and for a number of reasons she seemed to be clearly evocative, for John, of his sister. "I am headed into a terminus, and I suddenly see her coming toward me, on her way out. We pass, ignoring each other, even though we both recognize who we are. This happens again a few hours later, only with us walking the opposite way, she in, me out. She's dragging a suitcase on rollers. She stops. "Do you like the pursuit, the struggle, John?" I say that I do. We sit down at an outdoor area of a closed coffee shop inside the terminus and talk. It's good. We're both very charming and clearly interested in each other. She then says she has to go, and I leave the terminus, but now it has become a marina, and I get into a boat, where my brother is waiting to take me home. I tell him that I ran into her. "Oh, really? Is she coming too?" It's at this moment that I realize she isn't coming. And it's finally okay. I will see her again, or not. The story will continue, or not."

What struck me about John's dream was the image of his living brother, Andre, waiting in the boat to take him home. The image was with me when we both stayed at Andre's place in the Montreal suburb of Rosemère during the trial of Ugo Fredette. Sometimes, at night, I would curl myself into the corner chair in the living room with my laptop while the brothers prattled comfortably in the kitchen, talking about music, watching baseball, making inside jokes. There seemed to be a delicate repairing of their relationship going on. It had been strained by this book, by John's Quebec media appearances, by a quest that never ended, the older brother worrying that the younger one couldn't stop, as Theresa said (or so claimed a psychic), "stirring the pot."

Something about attending the Fredette trial had lifted John's spirits and shifted his focus. On his podcast he'd moved on to broader conversations about criminal justice, and he was deeply engaged with his city planning work back in Durham. The trial also corresponded with the end of this book, with a story finally fully told. Except, what story? Nothing ever ends, and there are always new beginnings. Coming to a summary close annoyed him. "In order for me to have closure, you'd have to pull an *Eternal Sunshine of the Spotless Mind* on me: zap the whole thing from my memory, and have me forget that it even happened. But then, practically every other good memory would get flushed along with it, and who wants that?" The untold stories about his daughters, and his theatre work, and the job he loves, and the red clay and catfish of the Carolinas, the Outer Banks and the Great Smoky Mountains.

So, "Closure. I've never heard a crime victim use that word. It always comes from the mouth of a journalist, or an inexperienced justice activist. They've heard someone else use it when discussing victims' issues, so they figure it must be right, 'What does closure look like for you?' Because they don't want to ask the question they should really put to themselves: *My god, faced with that experience, what would I do?*"

ACKNOWLEDGEMENTS

FROM JOHN ALLORE:

My three daughters are fond of reminding me that all my books are either about true crime or baseball. But my first love has always been baseball, so I'd like to borrow from Bill James, an author I admire who writes about both. My primary indebtedness for this book is first to the crime victims I have met along the journey; the warmest smiles, the most haunted eyes. And second, to those who have written about these crimes . . . these places and times so critical to this book. I can't name them all, but many went uncredited, particularly in the tabloid journals, *Allô Police* and *Photo Police*. Also to those good stewards of knowledge at the Bibliothèque et Archives nationales du Québec who set the example for public service.

Thank you for teaching me how to write a book, to my editors at Random House Canada, Craig Pyette and Anne Collins, and to my agent Richard Abate at 3 Arts Entertainment.

I have some very good friends I wish to thank for their support and guidance in putting this beast together. Each of you provided pieces to the puzzle; Mary Ainslie, Elisabeth Allore, Michael Arntfield, Eric Beauregard, Jean-Claude Bernheim, Ken Carriere, Suzanne DeRome, Chris Garbutt, Anna Grant, Kristian Gravenor, Any Guillemette, Manuelle Legare, Phillipe Legault, Grant Miller, CJ Perry, Mario Pompetti, Jean Pierre Rancourt, Sasha Reid, Annie Richard, Kim Rossmo, Tracy Wing, Kate Zernike.

To friends who helped me pick up the pieces: Gus Allen, Joanne Bayly, Solange Blais, Nathalie Bergeron, Stephane Berthomet, Pierre-Hugues Boisvenu, Daniel Desindes, Ray Dooley, Molly Eness, Marjean Fichtenberg, Kristy Fleming, Glen and Sherry Edmunds-Flett, Heidi Illingworth, Isabeau, Rob Jenkins, Bertha Johnson, Robert Lane, Stephane Levesque, Stephane Luce, Rachel Massicotte, Eden McCaffrey, Randy McCall, Areon Mobasher, Richard Pinter, Barb Pratt, Doreen, Moreen and Yvonne Prior, James Riordan, Sandy Roth, Diane Soucisse, Emily Thompson, Stephen Tobias, Rob Tripp, Patrick Vuillemin, Jo-Anne Wemmers, Arielle Yoder.

With gratitude to anyone who ever read my blog or listened to my podcast from the earliest of days. Thank you Daniel and Maritime Missy. Thank you Kevin, Chip Scheitlin and Garden Gremlin. I have left some clues for you in the book, I hope you find them rewarding.

Thank you to my three teachers: Amelia, Grace and Ava—you show me so many odd, funny, goofy and wonderful things.

I have a friend who has lived intensely inside my head for the last three years, and done it all without complaint. Always calm and witty, and with no drama. Thank you for making me a better writer, Patricia.

To my brother, Andre, my father, Robert, my mother, Marilyn, and mostly Theresa; we prevailed.

A final gratitude to anyone I have forgotten to thank, or anyone whose name I misspelled, or if I got your title wrong. It's a poor sort of memory . . .

FROM PATRICIA PEARSON:

I want to thank all those who agreed to be interviewed on such a painful subject, and who did so with candour and grace, in particular Marilyn and Andre Allore, Kathy deGroot, Vlad Kulich, Deborah Fernandez, Catherine Dawe, and Deb Horton. My gratitude as well to Andre and Bob Allore for allowing us to excerpt from their journals, and for hosting me in their homes.

In Calgary, I am grateful to Gail Weeks, Karen Venables, Sasha Reid and Detective Ken Carriere for their assistance and insight.

For expertise in various subject areas, I thank Dr. Candice Skrapec, Robert Martyn, Wolf Reidel, Melina Buckley, Joanna Bourke, Detective Éric Latour, Professor Eric Beauregard and Professor Kim Rossmo.

Carle Steele and the Access Copyright Foundation generously supported my reporting trip to Calgary and Vancouver to research victimized sex workers. The Canada Council for the Arts proved a godsend in supporting the writing of the manuscript.

Thanks to Craig, Anne, copy editor Sue Sumeraj and cover designer Lisa Jager. Love as always to my agent, Sarah Lazin, and gratitude to her assistant Catharine Strong.

Love to Ambrose, for his feedback and bent ear. And to Geoffrey for being curious, and loving, and leaving space.

Thanks to John Allore for being so flexible, self-aware and respectful as a co-author and co-investigator. We've shared a long road indeed, my friend.

And finally, a dedication of sorts to my mother, Landon, my daughter Clara Landon, and my sisters Hilary and Anne. It is time for us all to feel safe, and for our strengths to prevail.

NOTES

TWO: VIOLENCE BOILS IN THE GARDEN

27   He envisioned its dorms . . . : Sandy Sage, "Self-management Key to Compton Living," *Touchstone* (Champlain College), September 22, 1977.

34   "We may live in a small community . . .": Charles Bury, "Bish student attacked in parking lot," *Sherbrooke Record*, January 21, 1983.

34   On January 23, 1980, the *Sherbrooke Record* . . . : Nelson Wyatt, "It Was Busy Year for Coaticook QPF," *Sherbrooke Record*, January 23, 1980.

35   "The girl just had time . . .": Steve Kowch, "Kidnapped Girl Found Killed, Burly Man Sesen," *Gazette* (Montreal), July 15, 1972.

36   A duty officer "told me . . .": Albert Noel, "Daughter Kidnap Handling Delayed, Father Testifies," *Gazette*, March 28, 1973.

37   "The off-handed manner . . .": "Report Faults Brossard Police," *Gazette*, April 20, 1973.

37   A Champlain student was the victim . . . : Sandy Sage, "Co-eds Worry About Harassment Reports," *Touchstone*, February 16, 1978.

38   A mountain out of a mole hill . . . : Carolyn Rowell, "Police Ignore Assault Victims," *Campus* (Bishop's University), February 10, 1978.

38   "I find that I look at every stranger . . .": Sage, "Co-eds Worry About Harassment."

38   The *Touchstone* report continued . . . : Sage, "Co-eds Worry About Harassment."

38   Contacted by *The Campus* student newspaper . . . : Sage, "Co-eds Worry About Harassment."

38   The *Sherbrooke Record* ran a story . . . : Janet Cotton and Marilyn Mill, "Attempted Rape Unprobed," *Sherbrooke Record*, February 10, 1978.

38   On February 10, 1978, student journalist . . . : Rowell, "Police Ignore Assault Victim."

39   Jane Doe called the station . . . : Cotton and Mill, "Attempted Rape Unprobed."

39   To further the woman's feelings . . . : Rowell, "Police Ignore Assault Victim."

39   . . . "For more than a month, rumours . . .": *Record* Staff, "Lennoxville Police Shuffle Anticipated," *Sherbrooke Record*, February, 10, 1978.

40   A female student wrote an editorial . . . : "Police Action Needed," *Touchstone*, February 8, 1978.

40   "There has been as many as eight rapes . . .": Cotton and Mill, "Attempted Rape Unprobed."

41   I was invited to address . . . : Susan Brownmiller, *Against Our Will: Men, Women and Rape* (New York: Bantam Books, 1975), 409.

41   "Forcible rape is one of the most . . .": Brownmiller, *Against Our Will*, 408.

42   "From the 1970s onward," . . . : Joanna Bourke, *Rape: A History from 1860 to the Present* (London: Virago, 2007), 393.

42   But the most comprehensive study . . . : Liz Kelly, Jo Lovett and Linda Regan, *A Gap or Chasm? Attrition in Reported Rape Cases*, Home Office Research Study 293. (London: Home Office Research, Development and Statistics Directorate, 2005).

42   "Because the police are accustomed . . .": E.R. Galton, "Police Processing of Rape Complaints: A Case Study," *American Journal of Criminal Law* 4, no. 1 (1975–76): 15–30.

42   It's hard to summon . . . : *Photo Police*, February 8, 1975, 21.

43   "In the 1890s," wrote cultural historian Bourke . . . : Bourke, *Rape*, 25–26.

43   The influential forensic evidence expert . . . : John Henry Wigmore, *Wigmore on Evidence* (Boston: Little, Brown, 1970), 736.

44   Or, as the view of such experts . . . : Bourke, *Rape*, 34.

44 The director of scientific research . . . : David Abrahamsen, *The Psychology of Crime* (New York: Columbia University Press, 1960), 161.

44 The author of *Cry Rape* . . . : Hugo Paul, *Cry Rape: Anatomy of the Rapist* (New York: Dalhousie Press, 1967), 105.

44 . . . the 1969 US National Commission . . . : *Rape*, 73.

45 As Joanna Bourke argued . . . : Bourke, *Rape*, 75.

45 "In recent years, rape . . .": Brownmiller, *Against Our Will*, 390.

46 "The broad trend seems to be . . .": Bourke, *Rape*, 16.

THREE: WHISPER GAMES

48 "I was enraged," one wrote . . . : Patricia Pearson, "Who Killed Theresa?" *National Post*, August 10–12, 2002.

49 "For most boys and girls . . .": Pearson, "Who Killed Theresa?"

52 "I asked her what she was going to do . . .": Statement given to police in 1978, and contained in Theresa Allore's file. (Unless otherwise noted, all further student accounts are from police statements.)

53 Last year when *The Campus* investigated . . . : Carolyn Rowell, Editorial, *Campus*, November 3, 1978.

55 On November 7, the campus newspaper . . . : Mike Jette and Phil Sande, "Compton Confusion," *Touchstone*, November 9, 1978.

FOUR: THE DRUG THEORY

65 On November 4, the hunters reported . . . : "La jeune Allore toujours recherché," *La Tribune* (Sherbrooke), November 17, 1978.

68 ". . . in 1980, Gaudreault would come under fire . . . : "Proces de Belley: Le caporal Gaudreault reconnait avoir utilise 2 declarations fictives," *La Tribune*, October 10, 1980.

68 A witness predicted to Gaudreault . . . : Sainte-Thérèse cold-case file on Carole Dupont, reviewed by authors.

70 Now, out of nowhere, it announced . . . : "Disparition mystérieuse: une histoire de drogue?" *Journal de Montréal*, December 20, 1978.

74 In mid-February 1979, a six-man team . . . : "Three Arrested in Compton Raid," *Touchstone*, February 22, 1978.

74 Although Hamel publicly repudiated . . . : Serge Gosselin, "Disparition de Theresa Allore: mystère complet," *La Tribune*,

December 22, 1978. Hamel was asked by reporter Gosselin to respond to the December 20, 1978, *Journal de Montréal* article about Theresa's alleged involvement with drugs. Hamel stated, "There isn't any information at this point that would permit us to think that."

FIVE: THE GREEN AND THE BLUE

76   In Lachute, a town of fifteen thousand . . . : Ken Ernhofer, "Lachute Tried Not to Feel Bitter as Unemployment Rate Doubles," *Gazette*, March 17, 1977.

77   . . . "It was an election promise . . .": Steve Kowch, "Pay Rollbacks Anger Municipal Policemen," *Gazette*, January 11, 1977.

77   The province's mayors questioned . . . : Andrew Phillips, "Mayors Query $15 Million for Police," *Gazette*, January 13, 1977.

77   . . . where to put 100,000 confiscated copies . . . : Steve Kowch, "Morale of Top Police Brass Hits Rock Bottom," *Gazette*, April 4, 1977.

77   The proportion of major crimes . . . : Ken Ernhofer, "Unsolved Crime Up Last Year," *Gazette*, February 26, 1977.

78   A Quebec government study . . . : "Toronto Record Better/Police Suffer in Comparison," *Gazette*, January 27, 1978.

78   By the end of February 1977 . . . : "Two Young Women Found Murdered MUC Toll Now 24," *Gazette*, February 28, 1977.

78   . . . "the criminal in Quebec," . . . : "Toronto Record Better."

79   "Since Monday, police tactics . . .": Editorial, "Police Defiance Must Stop," *Gazette*, February 3, 1977.

79   "The slowdown has given Montrealers . . .": Editorial, "Police Overhaul Urgent," *Gazette*, February 4, 1977.

79   MUC officers during this time . . . : In August 1978, Maurice Houle, the fifty-one-year-old police chief of Repentigny, was charged by the Sûreté du Québec for the possession and cultivation of marijuana at his summer home in Lavaltrie ("Pot Charge Police Chief Suspended," *Gazette*, August 31, 1978). On August 25, 1978, an MUC policeman faced an illegal weapons charge after eighty weapons were seized by the RCMP at his home. Some of the guns had price tags on them ("Policeman May Face Illegal Weapons Charge," *Gazette*, August 25, 1978).

79   A 1982 inquiry into corruption . . . : The inquiry centred on what is widely known as "L'affaire Dupont," about the 1969 death of Trois-Rivières police officer Louis-Georges Dupont.

79   *Gazette* reporter Steve Kowch . . . : Kowch, "Morale of Top Police."

79   Newly appointed police chief . . . : "Police Four-Day Week Plan a Pressure Tactic: Vignola," *Gazette*, December 8, 1977.

80   At a news conference . . . : Bill Kokesch, "Vignola Begs Police to Obey His Orders," *Gazette*, December 30, 1997.

80   Mayor Edwin Briggs . . . : "Police Action 'Blackmail': Suburb Mayor," *Gazette*, January 5, 1978.

80   . . . many men called in sick . . . : "Police Give Up on Schedule but 'Vignola Flu' Spreads," *Gazette*, January 9, 1978.

80   In the midst of all this . . . : Albert Noel and Eddie Collister, "Levesque Accident Victim Alive When Car Hit Says Witness," *Gazette*, February 8, 1977.

81   About forty municipalities . . . : In February 1977, the Quebec Police Commission voiced its alarm at the number of municipalities electing to abolish their police forces to balance budgets ("Police Reductions Alarming: Judge," *Gazette*, February 17, 1977). The towns of Schefferville, Bois-des-Filion and Richelieu (across the river from Chambly) all cited layoffs to counter the elimination of provincial grants that formerly helped to pay for police services. Of the 1,400 incorporated municipalities in the province in 1977, 225 of them had their own police departments; the other 1,175 had police services provided by the Sûreté du Québec.

81   Colloquially, this expanding provincial force . . . : *Greens and blues* was a term given to us by the source Gilles, featured in later chapters: "Well, you won't find this with the new generation of SQ investigators . . . but they still have the green vs. blue."

81   In the early-morning hours . . . : Steve Kowch, "Death Rouses QPF Anger," *Gazette*, March 31, 1977.

81   In a rare display of police unity . . . : Bill Kokesch, "1,500 Police Officers Give Final Salute to Comrade," *Gazette*, April 4, 1977.

81   On March 23, 1977, twenty-year-old . . . : "Stupeur et consternation chez les proches de Louise Camirand," *La Tribune*, March 28, 1977.

82   On April 14, Jocelyne Houle . . . : "Rebondissements à prévoir dans le cas de l'infirmière violée et assassinée," *Progrès-dimanche*, April 24, 1977.

82   On June 29, thirty-eight-year-old . . . : "Month's First Slaying Claims Woman, 38," *Gazette*, June 20, 1977.

82   On July 30, Joanne Dorion . . . : "Girl's Body Is Found in Laval," *Gazette*, August 12, 1977.

83   The kidnappers tied . . . : Eddie Collister, "Airwaves Carry Only Clue to Kidnap," *Gazette*, August 10, 1977.

83   The abduction was similar . . . : Collister, "Airwaves Carry Only Clue."

83   Bank extortions involving hostages . . . : David Camp, "Kidnap-Extortions Spread Like Virus," *Gazette*, August 13, 1977.

83   . . . "Mr. Nebets wants to talk to Mr. Noiram": Collister, "Airwaves Carry Only Clue."

84   "I know my life isn't worth a million . . .": "'I Want to Live,' Kidnap Victim Says," *Gazette*, August 15, 1977.

84   . . . some speculated that the red matter looked more like ketchup: "'I Want to Live,'" *Gazette*.

84   On Wednesday, August 17, the SQ reported . . . : Steve Kowch, "Kidnappers Use Logo on Notes," *Gazette*, August 17, 1977.

84   But on August 19, the hostage wrote . . . : Steve Kowch, "Kidnappers of Marion Ask for Old $10 and $20 Bills," *Gazette*, August 22, 1977.

85   The kidnappers had decided . . . : Steve Kowch, "450 Police on Alert to Hunt for Marion," *Gazette*, September 14, 1977.

85   On September 10, on her eighteenth birthday . . . : "Une autre jeune fille victime d'un dépravé sexuel," *Allô Police*, September 25, 1977.

85   So intent was the SQ . . . : Steve Kowch, "Kidnappers Under Siege," *Gazette*, September 30, 1977.

86   If the ransom wasn't paid . . . : "You'll Get Only His Head Marion Abductors Warn," *Gazette*, September 21, 1977.

86   On September 20, thirty-three-year-old . . . : "Encore un maniaque sexuel!" *Allô Police*, October 2, 1977.

86   They received a communiqué that evening . . . : Bill Kokesch, "Police Take Radios in Marion Kidnap," *Gazette*, September 26, 1977.

87   It was later admitted . . . : Kokesch, "Police Take Radios."

87   *The Gazette* characterized . . . : Kokesch, "Police Take Radios."

87   "If you print that picture . . .": Steve Kowch, "Caisse Officials Want Marion Freed When Ransom Paid," *Gazette*, September 16, 1977.

87   On September 26, the skeletal remains . . . : "Un troisième cadavre a trouvé à Rawdon," *La Presse*, September 29, 1977.

88   Maltais and Poirier left the offices . . . : Steve Kowch, "Is Marion Still Alive? Only the Kidnappers Know," *Gazette*, October 1, 1977.

88   A Lennoxville local snorted . . . : Kowch, "Is Marion Still Alive?"

88   "We won't have to liquidate . . .": Steve Kowch, "Marion Kidnappers Want New Pair to Drop Cash," *Gazette*, October 5, 1977.

89   "I have been in this business . . .": Steve Kowch, "'No Tricks' Say Ransom Couriers," *Gazette*, October 6, 1977.

89   "Sell everything I have . . .": Bill Kokesch, "Marion's Captors Now Want $50,000," *Gazette*, October 22, 1977.

89   "He looked like he needed a bath," . . . : Steve Kowch, "Marion Freed Unhurt 92-Day Drama Ends," *Gazette*, October 28, 1977. The nurse who said this was the sister of Luc-Yoland Grégoire.

89   In a Halloween interview . . . : Bill Kokesch, "Marion Affair to Be Raised in Assembly," *Gazette*, October 31, 1977.

89   *The Gazette* reported . . . : "Marion Cases Raises Questions," *Gazette*, November 3, 1997.

90   On Monday, October 24th . . . : "Après Louise, Jocelyne, Johanne, Hélène et Catherine, c'est au tour de Denise, 23 ans," *Allô Police*, November 6, 1977.

90   The fellow was having a drink . . . : Janet Cotton, "The Verdict That Left a Mystery," *Maclean's*, January 15, 1979.

90   The officer went back to Disco René . . . : Cotton, "The Verdict That Left a Mystery."

91   Gaudreault also discovered . . . : "Desmarais on Snatch List," Canadian Press, November 17, 1978.

91   It was like "an overnight tourist attraction," . . . : "Sight-Seers Flock to Spot Where Marion Held," *Gazette*, July 7, 1978.

91   "That's one heck of a lot of witnesses": "Courtroom Marathon Looms as Marion Trial Begins Today," *Gazette*, October 2, 1978.

92   Under cross-examination, Marion admitted . . . : "Marion Involved in Own Kidnapping Defence Charges," *Gazette*, December 20, 1978.

92   He was, he said, punched repeatedly . . . : "Policemen Tortured Me
      Says Valence," *Gazette*, December 15, 1978.

93   In 1989, Valence was shot . . . : "Played a Key Part in 1977 Kidnapping,
      Man Shot to Death," *Gazette*, June 30, 1989.

93   A decade later, Charles Marion . . . : "1977 Kidnapping Victim Marion
      Is Found Dead," *Gazette*, December 3, 1999.

93   Grimard had been shot . . . : Claudia Bowers, "Laplante Murder Trial
      Opens," *Sherbrooke Record*, April 18, 1979.

93   SQ officer Réal Châteauneuf . . . : "Charland admet avoir menti à la
      police et au coroner," *La Tribune*, April 25, 1979.

93   . . . found a piece of paper on Grimard's body . . . : Yvon Rousseau,
      "Fernand Laplante accusé de trois meurtres au premier degré," *La
      Tribune*, December 29, 1978.

94   Charland honked the car horn . . . : "Laplante Trial: Crown
      Witnesses Challenge Charland," *Sherbrooke Record*, April 27, 1979.

94   Rancourt told the jury . . . : Claudia Bowers, "Charland Survives
      Credibility Test," *Sherbrooke Record*, April 25, 1979.

94   . . . they lied to him by pretending . . . : John McCaghey, "Laplante
      'Surprised' at Death," *Sherbrooke Record*, November 29, 1979.

95   Asked if this type of deception . . . : Claudia Bowers, "QPF Used
      Bogus Statement," *Sherbrooke Record*, April 26, 1979.

95   One of the witnesses said . . . : Claudia Bowers, "Laplante Trial
      Witnesses Ask Court's Protection," *Sherbrooke Record*, May 1, 1979.

95   No one was ever convicted . . . : Fernand Laplante was acquitted of
      Carole Fecteau's murder on December 4, 1979. That was the last
      mention of Fecteau in the media ("Les plus importantes causes de la
      décennie," *La Tribune*, January 2, 1980).

96   The second man on the ride . . . : "Laplante Trial: Crown Witnesses
      Challenge Charland," *Sherbrooke Record*, April 27, 1979.

96   Attorney Rancourt speculated . . . : Bernard Tetrault, *Me Jean-Pierre
      Rancourt - Les Confessions d'un Criminaliste* (Montreal, QC: Les
      Editions internationales Alain Stanke, 2015). In his biography,
      Rancourt devotes an entire chapter to the Laplante affaire, and the
      murders of Grimard, Bergeron and Fecteau. Concerning Laplante's
      involvement in the Grimard and Bergeron murders, he states, "In the

case of Laplante: I was convinced that he was not involved in the double murder."

96 ... private investigator Robert Beullac decided ... : "Local Police Accused of Lying, Intimidation," *Sherbrooke Record*, August 31, 1979.

96 "The problem is that provincial police ...": "Local Police Accused," *Sherbrooke Record*.

SIX: WHEN THE SNOW MELTED

102 "The pathologist, because of the state of decomposition ...": Serge Gosselin, "Theresa identifiée par son père," *La Tribune*, April 17, 1979.

102 It would be decades before *Gazette* journalist ... : The coroner's report referencing the marks of strangulation was faxed to John Allore by reporter Paul Cherry in the fall of 2002. For whatever reason, Cherry did not report it.

SEVEN: REMEMBER A DAY

112 "The piece, titled "Starlight" ... : Sarah Priestman, "Starlight," in *The Best American Essays 1992*, ed. Joyce Carol Oates and Robert Atwan (Boston: Ticknor and Fields, 1991).

114 In the summer of 1896 ... : Harold K. Bush, *Continuing Bonds with the Dead: Parental Grief and Nineteenth-Century American Authors* (Tuscaloosa: University of Alabama Press, 2016), 36.

115 In traumatic loss ... : Shelly Rambo, *Spirit and Trauma: A Theology of Remaining* (Louisville, KY: Westminster John Knox Press, 2010), 7.

EIGHT: BAD DREAM HOUSE

137 Years later, he confessed ... : Clarke Morrison, "Man Gets 27-Year Jail Term," *Asheville Citizen-Times*, March 27, 2010.

NINE: SENSE OF DOUBT

156 At first, the city brass dismissed ... : Robert Anthony Phillips, "Mayor: No Reward in Missing Hookers Case," APBNews.com, April 9, 1999.

156 The cost of excavating serial killer ... : Edward Butts, "Robert Pickton Case," *The Canadian Encyclopedia*, July 26, 2016, https://www.thecanadianencyclopedia.ca/en/article/robert-pickton-case.

157 "The murder is not necessarily...": Jean Proulx, Éric Beauregard, Maurice Cusson and Alexandre Nicole, eds., *Sexual Murderers: A Comparative Analysis and New Perspectives*, trans. Steven Sacks (Hoboken, NJ: John Wiley & Sons, 2007), 147.

160 With the discovery of the body...: Pierre Saint-Jacques, "Découverte d'un cadavre... peut-être Theresa Allore," *La Tribune*, April 14, 1979.

TEN: HEROES FOR GHOSTS (A TRIO OF MYSTERIES)

162 "Manon!" the girl called...: Janet Cotton, "Kidnappers Demand $25,000," *Sherbrooke Record*, January 30, 1978.

163 Investigators wondered if she had been struck...: Janet Cotton, "Dubé's Death Linked to Hit-and-Run," *Sherbrooke Record*, March 28, 1978.

165 Another theory bandied about...: Janet Cotton, "Kidnappers Demand $25,000," *Sherbrooke Record*, January 30, 1978.

165 In 1978, the Quebec crime magazine...: "Manon, 10 ans, a-t-elle été victime d'un maniaque?" *Allô Police*, February 12, 1978.

165 Another headline read...: "Victime d'un pédophile? On reprend l'enquête policière de A à Z," *Allô Police*, April 6, 2001.

165 The question of sexual murder...: In his report of March 24, 1978, Coroner Jean-Pierre Rivard noted "possibility of a sexual murder." In his report of May 17, 1978, Rivard determined that "the death of Manon Dubé is violent and the verdict concluded is VIOLENT DEATH with criminal negligence..." These details were never published in the media. Rivard served as the same coroner on the inquiries into the deaths of Carole Fecteau, Raymond Grimard and Manon Bergeron, which occurred later that year.

166 Beullac sent him a news clipping...: "Louise, 20 ans, violée et étranglée un mois avant son mariage," *Allô Police*, April 10, 1977.

170 They searched for a car...: "Louise, 20 ans," *Allô Police*.

170 (In Statistics Canada's 2005 report...): Mia Dauvergne and Geoffrey Li, "Homicide in Canada, 2005," *Juristat* 26, no. 6 (Ottawa: Statistics Canada, Canadian Centre for Justice Statistics, 2006), Catalogue no. 85-002-XIE.

171 "A plausible hypothesis...": "A-t-elle été victime d'un maniaque sexuel?" *Photo Police*, December 2, 1978.

172   "We will see this syndrome . . .": Bill James and Rachel McCarthy James, *The Man from the Train: The Solving of a Century-Old Serial Killer Mystery* (New York: Scribner, 2017), 25.

175   "I know now why . . .": Ms. Andersen, as reported in *Forsaken: The Report of the Missing Women Commission of Inquiry*, Executive Summary, the Honourable Wally T. Oppal, QC, Commissioner (British Columbia: Missing Women Commission of Inquiry, November 19, 2012), 32.

176   "I know it," she vowed to the police . . . : Ms. Andersen, as reported in *Forsaken*.

177   (Note that 93 percent . . .): D. Kim Rossmo, "Organizational Traps: Groupthink, Rumor, and Ego," chap. 3 in *Criminal Investigative Failures* (Boca Raton, FL: Taylor & Francis, 2009).

178   "If these numbers represented . . .": Rossmo, "Organizational Traps."

178   As the Commission of Inquiry . . . : *Forsaken*, 62.

179   "I feel very strongly . . .": *Forsaken*, 59.

179   On August 27, 1998, Shenher wrote . . . : *Forsaken*, 60.

180   "It is difficult to understand . . .": *Forsaken*, 62.

180   "Police officers start from the premise . . .": *Forsaken*, 62.

180   "A review of 1,400 killers . . .": *Forsaken*, 20.

ELEVEN: RIDDLES AND DARK WORDS

191   The bikers brazenly stole . . . : The tale is told in detail in Paul Cherry, *The Biker Trials: Bringing Down the Hells Angels* (Toronto: ECW Press, 2005).

TWELVE: RAVING AND DROOLING

206   In November 1982, a student . . . : Charles Bury, "Female Jogger Attacked; Friends Seek Assailant," *Sherbrooke Record*, November 17, 1981.

THIRTEEN: DOWNWARD SPIRAL (THE SUSPECT)

212   Silva had been working . . . : Bob Beaty, "Silva's Murderer in Court Again," *Calgary Herald*, September 9, 1994.

212   . . . on April 6, a sex worker . . . : Beaty, "Silva's Murderer in Court Again."

215   "He didn't need a weapon," . . . : Christina Mungan and Bob Beaty, "Profile of a Predator," *Calgary Herald*, June 29, 1994.

216   It is worth noting that around this time . . . : Luc Grégoire's address
        comes from his court documents for that era.

216   . . . one block away from the apartment . . . : Carole Fecteau's address
        comes from her coroner's report.

216   In May 1981, Luc Grégoire . . . : "Serge Gagnon cite a son process par
        un cheveu," *La Tribune*, August 5, 1981.

217   . . . one British parliamentarian clarified . . . : Hansard Debates,
        December 4, 1994, https://publications.parliament.uk/pa
        /cm199394/cmhansrd/1994-04-12/Debate-34.html.

217   "Grégoire had sequestered . . .": "Trois ans de prison pour Grégoire,"
        La Tribune, July 29, 1981.

217   By fighting and screaming . . . "Townships talk," *Sherbrooke Record*,
        May 27, 1981.

218   In another version filed . . . : "Grégoire attendra sa sentence encore
        une semaine," *La Tribune*, July 9, 1981.

218   Within months, as Nicole Couture . . . : Correctional Service of Canada,
        Internal Review/Investigation into Luc-Yoland Gregoire, June 14, 1993.

218   . . . the review's mandate was "to analyze . . .": Correctional Service of
        Canada, Internal Review.

219   "As regards your two previous acts . . ." : Decision Registry, Parole
        Board of Canada, in accordance with section 144 (2) of the
        Corrections and Conditional Release Act (CCRA).

219   Grégoire admitted the assault . . . : Decision Registry, Parole Board
        of Canada.

219   "So long as knowledge about sexual violence . . ." : Joanna Bourke,
        Rape: A History from 1860 to the Present (London: Virago, 2007), 366.

220   Retired Brigadier General Al Geddry . . . : John Nicol, "Mystery at
        Gagetown," *Maclean's*, July 13, 1998, 22. See also John Nicol and Brenda
        Branswell, "CFB Gagetown Rape Controversy," *The Canadian
        Encyclopedia*, March 17, 2003, https://www.thecanadianencyclopedia.ca
        /en/article/cfb-gagetown-rape-controversy.

220   His prison intake report identified . . . : Correctional Service of
        Canada, Internal Review.

221   In one 1986 study, college students . . . : William Henry George and
        G. Alan Marlatt, "The Effects of Alcohol and Anger on Interest in

Violence, Erotica and Deviance," *Journal of Abnormal Psychology* 95, no. 2 (June 1986): 150–58.

221 The 1978 book *Understanding Sexual Attacks* . . . : Bourke, *Rape*, 139.

221 "These schemes were designed . . .": Bourke, *Rape*, 177. See also Kurt Freund, Hal Scher and Stephen Hucker, "The Courtship Disorders," *Archives of Sexual Behaviour* 12, no. 5 (October 1983): 369–79.

221 In the 1950s, Nathan Roth . . . : Bourke, *Rape*, 187.

222 Yet, according to one major survey . . . : Bourke, *Rape*, 195.

222 The criminologist Dr. Candice Skrapec . . . : Personal correspondence between Patricia Pearson and Dr. Candice Skrapec.

222 A year after his brutal attack . . . : Decision Registry, Parole Board of Canada.

223 One possibility . . . : "A 20-year Murder Spree," Jane Davenport, *Gazette*, December 1, 2001.

223 "Apparently, offender Gregoire . . .": Decision Registry, Parole Board of Canada.

223 On March 28, a case management worker . . . : Decision Registry, Parole Board of Canada.

224 According to forensic psychologist . . . : Jean Proulx, Éric Beauregard, Maurice Cusson, and Alexandre Nicole, eds., *Sexual Murderers: A Comparative Analysis and New Perspectives*, trans. Steven Sacks (Hoboken, NJ: John Wiley & Sons, 2007), 94.

224 . . . there's no trace of him . . . : Correctional Service of Canada, Internal Review.

224 By May 1986, he'd been convicted . . . : Else Rempel, "Armed Fur-Coat Robber Given Seven-Year Term," *Edmonton Journal*, May 15, 1986.

224 As the Parole Board of Canada would say . . . : Decision Registry, Parole Board of Canada.

225 He would ultimately commit . . . : Correctional Service of Canada, Internal Review.

225 In August 1988, Grégoire underwent . . . : Correctional Service of Canada, Internal Review.

225 His mother, Claire, described him . . . : Mungan and Beaty, "Profile of a Predator."

225   Later that month, transferred . . . : Correctional Service of Canada, Internal Review.

226   . . . an assessment tool known as the Psychopathy Checklist (PCL): See, for example, Robert D. Hare, *Without Conscience: The Disturbing World of the Psychopaths Among Us* (London: Guildford Press, 1999).

226   . . . what psychiatrist Hervey Cleckley once called . . . : Hervey M. Cleckley, *The Mask of Sanity: An Attempt to Clarify Some Issues about the So-Called Psychopathic Personality* (New York: Plume Books, 1982).

226   . . . one of his UBC studies had found . . . : Danielle Egan, "Into the Mind of a Psychopath," *Discover*, May 2, 2016. Available at http://discovermagazine.com/2016/june/12-psychopath-and -the-hare.

227   In September 1989, he was assessed . . . : Correctional Service of Canada, Internal Review.

227   "There was no translation . . .": Correctional Service of Canada, Internal Review.

227   At a parole meeting in February . . . : Correctional Service of Canada, Internal Review.

228   The RCMP later reviewed . . . : Helen Plischke, "Calgary Slaying Interests Local Police," *Edmonton Journal*, May 8, 1993.

228   At his August supervision appointment . . . : Correctional Service of Canada, Internal Review.

228   Her body would be found . . . : Bob Beaty, "Cops Probe Teen Murder Link," *Calgary Herald*, October 16, 1991.

228   Another teen, Jennifer Janz . . . : Beaty, "Cops Probe Teen Murder Link."

228   Grégoire was due to be assessed . . . : Correctional Service of Canada, Internal Review.

229   Her family didn't know . . . : Jason van Rassel, "When the Trail Goes Cold," *Calgary Herald*, October 27, 2014.

229   There are no parole notes . . . : Correctional Service of Canada, Internal Review.

229   The first body found dumped . . . : van Rassel, "When the Trail Goes Cold."

230   In October, Grégoire headed . . . : Correctional Service of Canada, Internal Review.

230   Missing from the crime scene . . . : Ron Collins, "Mother Waits for
        Justice," *Calgary Herald*, April 17, 1993.

230   A December parole report . . . : Correctional Service of Canada,
        Internal Review.

231   Another stressor, likely related . . . : Mungan and Beaty, "Profile of a
        Predator."

231   Jeffrey Dahmer, for example, killed his first victim . . . : Michael
        Arntfield and Marcel Danesi, *Murder in Plain English: From
        Manifestos to Memes—Looking at Murder through the Words of Killers*
        (Amherst, NY: Prometheus Books, 2017), 117.

231   . . . Gregoire had been caught . . . : Correctional Service of Canada,
        Internal Review.

231   One pattern observed . . . : Personal correspondence between
        Patricia Pearson and Dr. Candice Skrapec.

231   Skrapec's perception was later . . . : Personal conversation between
        Sasha Reid and authors.

232   Two weeks later, a twenty-year-old . . . : Rick Mofina, "The Hunt for
        a Killer," *Calgary Herald*, May 9, 1993.

233   The police traced these clothes . . . : Mofina, "Hunt for a Killer."

233   "I squeeze her neck a little bit . . .": Beaty, "Silva's Murderer in Court Again."

234   . . . Gregoire "tries by all means possible . . . ": Correctional Service of
        Canada, Internal Review.

234   "Starting to celebrate," the officer noted . . . : Correctional Service of
        Canada, Internal Review.

234   There were seventy-two reported incidents . . . : Augustine
        Brannigan, *Victimization of Prostitutes in Calgary and Winnipeg*
        (Ottawa: Department of Justice Canada, Research, Statistics and
        Evaluation Directorate, 1996), Technical Report No. TR1996-15e.

FOURTEEN: ECHOES

235   In the *Sherbrooke Record* . . . : Bertrand Daigneault, "Letter Was
        Attack on Champlain College's Sterling Reputation," *Sherbrooke
        Record*, August 26, 2002.

236   "Violence just wasn't on the radar screen,": Sharon McCully, "Family
        Seeks Closure in Daughter's Murder," *Sherbrooke Record*, August 19, 2002.

236   Red Alert . . . : John Allore, "Champlain's Conduct Should Be Investigated," *Sherbrooke Record*, August 21, 2002.

237   "Many of the elements are still there . . .": Sharon McCully, "Homicide Investigator to Review Murder Files," *Sherbrooke Record*, August 21, 2002.

237   "Girl's Death in '79 Gets Second Look": "Girl's Death in '79 Gets Second Look," *Gazette*, November 14, 2002.

237   "Montreal SQ to Revisit Theresa Allore Case": Kate Shingler, "Montreal SQ to Revisit Theresa Allore Case," *Sherbrooke Record*, November 11, 2002.

237   That was home base . . . : Paul Cherry, "Man charged in '87 killing," *Gazette*, February 15, 2002.

238   ". . . Recently, another young woman . . .": René-Charles Quirion, "L'accusé nie le meurtre," *La Tribune*, September 24, 2002.

240   "There's a part of me . . .": Sherri Zickefoose, "Unsolved Murders Still Haunt Families and Police," *Calgary Herald*, May 15, 2011.

243   Police spokesman Jimmy Potvin . . . : Sidhartha Banerjee, "Murder Case Stays on Hold," *Gazette*, September 18, 2002.

243   John wrote a response in *The Gazette* . . . : John Allore, "Justice Delayed in Townships," *Gazette*, November 22, 2002.

245   No one articulated this sentiment . . . : Michael Benazon, "Unanswered Questions Remain on Death of Theresa Allore," *Sherbrooke Record*, September 19, 2002.

248   Within a year, this detective . . . : Marc Pigeon, "Sur la trace des pires criminels," *Journal de Montréal*, September 20, 2012.

260   At one point we noticed . . . : Many articles document the partnership between Gaudreault and investigator Luc Grégoire. Roch Gaudreault, Réal Châteauneuf, Guy Lessard and Luc Grégoire all continued to work together on the Townships SQ force through the 1980s. See, for example, Pierre Saint-Jacques, "Criblés de balles dans leur auto," *La Tribune*, August 29, 1984.

261   Luc's father, Roland . . . : Advertisement, "Soirée veille du jour de l'an," *La Tribune*, December 31, 1976.

261   "A close observer of the MH370 process . . .": William Langewiesche, "What Really Happened to Malaysia's Missing Airplane," *Atlantic*, June 17, 2019.

FIFTEEN: THE SEXUAL MURDERER

268 Years later, at a 2013 parole hearing . . . : Decision Registry, Parole Board of Canada, in accordance with section 144 (2) of the Corrections and Conditional Release Act (CCRA).

268 The board responded . . . : Decision Registry, Parole Board of Canada.

269 "DNA was handled much differently . . .": Interview with Calgary detective Ken Carriere, recorded on September 17, 2019.

273 One might well have been Robert Leblanc . . . : See, for example, James Mennie, "Jury Hears Tape of Suspect Confessing to Rape," *Gazette*, January 24, 1996. According to his parole records, Leblanc's adult criminal record began in Sherbrooke in 1976 when he robbed an elderly woman of her purse.

273 Most homicide investigators never . . . : See, for example, Jonathan James and Eric Beauregard, "Murder vs Investigator: Factors Influencing the Resolution of Sexual Homicide Cases," *Police Practise and Research* (October 2018). DOI: 10.1080/15614263.2018.1526683.

274 In 1998, Beauregard and his research colleagues . . . : Eric Beauregard and Melissa Martineau, *The Sexual Murderer: Offender Behavior and Implications for Practice*, Routledge Studies in Criminal Behavior (Boca Rotan, FL: CRC Press, 2018).

274 One example from Beauregard's research . . . : Beauregard and Martineau, *Sexual Murderer*, 206–07.

274 It is more likely with serial sexual murderers . . . : Beauregard and Martineau, *Sexual Murderer*, 103.

275 "Pre-crime anger," Beauregard found . . . : Jean Proulx, Éric Beauregard, Maurice Cusson and Alexandre Nicole, *Sexual Murderers: A Comparative Analysis and New Perspectives*, trans. Steven Sacks (Hoboken, NJ: John Wiley & Sons, 2007), 94.

275 They were also more likely to exhibit . . . : Proulx et al., *Sexual Murderers*, 42.

276 "Sexual crimes against women . . .": Proulx et al., *Sexual Murderers*, 44.

276 . . . sadistic aggressors have "a sexual preference for rape.": Proulx et al., *Sexual Murderers*, 120.

276 This was conceivably true of Grégoire . . . : Decision Registry, Parole Board of Canada.

276 "Deviant sexual fantasies . . .": Proulx et al., *Sexual Murderers*, 104.

277 "What plagues criminology . . .": Keith Soothill, Brian Francis, Barry Sanderson and Elizabeth Ackerley, "Sex Offenders: Specialists, Generalists—or Both?" *British Journal of Criminology* 40, no. 1 (January 2000): 57.

271 "I repressed so much of that incident . . .": Posted using moniker "Notforgetting" to Unsolved Canada, December 20, 2011, on the Tracey Maunder thread.

282 ". . . When I met Solange Blais . . .": "Missing Girl Found Dead," *Gazette*, June 5, 1978.

282 ". . . Sharron Prior's evidence . . .": Michelle Lalonde, "Families of Nine Murdered or Missing Local Women Demand Inquiry," *Gazette*, April 1, 2019.

282 It took detectives forty-six years . . . : Esmeralda Bermudez, "2 Sought in Possible Manson Killing," *Los Angeles Times*, September 11, 2016.

283 "There was the murder of Isabelle Bolduc . . .": Katherine Wilton, "Rape Accused Was on Parole," *Gazette*, July 12, 1996.

283 "You had the killing . . .": René-Charles Quirion, "L'accusé nie le meurtre," *La Tribune*, September 24, 2002.

284 Almost exactly forty years earlier . . . : "Une autre jeune fille victime d'un dépravé sexuel," *Allô Police*, September 25, 1977.

285 "A crazy person must have come . . .": Jesse Feith, "Cold Cases Leave Families in the Dark," *Gazette*, August 20, 2016.

285 On Monday, October 24, 1977 . . . : "Après Louise, Jocelyne, Johanne, Héléne et Catherine, c'est au tour de Denise, 23 ans," *Allô Police*, November 6, 1977.

286 Police theorized that the motive . . . : "Après Louise, Jocelyne, Johanne," *Allô Police*.

SIXTEEN: WHAT'S IN THE BOX?

291 On Thursday, September 14, 2017 . . . : "Alerte Amber à Saint-Eustache," TVA Nouvelles, September 14, 2017.

298 . . . he'd bootstrapped a film together . . . : See, for instance, "New Documentary Claims Serial Killer Might Be Behind Unsolved Child Murders," *Gazette*, August 5, 2016.

298   Neither film got a distribution deal . . . : Marie Poupart, "Le combat d'une vie," *Journal de Montréal*, January 31, 2015.

298   But this caught the imagination . . . : In an interview, Parent stated, "*À l'époque, certains avaient même surnommé le tueur comme étant le 'Bootlace killer'. . . car les victimes auraient vraisemblablement été étranglées avec leurs propres lacets de chaussures ou leur écharpe.*" ("At the time, some had even nicknamed the killer as the 'Bootlace killer' . . . because the victims were likely to have been strangled with their own shoe laces or their scarf.") Caroline Mireault, TV Hebdo, June 2, 2015.

305   "Fuck you. Shoot me . . .": Louis-Samuel Perron, "Ugo Fredette a utilisé un enfant comme 'bouclier' devant les policiers," *La Presse* (Montreal), September 19, 2019.

306   "She would have been one of the main cases . . .": In an interview, *7 Femmes* film supporter Marc Bellemare commented that he saw Véronique Barbe, and her son: "*Nous étions à Laval pour le tournage d'une séquence sur Joanne Dorion, disparue en 1977.*" ("We were in Laval for the filming of a sequence on Joanne Dorion, who disappeared in 1977.") Louise Leduc, "Ugo Fredette 'dévoué à la cause des victimes,' selon Marc Bellemare," *La Presse*, September 18, 2017.

308   "I'm in shock, really stunned . . .": Amélie St-Yves, "La famille d'une victime est choquée par un film," *Journal de Montréal*, December 3, 2017.

308   "I felt the need to express . . .": "Le réalisateur Stephan Parent s'engage à retirer les scènes de son film montrant Ugo Fredette, accusé de meurtre," *Journal de Montréal*, December 4, 2017.

308   "Parent pledged to reshoot . . .": "Le réalisateur Stephan Parent," *Journal de Montréal*.

308   "Very few people in Quebec . . .": Louise Leduc, "Ugo Fredette 'dévoué à la cause des victimes,' selon Marc Bellemare," *La Presse*, September 18, 2017.

312   Speaking with the wire service . . . : "Le réalisateur Stéphan Parent se sent trahi par Ugo Fredette," La Presse Canadienne, September 16, 2017.

312   Within a year he announced . . . : "New Documentary Will Explore Details of 1999 Julie Surprenant Cold Case," CBC News, November 18, 2018.

314 His and other cases are discussed . . . : Michael Arntfield and Marcel
     Danesi, *Murder in Plain English: From Manifestos to Memes—Looking
     at Murder Through the Words of Killers* (Amherst, NY: Prometheus
     Books, 2017).

314 As Arntfield and Danesi noted . . . : Arntfield and Danesi, *Murder in
     Plain English*, 250.

315 At that point, he asked them to stop . . . : Amélie St-Yves, "Le père de
     Cédrika Provencher arrête un documentaire sur sa fille," *Journal de
     Montréal*, May 16, 2017.

316 Lacasse's daughter, Jennifer, put it aptly . . . : Stéphanie Marin, "Ugo
     Fredette a été trouvé coupable de 2 meurtres au 1er degré," La Presse
     Canadienne, October 19, 2019.

INDEX

Allore, Theresa Marie, 13–16, 18–20.
See also Allore, Theresa:
murder of
at Champlain College, 48–52
on day of murder, 52–54
personality, 10, 15, 19–20, 51
and Vlad, 20–24
Allore, Theresa: murder of, 157–59
autopsy/coroner's report, 101–2,
109, 140–41, 157–58
case file, 250–54
drug use theories, 70–71, 74–75,
103–4, 107–9, 257
dump site, 2–4, 98–101, 146–47,
154–55, 185, 252–53
emotional repercussions, 114–17,
236–37
media response, 61, 63, 150, 171,
173, 237
reinvestigation, 237–38, 240–41,
243–44, 247
scarf, 3, 52, 127–28, 190, 252–53
Sûreté de Québec and, 2–4, 10,
24, 62, 67, 180
wallet, 10, 105–6, 182–83
Alouis, Tony, 208, 211–12, 214, 234
antisocial personality disorder,
225–26, 267
Archambault, Serge, 286
army. See Canadian Armed Forces
Arntfield, Michael, 231, 314

Barbe, Daniel, 307–8, 309, 313
Barbe, Véronique, 304, 306, 308, 311,
313, 315–16

Bazinet, Denise, 90, 285–86
Beauregard, Eric, 224, 273–77,
287–88
Bédard, Louise, 82
Bédard, Marc-André, 96–97
Bellemare, Marc, 298–99, 308–9
Benazon, Michael, 245–47
Bergeron, Manon, 93, 94, 95, 216
Beullac, Robert, 66–67, 70–75,
96–97, 102, 158, 172
and Andre's investigation,
123–25, 127
and John's investigation, 166, 245
Binette, Francine, 78
Bishop's University, 26–27, 46–47,
66. See also Champlain
College
student newspaper, 38, 46–47, 61
Blain, Paul Émile, 36
Blais, Lison, 282
Blais, Solange, 282
Blanchette, Lena, 83
Blasey Ford, Christine, 255–56
Boden, Wayne, 286
Boisvenu, Julie, 238, 246
Bolduc, Noël, 93
Bourke, Joanna, 42–43, 45–46,
219–20, 221
Boutilier, Rebecca "Becca", 232–33,
269–72
Boutilier, Sandy, 270
Bowie, David, 24
Brabant, Robert, 81
Braun, Daniel, 167, 170
Briggs, Edwin, 80

JOHN ALLORE is the creator and host of the podcast *Who Killed Theresa*, which centres on unsolved murders in Quebec, and other criminal and social justice issues. He launched one of the first crime blogs, and the website theresaallore.com not only documents the search for his sister's killer but is a trove of information on other unsolved cases in Canada and the US. In 2018, John was awarded the Senate of Canada's Sesquicentennial Medal for his work in victims advocacy. He lives with his family in Chapel Hill, North Carolina.

PATRICIA PEARSON is the author of six books, and a critically acclaimed journalist whose work has appeared in *The New York Times*, *The New Yorker*, *The Daily Beast*, *The Daily Telegraph*, *The Globe and Mail*, and more. Her book about what people experience when they die, *Opening Heaven's Door*, was a finalist for the BC National Book Award. She has also won three National Magazine Awards and the Arthur Ellis Award for best non-fiction crime book of 1998.